Send
Her
Down,
Hughie!

An Australian Experience

Send Her Down, Hughie!

An Australian Experience

Arthur Clifford

*With Illustrations
by the Author*

RIGBY LIMITED

Rigby Limited, Adelaide
Sydney, Melbourne, Brisbane, Perth
First published 1968
Copyright 1968 by A. Clifford
Library of Congress
Catalog Card Number 68-29171
National Library of Australia
Registry Number AUS 68-1353
All rights reserved
Printed at
The Griffin Press, Adelaide
for Rigby Limited
Registered in Australia
for transmission by post as a book

1

[This is the story of an American family in Australia. When we arrived, on a visit which was part of an educational journey round the world, we thought that we ought to be able to "do" the country, big as it is, during a couple of my daughter Candi's high-school holidays. We found that Australia was not only bigger than we had expected, but far more exciting and interesting than we had ever imagined. So we stayed for a closer and deeper look. This is the story of our first year's travels, interspersed with flash-backs, or rather "flash-aheads," to events, people, and observations made during our subsequent three years' residence, together with some letters written by Candi.]

"The picture was awful. It was just a series of these weak old-hat jokes all rigged into place like Bob Menzies epics always were. It wasn't even funny. For example they had this Italian migrant, who had just come to Australia, go into a hotel for no other reason than so this guy could shout him to a beer and they could have a joke on shouting. The whole thing was like that. Stella and Ian, who are dinkie die Aussies, liked it all right. Ian didn't have a word against it but Stella objected that some of the parts weren't true to life enough. For example Nino was going to get married and there was a sort of afternoon tea for him at the place where he'd been staying with this builder and his wife. Well all his friends, these three builder's labourers, sat there poking each other in the ribs so they would say something. Then a plate of meringues was passed around and they kept squashing them and the meringue would go everywhere.

"That was what made Stella so mad. They didn't know how to eat meringues. She reckoned that Australians knew as well how to eat meringues as anyone else. I suppose they did overdo it a bit with the meringues, but that was really one of the best parts, the

1

way the men all sat three in a row on this bench in their suits and didn't say anything, and the two wives sat at the table with Nino and the girl and tried to make conversation. That part looked pretty typical to me but I can see how an Australian would be offended by it.

"That was mainly the only thing Stella found wrong with the film. It would be sent overseas and in certain parts people would get a wrong impression of what Australians were like. However no one seemed to mind the way at the beginning Nino went to this real posh hotel in King's bloody Cross (which was an endless joke for the rest of the picture) and that the hotel staff just dropped everything to help him. For example he rang up this builder. The manager, the desk clerk, the switchboard girls, and everyone left customers just standing there and took up their extensions and listened in; and when he didn't know the meaning of a word they told him. I mean that wouldn't be exactly typical behaviour of Australians to an eye-tye immigrant, would it?"

DECEMBER 27: Early tomorrow morning we drive to Auckland in time to put the car on the ship. Communications to Australia are so bad across the Tasman that the only ship available is one picking up New Zealand passengers for a cruise to the Great Barrier Reef. We can get off at Sydney or Melbourne of course and drive to Adelaide, but we might not get another chance to see the tropical regions of Australia.

Our camp here in Whangarei is quite attractive, set in the Domain beside the river. The caretaker, Mr Kimber, is an elderly man who comes originally from the South Island but has lived in Australia.

You like New Zealand better? Ah yes. Why? There's more room. What do you mean? In Aussie every man is out to take you for everything you've got.

He told us how bad he'd found the mosquitoes while camping in Queensland. "How about snakes?" I asked nervously. They were bad too and extremely venomous. "Near Adelaide, close to the water? That's where we plan to camp when we get there." He didn't know about that. They might not bother us so much if we camped real close to the water. We'd be better off if we had a caravan though.

Most of the other campers here are in caravans, including two Englishmen from Kent. One brought a family, a Landrover, and a large caravan on the boat with him. The other has been here a week, after a year in Australia. Thinks this is heaven by comparison.

"just like the English midlands." Aussies, he says, hate Englishmen and they hate Yanks. They don't like anybody but themselves. "They say New Zealand is running down. The blacks have control of everything. Nobody has any ambition."

Young, who came from Surrey, deplored the indolence of the New Zealand workingman—starting late, quitting ten minutes early to wash for lunch, stretching the ten-minute tea breaks to twenty, loafing on the job. It was even worse in Australia. He quoted an Australian employer: "They'd do more in a 30-hour week than their present 40 hours, if they worked 30 hours." This, said Young, was the Labor Party's doing. "They penalize the highly skilled and the man who works hard and rely on compulsory unionism to raise campaign funds." "That's been done away with now, hasn't it?" "Legally, but take in the freezing works, a knife can slip. Your union dues are cheap insurance." I said apart from that did he like New Zealand. Yes; the easy relaxed atmosphere, the democratic relations between boss and man, in contrast to England's forelock pulling. "But compared to Australia?" Ah, there it was too free. No respect for authority whatever. A constable in Sydney of whom he asked directions: "What's on your mind, mate?" A bus driver, when he inquired whether the bus would take him to a certain place: "Hire a cab. That's what they're paid for."

DECEMBER 28: On the ship at 11.00, we found our baggage in two cabins: one with a bath and a long narrow corridor to a wash basin under a porthole to make it an "outside" cabin; the other an inside double without a bath. At present Candi is its only occupant. At 12.30 we had lunch and were interrupted by a call over a loudspeaker to announce "a friend" to see me. It was Anthony, too shy to ask for Candi. We hurriedly got out on deck to grab the last bit of rail space facing the terminal. Then one after another, the Harwoods, Gledhills, Meesons, Mrs Paul with Jennifer and Adrienne, the Davises, and the Brittons. A real send-off.

We watched Northland go past in the afternoon sun, cleaned up for dinner, and dined after eight. Most of the second sitting, as I observed while waiting outside the dining room for the first sitters to get up, the tables to empty, and the chimes to sound, were kiwis, destination Sydney, and desperately anxious to acquire a suntan. At lunch they appeared with every inch of spindly leg showing from sandal sole to skimpy shorts; and one had nothing on above the shorts but an undershirt—what they call a singlet.

4

The first sitters are just completing a cruise to Hawaii. Most of them would be Australians and all are well tanned.

I have observed that the stage American in New Zealand sounds like a cross between a movie cowboy and a teenage pop singer, dropping his g's and sounding his r's with a twang. The stage Australian shouts his lines as though he were hollering from the top of a rock. Thus kiwis pay tribute to the supposed greater vigour of the Aussie. I asked Mrs Britton and Mrs Paul what difference they saw between Aussies and NZedders. They conceded that Englishmen saw no difference and were not sure themselves what the difference was—except that Aussies were descended from convicts.

DECEMBER 29: Our table companions are two elderly kiwis, on for the full cruise, and a gentlewoman returning to Melbourne on the Hawaiian cruise. None of them has ever heard of Arthur Upfield. When I described his books and their central character, an Aboriginal police detective named Napoleon Bonaparte, Mrs Collins said it was the purest fantasy. No Aboriginal could conceivably be a detective inspector in the Australian C.I.D. She doubted that one was employed by the police in any capacity except possibly as a black tracker. "Yes," I said, "Upfield tells about them, how they can track a person days or weeks after he has been over the ground." All the same it was a let-down. Upfield has been virtually my only source of reference on Australia. If I can't have confidence in him. . . .

Mrs Collins, quite a patrician in looks and pleasant if somewhat unresponsive in speech, said I mustn't confuse the Aborigines with the Maoris of New Zealand. Even to become Australians, she said, the Aborigines have to be naturalized. She had no idea what the legal grounds might be for this. Like the kiwis about the Maoris, she is convinced they cannot drink safely, and cited the case of a famous painter Albert Namatjira who drank himself to death at the age of seventy. When I asked how I might see and get acquainted with them she said the only thing she could think was to go to their reserves in the outback. They have not apparently moved in any great numbers to the cities and they revert, she said, even when educated, to their primitive living conditions. Education leaves them outside both worlds, the Australian and the Aboriginal. She told of an educated Aboriginal nurse travelling with some of her people. Because she was naturalized she could stay at a hotel. The others couldn't.

We've had a very smooth trip. Peggy noticed some motion as we

5

cleared the northern tip of Ninety Mile Beach during the night; but I didn't. She also had her usual brief spate of seasickness and lay in a deck chair all morning sucking a piece of toast; but she was out in the afternoon again to do the number of turns around the ship that constitute a mile. This time Candi didn't accompany her, having found some other teenagers including a pimply youth from Geelong Grammar, which seems to be something rather special around Melbourne.

While Peggy was picking her way over half-clad bodies spread-eagled in the sun I had a drink with an ex-N.Z. Navy man who said he prefers N.Z. to Australia because it is smaller and less hectic. Yet he feels quite at home in London and has just returned from three months there. Hearing him speak of England as "home" I asked if he were English. No, he said, he was born in Wellington but every kiwi of his generation—around fifty years of age—thinks of England in that way. Would this also be true of Australia? In some parts, yes; definitely not in Sydney. "That's where you'll find yourself at home," he said smiling; "Sydney's quite Americanized."

May and Walter Woollaston came originally from western New South Wales, she from a stock farm and he from a small town whose single industry was cement. He never knew trees were green until he left; he always thought they were white. In the course of their young lives they have lived and worked in New Guinea and Britain. They also briefly visited the United States where Immigration officials, keeping them penned on their ship several hours before allowing them to go ashore at Miami, left them little taste for seeing the country again. In England they were both schoolteachers, and they lived in a 15th-century cottage in Little Ickford, surrounded by Ickford, in turn surrounded by Greater Ickford. Here they had their first introduction to English class distinctions. The old families of Little Ickford seemed hardly aware of outer Ickfordians, whether of the lower class living in Council houses or of the middle class in the suburbs. They acknowledged the existence of one of these creatures only when he might happen to be of use to them, as in changing a tyre or unstopping the drains or serving them over a counter.

Since their return after eleven years away from Australia the Woollastons complain of finding it too competitive, and the people too much concerned with owning a house, a washing machine, and a power mower. May said if she wasn't already familiar with the country she could have wondered if the plane

6

that brought them to Sydney had flown off course and landed its passengers in the United States. There were the same advertised brands of goods everywhere, the same drawling accents on movie and television screens, the same news of troops fighting Asians; the largest corporation—General Motors—was the same. There was even an attempted political assassination to greet them; the Leader of the Opposition in Parliament was shot point blank in the face. "But," she said, "after we were here a few days we got things sorted out. In America the news headlines would have been six inches high and editorials demanding the death penalty for the criminal. In Australia the papers hardly looked upon it as a crime at all." Though the gun was aimed at the politician from a distance of less than three feet, he was said to have been shot at rather than shot; and the assassin was released on $2,000 bail. Most of her friends, said May, seemed to think the bail was unreasonably high.

DECEMBER 30: After a day given over mainly to sunbathing we had afternoon tea with an attractive young Sydney couple, both hairdressers working the cruise. Barry went shooting kangaroos last year in Aboriginal country and found them a dirty shiftless lot. He was cautioned not to walk in his bare feet where they had been. The Government used to put up good homes for them but they built campfires right on the floor and burned them down. Now they live in sheet metal shacks the size of pup tents. They get a weekly Government allowance and spend it immediately on a meal and cheap wine. Outside the townships they still live a life scarcely different from the one Captain Cook discovered them in: unclothed, migratory (the walkabout is a general pulling up of stakes when a water hole goes dry or game gives out), primitive hunters and gatherers.

"They live in a tranquillity which is not disturbed by the inequality of conditions: the earth and the sea of their own accord furnish them with all things necessary for life . . . they live in a warm and fine climate and enjoy a very wholesome air so that they have very little need of clothing . . . They seemed to set no value upon anything we gave them, nor would they ever part with anything of their own." So wrote Captain Cook in 1769.

"What language do they speak?" I asked Barry. They had something which might be called a language, different dialects for different tribes. Many spoke English, but teachers who'd worked in their schools said they were almost unteachable. Perhaps a thousand live in Sydney, not segregated and not barred from buses and beaches. In the rural townships, however, they are excluded from all but two or three stores, and the hotels.

"I haven't heard you use words like 'bloke,' 'joker,' or 'blighter,' " I said.

"No," said Barry. "You seldom hear such language outside the rougher pubs." They didn't talk of chaps either, but "blot his copy book," "sorted out," and "mixed bag" were common in their speech. "Fellow" was frequently used, and "ah yeh" instead of New Zealand's "ah yiss."

They'd like to visit the United States but aren't sure they can get work permits and don't believe they could afford it otherwise. I assured them it's less costly to travel there than they were given to think. All of these people travel extensively to the different Australian States, and to New Zealand, England, the Continent, Hong Kong, Japan, even China. But America both fascinates and frightens them. If they went to the U.S. more than they do, more Americans would visit Australia.

My doctor in Manly got his degree at Northwestern University in Evanston; but though he spent eighteen months in Chicago he didn't care too much for it. On the other hand the chemist from whom I obtained the doctor's prescription had a rip-roaring time during the twelve months he and a friend spent in the U.S. back in 1936. They bought a used car in Los Angeles and drove it all over the country and down to Mexico City. The car had, as he put it, "several spills" and each time they would wire the insurance company to say they had had a terrible accident. A wire would come back instructing them to take the car to such and such a garage and get it fixed. This invariably meant a general overhaul and a complete new paint job, as the garage man was only too ready to get into the insurance company for all the money he could. One such spill occurred in Mexico where the car's insurance didn't reach, but they managed to get it limping back into the U.S., and from Albuquerque they wired that they'd had a terrible accident. Going into Mexico and back over very bad roads they wore out a set of new tyres but, since these were covered by a twelve-month guarantee, they got another set free—only the dealer wouldn't guarantee the new set. At the end of their year they'd had so many insurance claims the company cancelled their policy. When they squawked about this their full year's premium was returned. Finally after 48,000 miles they sold the car for $65 less than they'd paid for it. Which, as the chemist said, wasn't bad, was it?

8

2

DECEMBER 31: Immigration officials boarded the ship at the harbour heads at 6.30 this morning. We didn't have to be out that early but I was anyhow—to see whether Sydney Harbour lived up to its reputation. Of course I wasn't able to take it all in and what I have is a succession of individual impressions: the high, nearly vertical cliffs of the heads themselves and the surf dashing against them, some grey concrete boxes on the equally high opposite shore which someone said were gun emplacements commanding the harbour entrance. All the same a Japanese submarine did slip through during the war and sank one of the large ferries that run to the suburb of Manly. While I was hearing about this a ferry overtook and passed us heading for Sydney.

The city lay low on almost the only part of the shore that isn't a high wooded bluff. We passed a tiny white wooden lighthouse, a favourite roosting place for seagulls. Two kiwi ladies were eagerly calling each other's attention to landmarks they'd last seen several years ago. One identified the lighthouse as Pinchgut Island and marvelled at "how they've changed it." While she was going on about it the other looked ahead and saw the real Pinchgut Island, an old grey fortress with a grey stone wall around it, and she tried in vain to draw her friend's attention to it.

A large inchoate shape in concrete, bristling all over with cranes, came in view and both ladies had a good laugh over it. A middle-aged gentleman I had been talking to said disgustedly, "An eyesore. The best thing would be to put a bomb in it and blow it up." I asked, "What is it?" and he gaped at me. Was it possible anyone could fail to recognize Sydney's folly, trumpeted throughout the world? He had been saying proudly that he thought Australia would ultimately support a population of a hundred million or so. "After all, the United States is largely desert." He had been surprised to discover just how little good land there is there.

9

Australia might have to have its north populated by Asians. He wasn't too sure she was getting the best migrants now. "They all want to live in the cities." As for the country's falling birth rate, "young people are waiting until they have a home of their own. They can't raise children in flats." His own niece and nephew-in-law were a case in point. They wanted children but first they had to pay off on their block of land in order to obtain finance for building a house. Sydney's great need was for housing.

And then—as we passed the complex of concrete and cranes— "Look at that eyesore, the money and manpower wasted on it." The architect had really made suckers of Sydneysiders. "There's a supermarket in Norway or Denmark or one of those countries exactly like it. He entered the competition purely as a joke, never expected to be taken seriously, just made a rough sketch of this supermarket and sent it in. Somebody saw it and insisted it get the prize. Some American architect named Sorenson or Silverman."

It seemed to all boil down to a question of politics. Darrell Raineau, who was a Liberal, said the Sydney Opera House was being financed by a lottery, and the lottery was such a popular thing people queued up for tickets. Hence with money so easy to raise the architect kept thinking of improvements to spend it on. He got six per cent of everything spent and the cost had risen from an original estimate of $7,000,000 to $60,000,000 and no end in sight. Seeing a lifelong career for himself in this single project the architect had migrated to Sydney and built a home and workshop in the posh suburb of Palm Beach, where he kept coming up with clever schemes. Raineau didn't much fancy Sydney's Opera House. Melbourne's more conventional, and more conventionally financed, Art Centre was a far handsomer building in his opinion.

Herb Fitzroy on the other hand, who also lived in Melbourne but voted Labor, argued vehemently that "they must keep the Dane on the job. He's the only one who can finish it properly. It isn't costing the people anything. If they didn't have the Opera House Lottery to invest in they'd do their dough in the poker machines or at the races." Sydney to him was an unsightly city, dirty and scrappy looking, too much like pictures of the New York skyline. Its only redeeming feature was the Opera House. "And it isn't costing nobody nothing!"

My most lasting impression is of the solidity of the hills bordering the harbour, littered all over with the cubes and corners of houses, flats, and red roofs, yet remaining somehow green. And the

wide sweep of the city's skyline, not high and not inspiring but nice to look at in the low morning sun. As we turned to glide under the bridge everybody looked nervously up to see if we would clear it. Surely the Christmas tree lashed to the topmost mast . . . But we did and, breathing more easily, went in to breakfast and the Immigration line-up. Then for the big trek.

And it was a trek. Few taxis would cruise as far out of town as our ship found its berth. The Circular Quay is virtually in the city itself but, although there was no passenger ship there, we tied up in the sticks. Or rather I should say "the bush," which seems to be the Australian equivalent.

Bush *means forest in Australia as in Canada or any other part of the British Commonwealth. The bush, however, is peculiarly Australian, suggestive of swagmen, bullock drovers, tea boiled in a billy over an open fire, and the indigenous myth of mateship. The bush, as a concept, evokes in every "dinkum Aussie's" heart the nostalgia of his country's largely unrecorded past.*

11

The bush as a place, or up bush, *is wherever people are not—or relatively few. The desert, where there is of course no bush at all, is pre-eminently the bush, but so is any small town. To that great majority of Australians who dwell in or near large cities the entire countryside is the bush. "Sydney or the bush," an expression signifying that one's choices have narrowed to no more than two, implies this even of Melbourne.*

It was a long walk through twisting streets, up and down hills, inevitably finding ourselves lost in a neighbourhood called the Rocks that evidently dates back to the earliest white settlement of Australia. But it was worth it. I hadn't expected to see kangaroos springing about on Sydney sidewalks (called footpaths here) as some of the passengers seemed to think. But neither had I expected this, this clatter, this frenzy, this vigour. What I really expected, I guess, was simply a large edition of Auckland, and it was good on the eyes to see metropolitan bustle again: crowds milling everywhere. Cars, mostly taxis, darting swiftly into streets from every angle and missing one another by a whisker. Cranes creaking overhead, sidewalks excavated beneath our feet.

It was as well we walked it. We had leisure to examine the old buildings of the dockside area known as Pyrmont with their New Orleans-type wrought iron balconies, bricks, palms, and general look of tumble-down picturesqueness. Lived in, as they most certainly are—the balconies display almost as much laundry as they do in Hong Kong—they are slums, but looked at are quite lovely. Crowded side by side, each with its collection of chimney pots, and a church squeezed tightly in among them, they sound a note of history and great age that jars rather pleasantly in this youthful country.

Sydney's skyline has still to grow, and is growing. At present it seems to consist chiefly of cranes perched on top of scaffolding, and tall hoardings pasted over with posters attacking conscription or advertising salacious literature. Chalked on one fence: "Hands off Cuba," "LBJ means war," "World Federalism," "Peace," and "Down with zip flies!"

The famous harbour bridge, its roadway suspended from a high arch between two pairs of pillars, is still the first thing you catch sight of coming by sea. Amid the throngs of people, the traffic policemen on duty at busy intersections, tiny horse-drawn delivery wagons and towering double-decker buses, tinier shops that seem to have room for hardly any save the clerks, massive department stores that seem to have no clerks at all, and still more massive public buildings which look to have stood from the beginning of time, we also saw beggars—one in a wheelchair, one blind man singing *When Irish Eyes are Smiling,* and one terribly old and terribly bent woman with a hessian bag in which she was collecting bottles and other litter. We needed no headlines of ANOTHER SWITCH-BLADE KNIFING to reassure us that kangaroos were not the menace we had to fear on the streets of Sydney. Candi of course was delighted, but after we'd tramped the same streets several times hunting an elusive shoe store—Fay's, or was it Foy's? —all she wanted was a place to sit, with a cold bottle of pop (called fizzy or lolly water) and a bite to eat.

By now I was convinced Sydneysiders don't eat their lunches off a table. Girls from shops and offices sit on the grass and eat out of a paper bag from home. Male clerks and shop assistants stand at a bar in a pub, in one hand a glass of beer, in the other a newspaper-wrapped parcel of fish and chips, ripped open at one end. Shoppers and their infants eat on the run meat pies smothered in catsup (called to-mah-to soce) and ice-cream. In Hyde Park, where much of the eating goes on, the City Council and the New South Wales Opera Company were giving an open-air concert to an accompaniment of bus exhausts and drag-racing taxis in adjoining Park Street. They had a sound truck and a piano on the grass, and a microphone to give a boost to the singers' voices. People sat or stood, ate, and listened.

We settled at last for a Devonshire tea at the rear of a milk bar. A milk bar is a small and ubiquitous food (or tucker) shop, selling everything packageable except—more often than not—milk. A Devonshire tea I discovered consists of scones, butter, thick cream, jam, and tea or coffee. Except for the coffee this was satisfactory. The British seem lately to have taken to coffee as a fashionable substitute for tea. As fashionably served the waiter stands behind you and pours from two pewter pitchers. With a gesture you control the flow and get a hot-milk mixture; not coffee, but something vaguely familiar . . .

I've just remembered: Postum! Years ago the makers of this drink, brewed from toasted barley and hitherto offered as a substitute to sufferers from "coffee nerves," threw in the sponge and ran huge ads asserting: "Postum doesn't taste anything like coffee! It doesn't taste like tea! It has its own distinctive taste!"

Distinctive no longer. British (and Australian) coffee tastes exactly like Postum.

After one last and this time successful search for the store where Peggy and Candi had spotted the shoes they wanted to buy, we got out on the streets after five, in time to see and be jostled by crowds running to catch subway trains or standing patiently in line for buses. So, laden with their old shoes and a pair of tight long pants for Candi, we walked the long way back to the ship. A person attempting to flag a cab here is an object of public ridicule.

It was open sitting at dinner (tea in Australia). Our table companions were a very pukka sahib and his wife who've been six years in Mount Albert, New Zealand, but have sold their home and are moving to Melbourne. Pukka Sahib, complete to Rudyard Kipling moustache, described Auckland as the only memorial park which is illuminated; warned me our steward was angry because I had served myself salad; advised Peggy in the kindest way that her method of eating, changing hands on her fork as she did, was inefficient.

Over a dinner of steak, chips (french fries), mashed pumpkin, peas, and salad we listened to the invocation, heard the attendance figures and "President Bertie" as he introduced the Sergeant-at-arms. He in turn fined everyone 20 cents for not having had or, alternatively, having had a cold so far this year. We watched a U.S. Bureau of Standards film dealing with the sun. At the end we stood and faced the Queen's portrait (which looked like a Russian icon with its Byzantine background) and sang "the national anthem," holding in our hands our hitherto untouched glasses of water. I was surprised when I saw water being poured, and thought of some comment on its rarity at the Australian table. Just as well I didn't utter it. The water was not for drinking, just toasting.

The Rotarians all ate with both hands of course. I told Llewellyn the shoestore proprietor—short, bald, and energetic—I had by now mastered the art to the point where I could carry food with my left hand. This was hardly more than a good beginning. My knife was still idle most of the time and lay useless on the plate after it had performed its minimum task of cutting the steak. Peter the dentist, a picture of the tired-eyed, quiet-voiced Britisher though born in Australia, sat down after the rest of us had started; and again I was able to observe what excellent use can be made of the knife, both as a cutter of other foods than meat—potatoes and lettuce for instance—and as a loader.

We had peas. I slid the tines of my fork under them and carried them precariously up to my mouth. Most rolled off on the way. By leaning over the plate, lips protruding to the peas and my head coming forward to meet them, I secured one or two. Those that

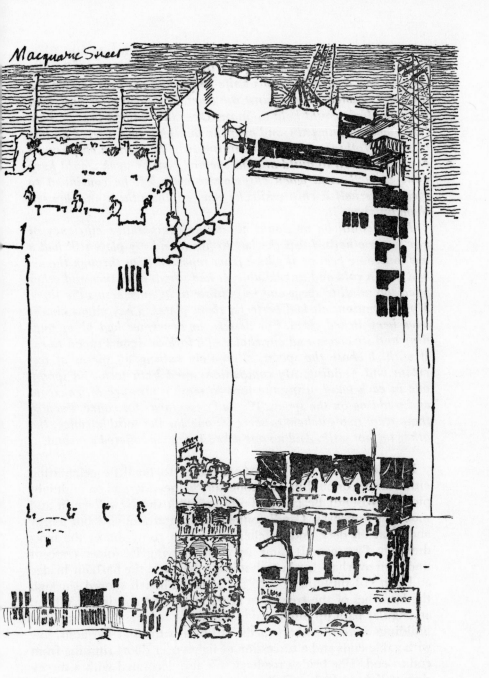

Macquarie Street

fell landed safely back on the plate rather than in my lap. Peter turned his fork over, standing the tines on the plate after having speared half a chip. With his knife he pushed the peas toward the fork and mashed them against the tines, knifeload after knifeload until the fork would hold no more. Over the mashed peas he plastered mashed pumpkin, and over the pumpkin he buttered on bits of salad. Nothing was ever lost in transit. The speared chip served as a foundation to build on, but speared peas or steak would have done as well. And when chips alone were left he continued to spear only half a chip while he mashed the others and pressed them on above it.

There could be no doubt about the comparative efficiency of our two methods. I was the last to finish and my plate still had a few lonesome peas on it which from repeated trips through the air had grown cold and unpalatable. It had shreds of lettuce and other salad too small to spear and impossible to balance across the tines. My companions all had perfectly clean plates. They might almost have been licked clean. For dessert, or sweet, we had plum pudding and ice-cream and our choice of a fork or dessert spoon to eat it with. I chose the spoon, alternately cutting off pieces of ice-cream and pudding. My companions used both fork and spoon, one in each hand, using the fork to mash a mixture of ice-cream and pudding on the spoon. We had demi-tasses for coffee. Even so there were two pitchers to serve it: one for the soluble coffee, the other for hot milk. And no one asked for or was offered a second.

It's New Year's Eve but there seems to be little celebrating either ashore or on ship. Someone said Sydneysiders go on midnight picnics to Bondi Beach or Manly to drink the New Year in and shoot off fireworks. Candi found some entertainment but Peggy and I sat on deck and watched the moon rise—one of the most dramatic I've seen. It came up, first showing its upper crescent under an overhanging branch midway between the harbour bridge and two tall buildings far to the south. Then it moved through the branches of the tree at an acute angle and continued still on an angular path up into the sky. Below the bridge, trees, and office buildings were the wharf sheds—all of a pattern at Pyrmont, low with gable ends and a succession of lights over doors running from end to end. The bridge roadway was also decorated with a succession of lights which were blue in late afternoon and twilight but seemingly pure white at night. (Is the colour of the moon really blue?) All these lights and the shadows which accompanied them were reflected in the water between the ship and the shore.

16

3

JANUARY 1: A lucky chance brought a taxi and a late-celebrating crew member out to Pyrmont wharf this morning just as we were setting off on our long trudge to the city. The driver told me to sit with him in front and give my daughter and granddaughter more room in back.

"Wife and daughter," I corrected him. He looked steadily at me.

"Nothing but thin steel walls between cabins on the ship," I explained. "Whistling, doors banging, coughing, tramping overhead all across the Tasman. Other passengers snoozed all day in the public lounges; I never learned how. My wife happens to be a scant three years younger than me."

He continued to look disbelieving. "If it was me, mate, I'd have a go at flying."

"This sitting in the front seat in a taxi," I probed. "They do it in New Zealand and nobody thinks anything about it; but I read six books about Australia in the ship's library: three by Englishmen and one each by a Frenchman, a Dane, and a Czech, and they all made a big thing of it. How democratic it is."

"Rubbish," said the driver. "The front seat is highest on the pecking order." It was my turn to look steadily at him.

"I'm a sociology student at Sydney University. This is my last trip on the shift."

"This pecking order."

"A man and a woman get in a cab, the man sits in front, naturally. They tell me that in America—" with a faint lilt of inquiry —"the women don't carry parcels, they don't push the baby's pram or the little cart in the supermarket, they don't even take the dog out for his walk. It's not that way in Australia." He pronounced his country's name with evident pride. "The man is boss."

"How about two men?"

17

"If one outranks the other, he sits in front."

"Doesn't a woman ever get to sit in front?"

"Yes, sometimes as a gesture of respect if she is elderly, and especially if she's wealthy, the man will offer her the front seat."

It's a toss-up which is the brightest jewel in Sydney's diadem, its harbour or its parkland. The harbour is one of the world's great natural wonders but the parkland is almost a greater miracle, that it should survive on the highest priced land in Australia. It is as large as the city's entire commercial area and immediately adjoins it, so that office workers and shop assistants need only cross the street at lunchtime. These parks, in an outdoor community like Sydney, are the venue of much civic activity. All official parades and welcoming receptions originate here. The Queen speaks to her subjects from the porch of the Art Gallery in the Domain. On Anzac Day veterans of the futile and bloody assault on Gallipoli, in what Australians still call the Great War, assemble in their different companies in allotted places in the Domain. From there they march through the city to commemorate the occasion when Australia ceased symbolically to be a British colony and became a nation. So our cabbie said before he dropped us at the Circular Quay.

"Last night I went to see Alan Seymour's One Day of the Year. *It was really marvellous. Or it would have been if it had finished at the end of the second act. I thought it had, actually, and when the curtain went down then I was ready to proclaim it a masterpiece. It was a perfect balance of humour and argument. The characters were real good too. They were really Australian—not that fake Australian either. They spoke almost like at the Basil's only a little cruder. The mother was especially good, in the way she poured the tea, washed the dishes, even how she pulled her cardigan around her; she really lived the part. Most kids liked the father and he was good too, only I thought a little too close to the prototype for comfort.*

"It is sort of the story of Anzac Day, the day Australians remember those who died in the first war in patriotism and reverence. The family is poor and their uni-student son looks down on his parents. He gets in with this girl snob from Sydney's North Shore and they decide to write an article showing the real Anzac Day— a universal booze-up. That is the general idea anyway, and in the first two acts both the pro and con of Anzac Day are presented about equally. And it is real funny.

"Then the third act came. Actually it has been a struggle to

18

remember how good I thought the first two acts were with the bitter taste of that last act still in my mouth. It spoiled the point of the whole play. Instead of being a logical question on the merits of Anzac Day it became the story of an inhuman son senselessly tormenting his parents. It's a sentimental psychiatric mess. The girl and boy turn into neurotic monsters and the old man, who seemed a jolly old fellow, a bit too fond of beer and the Australian adjective, turns into a poor martyr.

"I think what happened the author got worried that he hadn't come down hard enough on the side of Anzac Day; he'd left it sort of ambiguous whether it was a good thing or not. He was worried over his Aussie audience and what they might think. And it's true, I was the only one in our crowd who even liked the first two acts. They thought the third was far the best. Linda Highery couldn't stand the first act. I think it may have been because in that there was a lot of razzing of 'bloody poms and bloody eye-tyes' and she is one of the former (though not a bloody one, she is actually very nice). They also razzed the bloody Yanks though and I didn't mind. Meredith liked the third act best. Her favorite line was in the second though, when the father came home drunk and talked about his exploits on Anzac Day and he said, 'So I sez to him— good-ay you old bastard!' She says it is pure Broken Hill."

The Circular Quay is a much more impressive gateway to the city than Pyrmont. It has a new passenger terminal and new railway station, many new office buildings up or on the way up, and a wide mall and park along the waterfront. Jutting out from the mall like fingers are the busy wharves for harbour traffic. Ferries, double-ended for travel in either direction, were gliding in and out almost constantly, serving a score or more harbour-side suburbs. On Mrs Collins's advice, who said we must be sure not to miss it, we ferried over to Taronga Park Zoo and climbed a long hill to the zoo entrance, unaware that everyone else was going up by bus. Then down again past the exhibits and back by ferry and taxi to the ship for lunch. It was hot; and Candi, who had come to see the kangaroos, got dreadfully thirsty, so we didn't stay long or see much. It seems a pretty good zoo though and its setting must be the finest in the world. I found myself looking past the cages over trees, battleships, and freighters under various flags, to the ferries fanning out from Circular Quay, and to Sydney itself bright and sparkling in the morning sun. The young hairdressers compared Sydney to San Francisco and New York. I thought it far-fetched but looking at it over open water, rising suddenly with

19

no foreground litter and none of the roads, shacks, and billboards that announce other cities, it does resemble the Manhattan of Scott Fitzgerald's day. The buildings, not very tall and not distinguished architecturally, gain in impressiveness by being seen from bottom to top. As we zigzagged downhill the sun glinted from windows and threw brilliant and quickly disappearing reflections on the water. I hollered from the ferry to a crewman on the *Ostragoshk* out of Vladivostok, "Zdravsvuitye, tovarish." Either he didn't understand Russian or didn't hear me.

We lunched and came out just as we were casting away, breaking hundreds of coloured paper streamers. We again just managed to clear the bridge and passed the grinning moonface of something called Luna Park. We slipped silently by the tree-covered shores close to some picnickers on one of the points, past ships at berth, tugs pulling log rafts, Greek ships at anchor. The sun was high now but the distant houses, flats, and shops of the harbour suburbs were still jumbled together, not spectacularly slapped against a hillside as in Wellington or San Francisco, but rising in a steady solid climb, seeming to form a toothed monolith. The sky was clouding over. The Russian freighter with hammer and sickle on the stack was still in the stream, looking more Japanese than Russian. So were the *Auckland Star*, the *City of Wollongong*, and a Norwegian freighter with a first name *Olav*. And U.S. and Australian naval vessels at the entrance to the wharves of Woolloomooloo. We waved to some children on the Manly ferry and slid smoothly between the heads into the Tasman. In almost no time at all, what little skyline Sydney seemed to have was flattened out, leaving only the bridge showing when the land itself disappeared. Australia lies very low in the water. A small ship would need to run in very close to be able to sight it. This was no doubt the reason why, vast as it was, it was unlikely to be discovered even by the 16th-century Dutch who maintained a busy sailing schedule between Africa and south-east Asia. Unless it got stumbled over.

From Greek and Roman times theoretical geographers had been certain there was an Australia, and the Chinese appear to have visited and made a map of it some seventy years before Columbus discovered America. But though Australia spans 33 degrees of latitude—in Northern Hemisphere terms from Panama to Boston—it eluded European discovery until 1606. Late in that year the Spaniard Luis Vaez de Torres entered Torres Strait and passed within a few miles of it—yet failed to see it. Almost simultaneously the Dutchman Willem Jansz briefly landed on and was driven off the west coast of Cape York, the northernmost part of the continent. Thus, quite incidentally and still largely unnoticed, Australia was found.

Nowhere is the name of its discoverer preserved, either in a Mount Jansz, a Jansz River, Jansz Bay, Jansz Island, Jansz Peninsula, or Jansz Point. No tiny hamlet is called Jansz, no city has a Jansz Street, no anniversary of the discovery has ever been celebrated nor any postage stamp issued bearing the Jansz portrait. It goes without saying that there is no Jansz Day to keep company with the Queen's Birthday, Australia Day, Commonwealth Day, Anzac Day, Boxing Day, Easter Monday, and the other holidays that brighten the Australian calendar. No mythological goddess named Janszia is celebrated in Australian poetry; no anthem is sung to Janszia the Gem of the Ocean. *Not one Australian schoolchild in 10,000 knows the name. All believe their country was discovered by Captain Cook, though Cook didn't arrive for another 163 years.*

Meanwhile in 1611 the Dutch made a change in the trading route from Good Hope to the Indies. They stopped hugging the shore of Africa to go north and set off instead directly east from the Cape for 4,000 miles, taking advantage of winds which reduced the eighteen-month voyage to six. In 1616 Dirk Hartog went a bit too far east before turning and lo, there was Australia. The island he saw, about half-way up the west coast, is named after him. In 1642 Abel Tasman sailed half-way around the low-lying continent before sighting the mountains of Tasmania. So, in one way or another, the north and west coasts, and the south for 1,000 miles east of Cape Leeuwin, were observed, charted, and rejected. The British, last in the line of discovery, were the first to find a use for the land. It was a perfect exile for unwanted rogues.

In less than twenty years after Cook returned from his historic first voyage—during which he circumnavigated and charted the whole of New Zealand and explored nearly 2,000 miles of the hitherto unknown Australian east coast—convicts were settled at Sydney. This was in 1788. By 1825 all the principal seaports of the east and south, including Tasmania, were convict labour camps. Adelaide, founded in 1836 by the utopian economist E. G. Wakefield—himself an ex-convict—was the single exception. In less than six decades after 1810, when the rush really began, some 150,000 British convicts were landed in New South Wales, Queensland, Victoria, Tasmania, and Western Australia. This was to a group of colonies whose total white population, including free South Australia, amounted to only 190,000 in 1840.

4

"*You could pay 50 cents and stand on the mound of dirt around the oval or you could go posh and pay 60 cents and get in the part with the grandstand. We went posh. The stands were full but we stood on these concrete steps in front. Uncle George came all in his Sunday best suit and white shirt and tie, and I thought oh yeah, he probably hasn't had time to change from work. But all the men were dressed like that! They looked like they were going to church instead of a football match.*

"*It started with a burst of enthusiasm for the Centrals but Norths got a behind first and then Centrals did amid a roar of applause; and up to the first quarter they held a good lead. As soon as the players left the field at the end of the quarter all the little kids jumped the fence and crowded all over the field until they were pulled out by loud hailers and policemen. Everyone on the concrete steps sat down. The men spread out pocket handkerchiefs or programmes or newspaper to sit on but the ladies, who weren't so well dressed, sat on the bare steps. When the players came on again everyone stood up. The steps were about two feet wide but everyone stood on the very front edge of them.*

"*There was no pushing or shouting or rough house. Nothing like Auntie Bess had led me to expect when she told about the time she was up in Melbourne and it was Victoria versus Tazzie, and she sang out, 'Come on Tasmania!' A lady behind her promptly hit her over the head with a brolly, a man stood on her feet, and when she was leaving the match when it was over they just about beat her up. This one I went to on the other hand was very mild. All the people stood very still, reminding me of Seurat's picture of* La Grande Jatte, *except when a goal or a behind was kicked. Then there was applause.*

"*If you were very sporting like Uncle George you applauded whichever side kicked it even though he was grinding his teeth in the last breathtaking minutes hoping Centrals would win. Most people only applauded the side they were barracking for. It wasn't that they weren't keen though. You had to be keen to stand there two or three hours and not do anything but watch. And they really did enjoy it. Especially the Centrals barrackers. They practically breathed every breath with the team and knew everyone by name. I enjoyed it too.*

"Aussie Rules is real easy to understand and this one was a very lively game because the scores were so even. Centrals weren't really very good players. They were terribly quick and active but they consistently threw and kicked the ball right into Norths's hands. Norths on the other hand always kicked to one of their own players who wasn't covered by a Centrals player. They weren't too hard to find either because Centrals were too busy running around the field trying to get goals, to guard their men very well. In the last five minutes Norths were two goals and two behinds ahead, but then Centrals got three in a row to win by four points."

JANUARY 2: After a day which was cold and windy as we rounded Wilson's Promontory into Bass Strait that separates the mainland from the island of Tasmania, but which turned sunny, we entered Port Phillip Bay and docked at the Station Pier in Port Melbourne about six. We saw our car unloaded and made sure it went back on; and I talked to a boilermaker from Perth, fifty years old and born there of a father who was born there. Investing in a building and loan company which doubles his money in ten years, he has been using part of the proceeds for the cruise. He flies back to Perth tomorrow. With a movie camera strapped to his wrist he shot 800 feet of film on the voyage and tramped around Sydney shooting film till his wife's feet got sore. He chuckled over the swindlers charging ten cents for a five-cent roll of the coloured streamer paper they use here to farewell a ship. "You don't find people like that in Perth," I said.

"I'm one myself," he said proudly. "This money I make on building loans comes from the high interest rates—25 per cent— the people pay who buy homes. The loan company charges the interest but they couldn't if people like me didn't put their money in it."

"And don't forget. The same company will turn around and swindle you," I said. "They did it in California." This made him a little uncomfortable but he asserted he could get his money out any time he liked. I told him from what I'd seen of Sydney, American products for sale everywhere I looked, we seemed about to take the country over. He said, "We'd rather you'd take us over than the poms" (pronouncing it pawms). "Do you get a lot of poms in Perth?" "A lot of what?" "Didn't you call the English migrants poms?" "Oh, pawms! Woodbines if you'd rather."

"Miss Petunia had her usual collection of professional discussers. There was this one absolutely typical pom woman of about thirty, good looking, with the usual black-rimmed glasses, who is part of a publishing firm or something and couldn't bear to do her own washing or anything that menial, and had the most atrocious accent. She was so typically fake, though, I mean almost the stereotype fake, that you wondered at Miss Petunia inviting her.

"And then this silly Yank who really made you blush for your country. There was nothing fake about her but she was just sort of feather-brained. She would get so excited she would lose her voice and squeak, and her accent made me blush; and all she seemed to be able to say, or rather scream, was that American women took active part in civil government and got elected to school boards and DID things.

"The whole panel was just a collection of discontented émigrés: a Scottish obstetrician, the Yank, the pom, all deploring the plight of the woman in Australia and rubbishing Australia in general. It sure is funny. If a pom of the lower classes migrates over here and starts griping, everyone hates him and tells him to go back if he doesn't like it. But these upper class ones, or rather these 'intellectual' class ones, they can tear the country to pieces and everyone sits there gaga-eyed and applauds the more insulting they are.

"And they were such clichés that they said anyway, like the men going over to one side of the room at a party and the women to another. I think the reason the Yanks can get away with it more is they aren't very often lower class ones that come out here. But oh, if you heard that 'gal'! (She kept on saying 'gal' instead of 'woman' or 'lady.') She was just so loud and so dogmatic and such a woman with a cardboard cause, like schoolboard running, because she didn't have enough up top to look around her and see what really needed protesting about and thinking about."

JANUARY 3: Last evening was noisy with visiting Melbournians running and shouting in the halls; and every Australian male who went to bed after the bars closed whistling his way first to his room, then to the lavatories and back to his room again. We breakfasted early today. Then to town by taxi, finding Melbourne far less frenzied than Sydney but at the same time more metropolitan.

Its skyline of tall buildings is compact and even rather venerable, with a serene and substantial look as though it meant to stay. The streets are wide and straight; and one in particular, Collins, is quite lovely. Lined with trees and fine, well-kept 19th-century stone façades of columns and arches, it goes uphill to a pair of old stone public buildings set in a large park.

Melbourne is evidently a city, though, that has to be lived in to be fully appreciated. A quick visit won't do, as it will for Sydney, to account for the fierce loyalty of its residents. Our cabbie said he wouldn't live anywhere else, and certainly not Sydney. Sydney was always just going to be a city and never quite making it—though he granted its environs, and especially the harbour shores, might be a point in Sydney's favour. But a veteran guard on one of the Victorian Railways suburban lines would not concede even this. Melbourne was prettier all round; its parks were bigger and more colourful; its streets wider; its restaurants served better meals; its population now was even growing faster.

A lot of British migrants settled in Sydney, I reminded him. He said he thought they probably liked that way of life better, more night life, more competitive, more in the rat race, more cutting the other bloke's throat, more . . . "You mean more like an American city?" "I wasn't going to say so," he replied diplomatically, "but that's it in a nutshell. We're more easy going here in Melbourne. We take life easier."

"Even at the footy?" I said quizzically. "Isn't there any truth in these stories I've heard about Melbourne's near-hysteria in the football season? The battles with flour bombs? Mayhem on and off the field?"

"Ah, the footy. Well, that's different."

The game was Aussie Rules, a Victorian creation played in all save two Australian States. New South Wales favoured Rugby League, probably for the same reason that its railway gauge was different than Victoria's, and Queensland followed suit. There were 18 players to each side, plus two reserves which, like the spare tyres on a car, had to last. When they got used up there would be no more. A player once taken out of a game could not go back in and his team must, if necessary, play short-handed.

The oval-shaped field was extremely large, as it perhaps needed to be to accommodate so many players, together with several umpires who were often in the very thick of the fray; and fray it was sometimes with tempers snapping and fights breaking out to the immense delight of the spectators. Two pairs of goal posts were set at each end of the oval, one pair very tall and spaced about the same distance as in soccer. A ball kicked squarely between the two inner posts scored six points and was called a goal. A typical game might have twelve or more goals to each side. A second and shorter pair of posts, outside the first, formed a wider goal to accommodate near misses as when an angle kick, just missing a goal, sailed behind the goal post. Such a near miss, worth one point, was called quite properly a behind. The score was tabulated in goals and behinds—each evoking a cheer and a groan—and total points determined the winner.

The numerous scores, the multitude of players, the size of their arena, and the mobility of play—as the teams surged, not merely up and down field, but in every direction over the vast oval— made an attractive game to watch. But the chief ingredient of the footy's popularity, I believe, is its chanciness. It is by no means certain that the best team will win. On form the visiting Wombats were the best team today. In the early afternoon preliminary between the B teams they easily downed the Galahs. And when the main contest commenced it was readily apparent they would win, simply by keeping the ball in Galah territory and kicking it to one of their own men—or better say to a group of players in which their men outnumbered their opponents.

The general strategy of the game called for pairing opposing players. Each Wombat had his Galah twin and they went everywhere together. But in the mêlée and among so many some were bound to be separated and a knot of men would consist of, say, six Wombats and four Galahs—or vice versa. The difference between the teams was that Wombats kickers aimed at knots in which their men held a majority, giving them a better than even chance of catching—or marking—the ball. The Galahs simply kicked in the direction of the Wombats' goal and, as often as not, this would be at a cluster in which their opponents predominated. For Wombats kickers, who took the trouble to select their clusters, the proportion of enemy marks, or catches, was about 40 per cent, or 60 per cent in the Wombats' favour. For Galah kickers it should have been 50-50, except that chance was on the Galahs' side today. Many a Galah kick, aimed blindly at a group in which Galahs were outnumbered, was caught by a Galah man; and three in particular were crucial marks directly in front of the goal.

After such a mark a player has time for a leisurely drop-kick while the personnel of both teams take positions ahead of him to deflect the ball or prevent its being deflected. Other kicks, not

26

from a mark, are made freely in play—as in soccer—and free kicks, similar to marks, are also lavishly awarded as penalties.

Today's game, attended by 40,000 or so screaming barrackers, was a model of everything that footy should be. The Wombats early established their superiority by rolling up three goals to none. The Galahs fought harder than the Wombats felt like fighting after having demonstrated their ability to turn on a score at will, and gradually came within striking distance. Then chance took over and the Galahs went ahead. The Wombats settled down again to serious play and clicked the goals and behinds off like clockwork—especially behinds which, though counting little, could easily have been goals. Ultimately, with so many of them, one or more would. But time ran out on the Wombats and they lost the game by one point: a made-to-order finish for the largely pro-Galah crowd.

If the footy were played with a round soccer ball or, like another game it resembles, a basketball, much of the chance would be taken out of it. But the long, tapered, sausage-shaped ball, almost never carried but kicked and batted constantly, may fly in any direction off the foot and off the ground. It is even put in play by the umpire bouncing it off the ground in a ten-foot circle in the center of the oval. It is pre-eminently a children's game.

The match between the Wombats and Galahs was by no means the only game played in Melbourne this Saturday. There were five other big ones, with gates of 10,000 or more, and dozens of smaller ones in the outer suburbs and throughout Victoria. This goes on every week in the autumn and winter. The six leading games are broadcast play by play over radio, then later re-broadcast by television; and all week long the sport sections of Melbourne's newspapers are filled with pictures and gossip of footy personalities.

And still I don't think the game will last. It will pass with the youth and innocence of the country. British and European migrants, impatient with a game so lacking in "science," will have their way in the end, and the comparative dullness of soccer and rugby will triumph. Australia, facing its international responsibilities and becoming a great nation among great nations, will accept the sobering reality and admit that even in its play it must take itself more seriously.

Every successful Galah mark or kick during the game was greeted with blowing of horns, ringing of cowbells, and cries of "Lovely!" or "Bloody lovely!" Shuffling out at the end through an ankle-high carpet of food wrappings and beer cans I heard the match neatly summarized: "It was bloody beautiful, wasn't it?"

27

5

It was Sunday, so life in Melbourne was easier than usual, and a typical Melbourne Sunday, I was assured. The footpaths were deserted save for an occasional shabbily dressed man. The famous Flinders Street railway station—said on weekdays to be the busiest in the Southern Hemisphere—was filled with nothing but echoes and a few confectionery shops, garishly lighted in the vast gloom. No theatres, concerts, or motion pictures; no Sunday newspapers, and definitely no bars. If you desperately wanted diversion, and your favorite church did not open its doors until 7.30 in the evening, there were unattended stacks of magazines at convenient distances on the footpaths. You evidently took one off the stack and hunted for some receptacle to drop your money into. Or—it just occurs to me—perhaps one of the shabbily dressed men, perceiving your interest, would sidle up and let you pay him. Buying the *Australian Woman's Weekly* could thus have some of the conspiratorial excitement of filthy postcards in Paris or a fix in Harlem. Apparently nothing is allowed to be sold on Sunday except sweets, rancid coffee, and roasted peanuts. So we bought a bag of peanuts and shelled them beside one litter basket after another as we plodded the melancholy streets. This was our lunch.

I suppose Melbourne would receive as many Sunday visitors as any other port city of two million—from ships and overnight trains if not from Sunday drivers. It speaks volumes for the self-assurance of the people that they can have so little concern over making a good impression. Its port, in contrast to the colour, activity, and intimacy of Sydney Harbour, is a great grey beach—unattractive to surfers or picnickers, and rimmed by factory smokestacks; you take a train to get there. Its parks—the banks of the Yarra River, Fitzroy Gardens, and the grounds of the Mexican mausoleum which constitutes its War Memorial—are far from the

28

centre of town. Yet this very unconcern over the impression it makes could be part of the secret of Melbourne's impressiveness.

What the harbour ferries are to Sydney the electric railways are to Melbourne. From mid-city they reach out everywhere, down to Port Phillip Bay, deeper down into Mornington Peninsula where we were going, eastward to the Dandenong Mountains, north and west through vast stretches of wattle-fenced, red-roofed bungalows. Our guard had come from Holland fifteen or more years ago: the Dutch and certain east European refugees were the first non-British migrants since German Lutherans brought exotic cuttings to the Barossa Valley vineyards of South Australia early in the 19th century.

When the Yugoslav Michael arrived in Melbourne and sought a room the landlady asked, "Are you a Balt?" "Yes, I'm a Balt," he replied and got the room. Months later at a party he confessed, "I'm not a Balt." She was astounded. "You're not a Balt?" "You wouldn't have taken me in if I'd said I wasn't, but am I any different? You knew a few Balts and liked them but you didn't know other foreigners and so didn't like them. But you can't judge a whole nation by a few people." She kept shaking her head in wonder. "You're not a Balt."

Michael was a lieutenant in the Yugoslav army, fought the Germans when they invaded, became a guerrilla under Michailovic in the chetniks and continued to fight alongside the partisans under Tito until Tito and Michailovic split up. Then he fought on the Germans' side until the partisans drove him into Italy. He became a British prisoner of war there and was screened at Tito's request because the prison camp was suspected of harbouring war criminals. After screening—black, grey, and white (he was grey)—the blacks (mostly officers) were told by the British commandant, "You will be sent back home for trial, but I can't watch you all the time." Every night thereafter small groups escaped until there were no blacks among the prisoners at all. They infiltrated displaced persons camps, posing as civilian refugees. Michael himself was transferred to a D.P. camp in Germany, where he bunked with other men in a small hut and lined up for meals, going out to work from there or doing a certain amount of required work in the camp itself. "How did this life affect your morale?" I asked. "The real blow to my morale," he said, "was to come to Australia and be put into exactly the same kind of a camp."

This was in 1950. Recruiters from Canada, Australia, and France came to the refugee camps and interviewed them. His first

choice was Canada but he lacked sufficient teeth. He'd lost four. He saw no future working in France. The Australians, learning he was a pilot and still only twenty-eight, moved him over the heads of all the others to the front of the line. "We need pilots desperately," they told him. But when he arrived in Australia they put him to work in a timber mill and he had to take it, having signed a two-year contract. At the end of his two-year stint he was too old to become an Australian pilot; twenty-eight was the oldest a recruit could be.

The news was bad again out of South-East Asia. Our Dutch guard said he'd got out the atlas and learned how close the fighting actually is to Australia. "You got a quick lesson in geography." "Too right I did. I was plain scared. I told the wife I reckoned we'd go out on the Nullarbor Plain." "And kick an Aborigine out of his humpy?" "My word! He doesn't know the value of his atom bomb shelter as well as I do." But he thought there'd be no nuclear war. His real concern was the injustice of the have toward the have-not nations, breeding revolutions.

"I fought for the Dutch resistance. My men were no good until the last six months when their children began to starve. Now they are starving in Indonesia and we with our white Australia policy —it's no good. Let them come in and work and go back with maybe £250. It's a fortune to them. My father shot the niggers in

Mombasa. He was supposed to be a good Christian but they were better Christians than he was." He stopped to slide open the door of his cab and lean out over the elevated platform we were approaching. The train slid smoothly to a halt and passengers spilled from the sides of the cars, others taking their places.

There are no conductors on these long suburban trains; the driver sits at one end and the guard at the other, though the guard may be said to sit only in a theoretical way. He has a seat, up a small flight of stairs, from which he can look ahead down the track and spot any red or yellow signals the driver fails to observe. But the suburbs follow so fast on one another—each with its yellow-brick station and long bitumen-paved platform decorated with half-sheet posters advertising silently flushing cisterns, the copper-tone baby with its pants down, wartine for warts, and "alcohol a menace—abstain"—and the guard has so many other duties hand-ling baggage and finding room in his small van for travelling policemen and homeward bound railway employees, that the signals get little extra watching. There are ramps from every plat-form running over or under the tracks, and a baggily uniformed station master or mistress to keep the exit gate locked until the train leaves, then to collect tickets when the passengers are allowed through. Many of the station masters, who also sell tickets and announce the trains, are new Australians—and the ultimate in the unintelligibility so highly prized in station announcing is reached when it is done in a pronounced foreign accent.

Our guard fitted a key into a cross-shaped slot in the doorjamb, blew a whistle, gave the key two twists answered by a short whistle blast at the other end of the train, and we were off again. He closed the door and picked up the conversational thread, his Aus-tralian idiom all the more piquant for being overlaid with a Dutch accent.

"In America you have many unemployed. If you have too many, there is trouble. My word! So you have things to sell, and if you'll pardon my saying so you don't care what you do to sell them. Not you," with a gesture to suppress an outburst, "but your big men. That is why America wants war." "Do you mean you think we want to start a war in Vietnam?" "My word! Look how you did with Hitler in 1937 and 1939. We could see war coming, but you . . ." His sentence trailed off then in the rush of a passing train. "Now Germany is still paying you for that war. Did you know

Germany was still paying you?" "I thought we were paying Germany." He smiled mysteriously.

Long as he had lived in Australia he was still of half a mind to return to Holland. There he could look forward to an old age pension equal to 80 per cent of his wage, to unemployment benefits without time limit equal to 60 per cent, and medical benefits far in advance of Australia. But, he added ruefully, the Dutch Government prefers to pay a migrant's passage back to Australia a second time—"and one man I know is putting in for a third"— rather than be saddled with unemployment benefits indefinitely.

We caught a red train with a cheerful guard, an Australian Tom Lloyd, who had been with the railways thirty-four years, having started as an apprentice at seventeen. This included war service time in Palestine. He had 22 units of superannuation, half his own contribution and half the Department's, which would entitle him to 42 dollars a week at the age of sixty-five when he retired. He also had twelve months of unused long service leave which he'd be paid for and 200 days of unused sick leave which he'd lose altogether unless he got crook some time in the next fourteen years. Instead of a pension he had the option of taking a lump sum consisting of all of his own contributions to the fund plus 44 dollars for every year of service. He hadn't made up his mind what to do. If he took the lump sum he'd spend all but 5,000 dollars of it on a trip and become a pensioner. Under the means test he was allowed to own 5,000 dollars, a home, and a car, and he thought the pension was 13 dollars a week and he and his wife could manage on that. When she reached sixty it would be $23.50; their medical care would be free.

I don't know how we got on the subject of horses but he said he didn't bet or gamble except to invest in Tattersall's. Recently he'd won ten dollars and he put it all back into Tatts tickets. What could he do with five quid? He hadn't made up his mind what he'd do if he won the big prize. "You'd get your name in the papers." "I'd have lots of fair weather friends." Oh, he'd spend a couple of thousand pounds modernizing the house, "give Mum everything in the kitchen that opens and shuts," and they'd take a trip around Australia; but there wasn't anything he wanted. He never had yearned for anything that he didn't have.

On the platform at Frankston waiting for the bus an Italian fellow passenger introduced himself as Luigi and said he owned a restaurant in Richmond. He has tried Australia repeatedly, turning his hand at everything from gold mining to seafaring, in all parts of the country. Once he stayed only a month, went back to Messina and stayed there a month. Now he's determined to stick it out for five years when he hopes to have saved enough to return to Spain perhaps, not Italy. "You're a bigger man in a foreign country. Back home they know you and think you should stay down where you were when you left."

His first trip home was for seven months but "life is so easy here in Australia your brain gets soft. You can't think as quick as the people around you do. You get shoved aside." His savings all gone he borrowed the fare back to Australia from a friend still here. A day or two before sailing he saw an American woman in Milan with a box of oranges which she set down while she unlocked her car. A thief grabbed them. Luigi thought: "I ought to stop him. But why? I have no money. I'm hungry. Maybe he's hungry too or he sells the oranges to get money. She is not hungry." When the woman discovered her loss and told Luigi he should have stopped the thief, Luigi said, "Lady, those aren't my oranges."

On his last trip back he met a girl from the south of Italy, one of a half dozen he could choose from, and picked her. "It's best to have the south Italian girl for a wife. She has no ideas of marriage being a 50-50 business. A 50-50 business don't work, even a partnership. You got to have a boss. I bring her up the way I want a wife to be. She helps me in the restaurant."

"She's very pretty," I said, looking at the young woman holding a baby on the bench behind him.

"Thank you. She used to be ugly when I met her. But I tell her what to wear, how to fix her hair. She is what I make her."

I asked about Italian social life in Australia. "There is very little. Most of the Italians here are from the south. They have no culture. They think only of making money. In five years they can save two-three thousand quid. This would be a fortune in Italy" —some millions of lire as I recall. "If they wish to go back they can be one of the upper class." "Maybe even mayor of their home town," I suggested and he agreed.

When Luigi goes back to Europe, and it must be before their three-months-old son enters school, he will take it easy. "Maybe somebody wants me to come into business. I look it over. I have the money. I make up my mind on my own terms." "You might buy an olive grove in the south of Italy." "No. I don't do that. Too much work. With 5,000 quid I can take it easy the rest of my life if I want to. But if I see a business I like I might go into it."

Moving closer he told me confidentially, "In Australia the flowers, they have no smell. The birds, they have no song. And the women, they have no ———." He closed one eye suggestively and showed a row of gold teeth. "But it's all right if you're young. I was too old when I first came here. It looks like there'll be a war too," he added seriously.

6

"By 1880," writes the historian Douglas Pike, "Melbourne's roads, bridges, harbour, gasworks, water supply, and public buildings were on a grand scale. They helped give an air of permanence to what had previously been improvised . . . Melbourne's influence reached far beyond Victoria's borders . . . From farms and goldfields the sons and daughters of selectors and miners flocked to 'Marvellous Melbourne.' Its size and population doubled in a decade as it sprawled unevenly over a hundred square miles. The rapid spread of straight streets and tin roofs brought new suburbs." On Elizabeth Street rose the Australian Building, a towering twelve-story giant that dwarfed New York's tallest skyscraper. Wrote Mark Twain five years later:

"It is a stately city architecturally as well as in magnitude. It has an elaborate system of cable-car service; it has museums, and colleges, and schools, and public gardens, and electricity, and gas, and libraries, and theatres, and mining centres, and centres of the arts and sciences, and boards of trade, and ships, and railroads, and a harbour, and social clubs, and journalistic clubs, and racing clubs, and a squatter club sumptuously housed and appointed, and as many churches and banks as can make a living. In a word, it is equipped with everything that goes to make a modern great city. It is the largest city of Australasia, and fills the post with honour and credit."

But in the 1911 census Sydney's population moved ahead of Melbourne's by 40,000 to 629,000, give or take a few thousand. More important, Sydney with its splendid harbour and more favourable location for air traffic became the major gateway to Australia. And Sydney with its winter sunshine, its ocean beaches, and its vitality—in contrast to Melbourne with its dignity, its stateliness, and its Victorian gentility—became the city to project Australia's image to the outside world.

35

From Frankston we continued by bus down to the tip of the peninsula which ends at one of the heads of Melbourne's vast harbour. The Nepean Highway rolled inland over easy hills. It turned back at the water to be confronted by the most extensive concourse of canvas I have ever seen: mile after mile after mile of tents so closely packed together they practically touch one another. They fill the entire foreshore from highway to water, are virtual summer residences, and have signs with family names on them nailed to the trees to direct visitors through the maze of narrow paths. Their centre is a town called Rosebud in which all the business activity, noise, and frivolity so noticeably missing from Melbourne's Sunday were concentrated.

Each year in the pre-Lenten season Melbourne sponsors a two-week carnival called Moomba, with parades, theatricals, concerts, outdoor and indoor displays and exhibitions. Like Sydney's Waratah and similar affairs in the other capitals, it's a kind of Australian Mardi Gras, a gay and festive public occasion. But, our driver said, compared to Rosebud on New Year's Eve, Melbourne's Moomba is a funeral procession.

Well, you'd have to have listened to people telling you what a wonderful thing this Waratah Spring Festival parade was. I muttered something about the Tournament of Roses parade in Pasadena. It, well, yes, it was all right, but Waratah—there was something! So we went.

For the most part it consisted of marching girls and marching bands, all from Bankstown. Then we saw a dozen or so Volkswagens. Some firm had a station wagon with its name on the side, and there was the usual run of floats—girls with wands and crowns—from the Departments of Health, Railways, Motor Transport, Water, and Electric Power. The most interesting thing was a group of boys pedalling by on bicycles.

We were so closely hedged in by the crowd that we had little more than peep holes to look through between people's heads. However after we managed to pull out of our trap we walked backwards along the route and saw the thousands and thousands—three-quarters of a million was the newspaper estimate—who had come out to see the parade; and they all enjoyed it.

Our guard on the return train journey was a friendly Ukrainian. "The Ukraine is part of Russia, isn't it?" I asked politely. "Never!" he declared. "The Ukraine is under Russian domination. But we'll be free when big explosion comes." Though still

quite young he was a well-cultured man who could discuss painting and sculpture, and who read Ukrainian poetry in his limited
free time. Like all Australians he works overtime. I asked him how
he liked Yevtushenko. He said his *Babii Yar* was a great poem but
was too outspoken. Hence the Government had, "as we say, shot
him," by which he meant shut him up. "Those people are trained
psychologists. They know the very minute a writer steps out of
line."

Of the big three in Australian painting—Sydney Nolan, Russell
Drysdale, and Arthur Boyd—he thinks Boyd is very much the
most skilful painter but that he substitutes skill for creative fervour. He has no high opinion of Nolan and wonders why he
should be rated Australia's leading painter. I suggested it might be
because London critics, who evidently still determine Australian
standards of taste, had rated him so. But he didn't care much for
our Jackson Pollock either. "How can you tell when you never see
his pictures over here?" "No, I've seen several, all of the good
ones. I don't like how he throws the paint on," and he demonstrated with a mythical can of paint in his hands. He likes the
sculptor Archipenko. "He's another Ukrainian, the greatest sculptor since Rodin." But he doesn't like Pasternak. "He brings in too
many people. He doesn't deserve the Nobel Prize for that book."

Such is the conversation with a Victorian Railways guard, who
escaped from the Ukraine during the Second World War by going
west. His Ukrainian wife, whom he met here, escaped by going
east: sent as a child with her family to Siberia, then to Iran, Iraq,
India, and eventually to Australia. Opening his door as we
approached another suburban station—they run no more than two
minutes apart all along the line—he pointed to the houses, separate and distinct, but all very much alike and all precisely the
same height, marshalled in rows and files out over the flat land. He
commented on their solid, square, characterless look. "Is going the
same way what used to be going hundred years ago," he said.

*The Australian suburban look is uniform and unmistakable, in
Adelaide's Unley, Sydney's Balgowlah, Melbourne's Moorabbin:
green, well cared-for lawns; new and well-built if somewhat
chunky bungalows; moderately well-to-do people finding an excuse
in weekend garden and car-washing chores to get out in the sun.
The* Saturday Evening Post *covers in the days of George Horace
Lorimer and the old black and white movies used to show it in
their impressions of American suburbia. One only needs to substitute an English landscape of sturdy English cottages, cap the*

37

cottages with hipped roofs, not all tin or tile or all red but near enough, set them on treeless streets, and surround them with fenced yards, to recognize middle-class urban Australia anywhere across the continent west of Woolloomooloo.

In the rear and down the sides the fence is homely and utilitarian of five-foot-high corrugated iron, unpainted vertical boards set tight together, or wattle—long straight branches, an inch in diameter, closely packed so as to leave no chinks between them. Around and across the front is a lower fence, of slight practical value for keeping out dogs and prying eyes, with a gate across the driveway. But this front fence nevertheless, so seemingly useless, is of immense importance as an expression of the home-owner's individuality. There are outbuildings in the back and side yards which he simply throws together. There is a mailbox, for which his wife will search in the deepest recesses of Australia's mammoth department stores to find something different than her neighbours'; and there is an occasional name, like D. H. Lawrence's celebrated Torestin, spelled out in fretwork script.

On a street of nearly indistinguishable residences and lawns the front fences may be of wooden palings, iron pipe, brick, concrete posts and rails, discarded bottles, boulders, stucco, privet, wire, or weatherboard: whatever materials seem best fitted for the twin purpose of erecting a barrier between the householder and the outside world, and at the same time projecting an image of himself. In its design and construction are compressed the whole of his usually stifled urge to be a handyman as, with a fund of unsuspected ingenuity, he creates, once and for all, a thing entirely his own, a work of art, a latter-day variant of the iron deer or ball-balancing seal.

His cousin in California screens the mediocrity of his dwelling with vines and other plantings—a pusillanimous compromise but quite in character with a male whom all the world knows as merely his wife's consort. The Australian, who considers gardening along with shopping, pram-pushing, and dish-washing as strictly woman's work, meets the problem head-on with an eye-catching front fence that is sometimes rude but always remarkable.

Virtually every suburb, however small, supports a chemist's shop, pastry shop, toy shop and stationer, haberdasher, tea room serving hot meals, fish and chips shop, lending library, betting shop, shoe repairman, dry cleaner, pet food shop, wool and dress materials shop, and several banks. Most are as small as the shops on Sydney's Pitt Street and all have permanent canopies reaching across the wide asphalt footpath to the street. Each shop is easily

identifiable. Across a newsagent's front is a row of mounted posters
printed in large type with such terse messages as: "THE PILL,"
"RECTOR CHILD BRIDE SCANDAL," "LATEST KNIT
FASHIONS," "RAPE GANG TERROR," "60 LOW-CALORIE
MEALS," and "MORE OIL FOUND." A grocer has smaller sheets
stuck on the window featuring specials at, to American eyes, fan-
tastically small discounts. The sheets on a milk bar's window look
to have gone up when the window did. Butchers' windows invari-
ably have, among the various cuts of meat on display, a tray of
chopped-up beef and kidney. Appliance shop windows have
chalked on: "Used vacs from $10," "Used frigs from $30." Fruit
and vegetable sellers do without a window altogether, seizing upon
its absence to push some of their overflow out onto the footpath.
So it is in all suburbs; and if the shops can be told apart, the
shopping centres cannot.

In the city in late afternoon we again searched for something to
eat besides peanuts, but without seeing even a milk bar. There
were downtown butchers, grocers, and fruit markets, innumerable
banks, dress shops, shoe stores, and several large department stores
including one which our cabbie had told us was the fourth largest
in the world. He didn't know the other three. Barry and Elaine,
however, are convinced no store in Melbourne can equal what
they have in Sydney; and they mentioned one in particular which
we'd failed to visit. In general, my impression was that Sydney
shops tend to be smaller, more numerous, and more scattered than
in Melbourne. Anyhow, people were now out in large numbers,
window-shopping and enjoying the hot weather. It was too hot for
us. Candi's ill-fitting new shoes were torturing her feet, and the
flies, one of which actually flew into her mouth, were adding to
her misery.

Looking across the street you could see them dancing around in
the air like black snow flakes; and even on the opposite footpath
they were plainly visible clustered around people's heads like a
character that once appeared in the *Dick Tracy* comic strip called
Flyface. I used to think Flyface purely a creature of the cartoon-
ist's imagination; now I wonder whether he got the idea on a visit
to Australia. The flies were bad everywhere, but especially at street
intersections where crowds were massed, docilely waiting for the
traffic lights to tell them to WALK.

We were finally directed to a delly—a milk bar or delicatessen
reflecting the influence of Melbourne's European migrants—and
had scones, jam, and—all right, I surrender—tea. I refuse to look

39

at another cup of this souped-up Postum. Had we been more adventurous we could also have eaten sweet corn sandwiches, fruit salad sandwiches, or spaghetti sandwiches—all made up and on display in the delly's window. Not to mention curried rice pie with sauce.

"Don't serve dill pickles to Australians, Mom. They've never tried them and they never will."

"How come they sell them in the stores then?"

"They're for the German, Dutch, Italian, and American migrants."

"How about Greeks?"

"Yeah, the Greeks."

"The Poles?"

"The Poles too."

"Yugoslavs?"

"Yeah, and Hungarians and Czechs."

"Are there any Czechs?"

"There are a few. Anyhow, don't try to get Australians to eat dill pickles."

40

7

*You could fairly say that all Australians, however they may try
to hide it—and many don't try very hard—hate poms. I don't
believe they hate them as persons though, or even because they're
"different"—which they aren't. Next to the kiwis, Australians are
the most English of any people outside England, and nothing that
European immigration or American political influence can do will
ever change this. So they don't hate poms as native Americans
used to hate wops, dagoes, and hunkies; and they don't hate Englishmen or any other people who come to Australia because they
are attracted by it and want to grow with it and contribute to its
development. What they hate are the poms who were brought to
Australia and would not have come if it cost them more than the
$25 they paid in fares, children free. To a degree therefore the
poms resemble the convicts who were transported here.*

*In the later period of convict settlement it was not so much a
matter of Britain wanting to get rid of her felons as of Australian
employers eager to get them for cheap labour. Free Australian
labourers resented them, and their resentment grew until in Melbourne they forcibly prevented two convict ships from landing,
one in 1849, a second in 1850. Had the Australian War of
Independence broken out over either of these incidents it would
have gone down in history alongside the Boston Tea Party. The
ships went up to Sydney where, in the face of further demonstrations, the Governor waved them on; and finally, I believe, got
rid of their unwelcome cargoes somewhere near Brisbane. The
memory of Bunker Hill and Lexington was too fresh in Whitehall
minds to risk a revolution for the sake of a few squatters. Hence-
forth convicts were delivered only to Tasmania and Western Australia, until at last the trade was put to an end even in those
remote places. The poms today aren't convicts of course; but just
as Americans were put off tea by what happened in Boston and*

41

have never much cared for it since, so Australians cannot reconcile themselves to settlers being dragged to their country, in chains or not.

JANUARY 5: It was cold and damp much of yesterday, with the sun peeking out only now and then and a sharp chill wind blowing from the south. We heard many a rueful remark about Melbourne's brief summer (Sunday only) as the weather lived up to its reputation. The crowd at Rosebud Sunday wore little else but skin, whereas on Monday I saw several women in thick cloth coats —and what must be the distinctively Australasian felt turban.

We stayed on the ship all morning and finished our stay in Melbourne with an afternoon visit to the Collinses. Mrs Collins and her son Peter—thin, bearded, spectacled, and a graduate student at Melbourne University—picked us up in their station wagon and drove us around Melbourne before taking us to their house in Toorak. We went first along the waterfront to St Kilda, formerly a fashionable bayside suburb, now occupied largely by Italian and Greek migrants and Jews. The esplanade running from our wharf to St Kilda is lighted up at night and this, I think, was what we saw from the ship as we sailed out of the harbour late last evening. From St Kilda we got onto St Kilda Road, a wide thoroughfare with tram cars down the middle, and fine old mansions on either side now being turned into professional and business offices. We had been told that we must see this road for its beauty, but the Collinses said it was no longer as beautiful as it used to be with magnificent trees on the strips between avenue and carriageways, their branches reaching almost to the trolley wires. The city authorities have a mania for pruning trees to their bare trunks and would, if they felt they could get away with it, cut them down altogether.

Mr Ratner tramped heavily along beside me talking about football and why he preferred to live in Melbourne, but it wasn't Melbourne itself so much he liked as the suburbs. "Yes," I agreed looking around, "on account of the trees." "I wasn't wrapped up in Sydney. I wasn't wrapped up in Brisbane. I've been to the Gold Coast and Surfers and I wasn't wrapped up in them either." "A good place to spend your money." "And you spend it very quick too. Adelaide is a nice town though. It's a pretty place. But don't get me wrong. I'm not wrapped up in Melbourne itself, just the suburbs." "It's the trees that make Adelaide and the suburbs of Melbourne so nice looking." "I don't like big trees. Shrubs look

42

nice. *I've got two big trees in my paddock and before I go to work I have to spend half a day raking up the leaves."* We came to a house with a splendid maple towering above it, its leaves turning red and gold in a way to pull at my Middle Western heartstrings. *"Just look at that ugly thing,"* said Mr Ratner. *"Look at the mess on the ground. All those leaves."*

We passed a number of public schools, most of which one or more of the Collins children had attended. Two, Melbourne Grammar and Scotch College, have produced a significantly high proportion of Australia's business and political leaders. In contrast to Sydney, where well-to-do parents may send their girls to a private school to make young ladies of them but their boys to a State school for the better education, Melbourne parents will make almost any sacrifice to keep their children—boys as well as girls—out of the State schools. The so-called public school is a must for every child whose parents can afford it—and even for many who can't. But, Mrs Collins said, each new State and Federal election makes it a bit easier to afford the public school, as the two major parties vie with each other in grants and tax rebates to woo the parochial school vote. Few of the pupils are boarders. The benefits

—apart from religious instruction in the church schools—are intangible but none the less real.

We saw the rising structure of Melbourne's new art gallery and concert hall, the first World War Memorial that looks like a Mexican pyramid, an open-air theatre similar to Hollywood Bowl and, across the grassy Domain—almost empty of strollers and bench-sitters on this frosty day—the Botanic Gardens which Peter said were the finest in the world. Those at Kew rank second because they lack the hilly character of Melbourne's. We went in only as far as the gate to Government House. Government House, where Victoria's British governor lives—and every Australian State has such a governor and such a house in addition to those for the Governor-General of the country as a whole—is a large white edifice set in some incredible number of acres of hilly open land alongside the Botanic Gardens. An iron fence is all that separates the two and people who have free use of the Botanic Gardens may also enjoy the illusion that by climbing the fence they could romp and have picnics in the spacious grounds of Government House. They aren't apt to get in any other way. Two policemen stand guard at the gate and even the Collinses didn't presume to ask permission to show us around.

"There was a lot of noise outside and then one of the library guards came and opened the doors right near us. This got everybody excited. The guys facing the aisle on each side stood little sixpenny Union Jacks, that they bought for the purpose, in their lights. I had heard one of them on the library steps telling his mates about it: 'Ev cawse eh bote it specialeh, eld chop,' with such a precious accent I had to look twice to make sure it wasn't our English prof.

"When the Governor-General walked through everything was quiet. He was a white-haired, sour-looking little man and he ignored everybody in the library as he walked through. Then a most surprising thing happened. I always thought our uni students were the deadest and least principled of a dead lot, but when the G-G got to the doorway the silence was broken by a loud hiss. This was picked up by the crowd outside and, though I couldn't see what was going on on account of the mob at the doorway, I could hear a lot of hissing and laughter."

We crossed the Yarra River, as serene and placid as Melbourne itself, and went up Swanston Street past the old library and art gallery, into and around the campus of Melbourne University, and back down again for a long and admiring look at Melbourne Cricket Ground, a heritage from the Olympic Games. Cricket is played here at this time of year but the biggest crowds are attracted to the footy in autumn and winter. We came again to the Yarra and followed it back to the city, a very pretty drive, with glimpses of the skyline amid the trees that line the banks. Returning on a similar drive along the other bank of the river we entered an unbroken stream of car and truck traffic which, owing to an absence of traffic lights, makes this winding parklands drive far and away the busiest thoroughfare in Melbourne. Thence along Toorak Road and through Toorak Village, which somewhat resembles Beverly Hills, but only somewhat.

Almost from Melbourne's earliest times Toorak has been the home of Victorian aristocracy. In the era of the gold rush it was also the seat of colonial government. From his residence in Toorak in December, 1854, Governor Hotham directed the military operations against Australia's only armed battle for independence, the Eureka Stockade uprising in Ballarat.

"The disaffected miners formed themselves into Corps, elected their leader, and commenced drilling; they possessed themselves of all the arms and ammunition which were within their reach, they established Patrols, and placed parties on the high roads leading to Melbourne and Geelong; searched all carts, and drays for weapons, coerced the well affected, issued orders, signed by the 'Secretary to the Commander in Chief of Diggers under Arms,' dispatched emissaries to the other diggings to excite the miners, and held a meeting whereat the Australian flag of independence was solemnly consecrated, and vows proffered for its defence."—Lieut.-Gov. Sir Charles Hotham to Sir George Grey.

Most of the former estates have been cut up into small blocks for homes which, though new, are quite old-fashioned looking. The Collins property is still fairly large, with a house that grew as the family grew: a rambling brick structure bristling with tall chimneys, each leading from a fireplace in one of a dozen or more ample rooms. The house is surrounded by camellia bushes and trees, including one old pepper tree dating back to the days when the land was part of a sheep station. Yet it is only about five miles from the centre of Melbourne.

They had a flag of "silk, blue ground, with a large silver cross similar to the one in our southern firmament," and a flagstaff, "a very splendid pole, eighty feet in length, and straight as an arrow." They lacked both a leader and a clear idea what they were fighting for, or against. It was preposterous that they would fight at all, as young Lord Robert Cecil found when he visited the Victorian goldfields in 1852:

"We met two diggers, each with a sack of earth on his back which they were taking to some waterhole to wash. They were 'prospecting' as the phrase goes; that is, they were raising and washing earth in various spots, in the hope of discovering some valuable auriferous vein. But by the regulations of the police all work is forbidden on Sunday: so that this prospecting was a violation of the law. Mr Armstrong (superintendent of police) dismounted, gave his horse and whip to one of the offenders to hold, took the two sacks, and scattered all the valuable earth upon the road ... They neither made resistance nor showed any discontent. One of them only said, 'Well, Sir, I hope never to do it again.' I at first stood quite aghast at this specimen of submissiveness in Anglo-Saxons and colonists, especially after all that I had heard of their independent and unruly dispositions."

Nevertheless the flag did appear, late in November, 1854, flying from its 80-foot staff above a crowd of 10,000 to 15,000 miners assembled on Bakery Hill in Ballarat. "The day was very hot," wrote Carboni Raffaello, one of the miners present, "the sun was almost burning. Timothy Hayes, the chairman, spoke like a man as follows:

" 'Should any member of the League be dragged to the lock-up for not having the licence, will a thousand of you volunteer to liberate the man?' 'Yes! Yes!' 'Will 2,000 of you come forward?' 'Yes! Yes! Yes!' 'Will 4,000 of you volunteer to march up to the Camp, and open the lock-up to liberate the man?' 'Yes! Yes!' (The clamour was really deafening.) 'Are you ready to die?' shouted our worthy chairman, stretching forth his right hand, clenched all the while: 'Are you ready to die?' 'Yes! Yes! Hurrah!' This general decided clamour put our Tim in such good spirits that, in spite of the heat of the sun and the excitement of the day, he launched in the realm of crowned poets, and bawled as loud as if he wanted the head butler at Toorak to take him a quart pot of small beer—

" 'On to the field, our doom is sealed,
    To conquer or be slaves;
    The sun shall see our country free
    Or set upon our graves.' "

The announced purpose of the assembly was to receive the answer to a petition to pardon three men arrested for burning down the Eureka Hotel. But they had other grievances to air. One, markedly similar to the Stamp Tax of King George III's Parliament, was a licence fee of 30 shillings a month levied on every miner. As with the Stamp Tax it was less the tax itself than the way the British authorities set about enforcing it that provoked the greatest discontent.

"He asked him if he had a licence," wrote Cecil, "and the digger's replying in the negative, he said, 'Come up, then, my good fellow, and I will give you a licence,' and at the moment the digger had emerged from his hole on this invitation he clutched him by the collar saying, 'I arrest you in the Queen's name for not having a licence.' Such things seem to create more ill will than tent burning or arbitrary fines." And yet I can no more imagine their producing a Southern Cross Flag of the Republic of Australia than the Stamp Tax setting Betsy Ross to sewing the Stars and Stripes.

The real difficulty at Bakery Hill was that the men who were behind the flag and the idea of a republic were unwilling to assume leadership. There were the refugees from the European Revolutions of 1848, Raffaello and Friedrich Vern; a priest, Father Patrick Smyth; an editor, George Black; an American Negro, John Joseph; and another American, James McGill and the Independent Californian Rangers' Revolver Brigade. But nowhere in Ballarat or Victoria was there a John Hancock, a Patrick Henry, or a Tom Paine. The miners had to settle for one Peter Lalor (pronounced like Lawlor). As he himself explained:

"The diggers rushed to their tents for arms, and crowded on Bakery Hill. They wanted a leader. No one came forward, and confusion was the consequence. I mounted the stump where you saw me, and called on the people to fall in into divisions according to the firearms they had got, and to choose their own captains out of the best men they had among themselves. My call was answered with unanimous acclamation, and complied to with willing obedience."

What the outcome of the Eureka Stockade revolt would have been with a better, or at any rate more principled, leader is difficult to say. It might have been crushed as easily as it was when, at dawn on Sunday, December 3—in the words of Raffaello—"the old command, 'Charge' was distinctly heard, and the red-coats rushed with fixed bayonets to storm the stockade. A few cuts, kicks, and pulling down, and the job was done too quickly for their wonted ardour, for they actually thrust their bayonets on the body of the dead and wounded strewed about on the ground. A wild 'hurrah!' burst out, and 'the Southern Cross' was torn down, I should say, among their laughter, such as if it had been a prize from a May-pole. Of the armed diggers, some made off the best way they could, others surrendered themselves prisoners, and were collected in groups and marched down the gully. The Indian dragoons, sword in hand, rifle-pistols cocked, took charge of them all, and brought them in chains to the lock-up."

Had the insurrection succeeded, Lalor, the fiery leader who had presided over the forming of "the army of the revolution" and who was among those who "made off the best way they could," leaving thirty or forty of his soldiers dead or dying, would willingly have become its George Washington. When it failed he easily disowned republicanism and later refused even to be counted a democrat unless the meaning of the word could be made to cover "opposition to a tyrannical people." None of the defendants at the subsequent trial would confess to having fought for a free and independent Australia. They maintained, with Raffaello, that amongst the rebels "there was no democratic feeling, but merely a spirit of resistance to the licence fee." The Government was quite content with this. "If his Excellency punished these men, it would be calling into existence an agitation which would, we feared, end in civil commotion, if not in the disseverance of the colony from the mother country."

8

We picnicked and talked, first with Geoff about the book trade, and then generally about Australia and England. Our American style picnic mystified them. The children didn't know what potato salad was and their mother had to assure them it was a salad. Even then Karen wouldn't eat hers. Peggy had gone to great lengths to obtain hot dog rolls for the frankfurters and served them cut, buttered, and with mustard on. But when she was about to put the hot franks inside the rolls they said they'd prefer having them on their plates to eat separately. Geraldine, knowing they wouldn't be able to eat anything uncut, borrowed Geoff's pocket knife and cut their franks into bite-size morsels. They all ate the rolls separately and must have wondered at their being flavoured with mustard. But the picnic came to a happy end when—seeing the look of horror on every face at the thought of eating pumpkin pie—Peggy produced an orange sponge she had bought ready-made from a pastry shop. I suspect, though, when they got home they welcomed some proper food to eat. I had asked Peggy not to boast about this being American food and she took me to mean not to say anything at all about it. So they were never reassured as they might have been if she had told them this was exactly the lunch President Roosevelt served King George and Queen Mary when they visited him at Hyde Park.

In 1952 Geoff and Geraldine Lyons—Geoff in particular—decided to leave England. He called around at the consulates of Canada, South Africa, and New Zealand. New Zealand asked him what he did; they had a great need for tradesmen. Was he a bricklayer, a plumber, a carpenter? Somewhat shamefacedly Geoff said he sold books. New Zealand wasn't interested, but at Australia House a cheerful official shoved a bunch of brochures in his hands and a list of booksellers to write to. He received encouraging replies from all of them. Along about that time a visitor from

49

Tasmania called at the shop where he worked and was told that "our Mr Lyons is thinking of going to Tasmania." With the instinctive cordiality of Australians the visitor left her name and address so that Geoff could look her up. This friendly gesture decided him— or almost did. The finally decisive factor and the factor, he said, decisive for most migrants was Australia's willingness to pay his passage.

Geraldine said Englishmen were more reserved than Australians, less callous toward dumb animals. Australians kept their dogs out of the house; Englishmen wouldn't dream of it. But these were about the only differences. Oh, and there was more freedom in Australia; the air was fresher; people flocked to the beach. "Don't they in England when they can?" asked Geoff. She thought the speech was similar. Aussies often said to her: "You can't be English. You don't have an accent." Food, houses, habits, opinions were much the same—except Australians never walked; on the shortest errand they used a car; thought she and Geoff mad when they saw them walking. The warm friendly atmosphere of the English pub—which migrants made so much of—was only a fringe part of life, and better in memory than it actually was. So when Geoff talked, as he sometimes did, of going back to England she honestly couldn't see why. Geoff himself couldn't explain. He said Australians asked him, "Your children born here?" "Yes." "Aw, you're hooked, son. You'll never go back. Anyhow you're in a good spot."

JANUARY 6: Last night was the Welcome Ball. There are about 850 passengers, nearly two-thirds from Melbourne and Victoria, and almost all were crowded in the ballroom, along with the Captain and his chief officers dressed in white. Dancing was followed by a floor show and more dancing, followed at midnight by a cold buffet. Such was the press of diners we did not get fed for nearly an hour, and so again to bed late, but up early as usual today. A Sydney building contractor told me the reason there are so many Victorians on the cruise was that they are more used to travelling, having regularly to flee from the Melbourne winter. Sydneysiders have nothing to get away from. We've met several other new people including a man of eighty-six whose sight is so seriously affected by age that he collects a pension of 40 dollars a month which he uses to pay taxi fares to his various clubs. His son, who succeeded him in his paper business, is worth a few million dollars. Despite his age he is bright and alert like the other two old fellows at our table.

JANUARY 7: At the Captain's cocktail party this morning we met an elderly lady travelling with her daughter and infant grand-daughter. From them we learned that Victorians are called gum-suckers, South Australians are crow-eaters, West Australians are sand-gropers, and Tasmanians are taswegians. Mrs Thorne lives in Victoria but was born in Sydney in Woolloomooloo, an area much like Pyrmont with its row houses and ironwork balconies. The 'Loo, she says, was a slum then but the old houses have been reno-vated and it's fashionable to live there now. For all she's a native of Sydney I think of her in some ways typifying Melbourne, with her keen mind and hardy constitution. (She has survived two cere-bral haemmorhages; one only a few weeks ago.) She looks very fit and complained only of the oiliness of the food on this Italian ship —a common enough complaint amongst Australians. That and the over-riding necessity of being tested for TB every time she returns to hospital. It does no good to protest she has been chest x-rayed only a few months ago. TB must be stamped out in Australia even if the entire population comes down with radiation sickness. And, as Mrs Thorne said, at the first sign of TB they rush you to a sana-torium and give you 12 dollars a week whether you want it or not.

Shirley Hunter told Peggy that before she married Doug she had been a nurse. She came to Australia eighteen years ago, settled first in Adelaide, and found everyone friendly. They included her in their activities, invited her to parties, hardly left her with a moment's free time. Then she went to work in a sanatorium and they dropped her at once like a hot potato. Nobody called her, and when she called them they were always busy. She became a pariah. Only later did she discover the reason in the Australian phobia about TB. She thought the compulsory annual x-ray might have created this state of mind, but whatever it was, TB to Aus-tralians was the Black Death and bubonic plague rolled into one.
She and her husband were cattle ranchers (station owners in Australian terminology) on the Birdsville Track in South Aus-tralia. The station had cost $45,000 plus $60 apiece for 3,000 cattle and in ten years they had earned almost all of it back. There was an 18-inch bore on the property which ran constantly, shooting out a stream of steaming hot water twelve to twenty feet long. It formed a river which had to be crossed six times on the way to the homestead, ending in a kind of swamp. Basins a mile or so apart also caught some of the water which produced the grass on which the cows fed. The water's heat and steam were generated by fric-tion as it ran through the pipe. Such was Peggy's understanding.

time to
save!

THE
STATE SAVINGS BANK
OF VICTORIA

Shirley said the Americans would only allow point 000 some-
thing of DDT in the meat they imported. They claimed it got into
the fat but she couldn't see how it got through the hide and into
the fat. "And everybody said, 'Oh, bother the Americans!' That
was how they felt about it, but anyway they can't sell their meat so
they have to bother. They have an entomologist friend who tests
their dip for them in Adelaide, and they bring him the samples of
these new dips that they keep trying, but they have to dip them
every 18 weeks because of the ticks. Well, the ticks take that long
to mature. Then they drop off. And if they use other dips instead
of DDT they have to dip them every 18 weeks, but DDT lasts for
six months or so."

"Right, and the only people who suffer are the ones who eat the
meat," I said.

"Yeah," Peggy agreed, "and they didn't give a darn about that."

As for the TB it is responsible for less than one-half of one per
cent of Australian deaths, compared to two per cent due to sui-
cide, three per cent to motor vehicles, and over two per cent to
lung cancer; and half the TB deaths are in the over-65 age group.
So few are the new cases revealed by the mass x-raying (less than
half the incidence of gonorrhea or hepatitis, which no special
effort is made to track down) that the cost per discovery comes to
nearly $4,000. The total Commonwealth expenditure for TB
sleuthing is 40 per cent higher than its subsidy on milk for school
children.

Aborigines are the greatest sufferers from tuberculosis. It is
responsible for one adult Aboriginal death in every five, largely
as the result of overcrowding on the Government Welfare settle-
ments. The same conditions saddled Australia's Aborigines with
the highest leprosy rate in the world: 36 per 1,000 compared to 20
per 1,000 in India, 2 per 1,000 in Paraguay and Brazil, and less
than 1 per 1,000 in Cuba.

We talked a bit about the Aborigines who, though they are
dirty and shiftless, she nevertheless thinks are the real Australia.
Also about books including D. H. Lawrence's *Kangaroo* which
I've just read. She said she wasn't wrapped up in it, and I think I
can understand why. English visitors, including J. D. Pringle
whose own *Australian Accent* is largely a footnote to *Kangaroo*,
rate it the best book ever written about Australia. They attribute
this to Lawrence's genius, as they'd just about have to, seeing as
how he spent a mere two weeks at Darlington near Perth in May
1922, took ship for Sydney where he stayed a weekend (May 26-27),

then settled in Thirroul, 30 miles south of Sydney, until his ship sailed in July or August. During all of this time he was busy writing the 150,000 words of the book. There are, it is true, some wonderful physical descriptions of the sky, the bush, the rising sun, of a Sydney evening; but his Australians are people he only heard about. Or read about in books that Englishmen have been writing on colonials for the last 350 years. The subject of *Kangaroo* is not Australia but an immigrant's response to Australia, specially a British immigrant. This is what makes the book so real to Britishers. They think they see the real Australia in it when what they see is their own reaction to Australia.

"The Englishman proper is the pugilist of the world," writes Tom Collins in Such is Life. *"The Australian or American maxima may be as brutal, or even more so, but the average efficiency in smiting with the fist of wickedness is, beyond all question, on the English side. 'English fair-play' is a fine expression. It justifies the bashing of the puny draper's assistant by the big, hairy blacksmith; and this to the perfect satisfaction of both parties, if they are worthy the name of Englishmen. Also, the English gentleman may take off his coat to the potsherd of the earth; and so excellent is his discrimination that the combat will surely end even as your novelist describes; simply because no worshipper can make headway against his god, when the divinity hits back.*

". . . But English fair-play doesn't stand transplantation to Australia, except in patches of suitable soil. For instance, when barloafer meets pimp, at £1 a side, then comes the raw-meat business. The back-country man, though saturnine, is very rarely quarrelsome, and almost never a pugilist; nevertheless, his foot on his native salt-bush, it is not advisable to assault him with any feebler weapon than rifle and bayonet. There is a radical difference, without verbal distinction, between him and the Englishman's notions of fair-play. Each is willing to content himself with the weapons provided by nature; but the Southern barbarian prefers a natural product about three feet long, and the thickness of your wrist at the butt—his conception of fair-play being qualified by a fixed resolution to prove himself the better counterfeit."

Tonight the ship is giving a Tahitian party, but Peggy and I think we'll skip it in favour of the movies—and perhaps get to bed earlier as well. After the party, and every night during the cruise, the ship will conduct a night club from midnight till four in the morning.

January 8: Candi had a fine time at the party which turned out, from the costumes worn, to look more Mexican than Tahitian. The ship had distributed grass skirts but few of the women would wear them. On our way to the movie we were stopped by a Melbourne bank manager who told me how dependent Australia is on America, especially American money and American know-how. He would also like to see more Americans settle here because it is his opinion that the country needs new blood, to be less predominantly English. He says the English migrants expect too much from Australia; they don't want to give anything. This seems to be a very widely held opinion. He would like to see America use more wool and he thinks the British firms which own the big cattle stations in the north are primarily interested in promoting the cattle ranches they also own in Argentina, and that they hold on to the Australian properties only to keep them out of some competitor's hands.

The movie for me was mainly worth seeing because the scenes of London were so remarkably like Sydney—though with a heavier emphasis on row houses or terraces. The occasional cottage nevertheless had its dominant hipped roof; public buildings went to domes and columns as in Sydney; new office buildings were similarly squarish and anonymous; shop windows, a few slightly more picturesque, but the generality were also the same. There was a London short as well which confirmed these impressions and added a great Coca Cola sign which Sydney as yet hasn't altogether adopted. There is no harbour in London to be sure, and the scenes along the Thames and—I believe—the Serpentine are more like Melbourne. There are double-decker buses, but more brightly painted, and river traffic similar to the harbour. Even Sydney Harbour bridge turns out to be an up-to-date (somewhat) London bridge—pylons and all. And both cities have a low skyline.

9

Finally we saw the lights of a car moving slowly up Fairlight Crescent. It stopped in front and, after a long interval, a man got out and walked down our drive. "Do you think he looks like a solicitor?" I thought perhaps he did. But this was Seymour Montague, as leisurely and easy-going as you could possibly imagine. He seemed exceptionally young, with a fine even-featured face, hair perfectly parted on the left, and a diffident but eager manner: much like an ad agency account executive in his first tentative interview with an older client. He talked about the law and the legal profession, the "life in the raw" human interest to be seen in the courthouse on Liverpool Street—an old Victorian building where you go up some steps to a central foyer 30 by 30 feet, floored with black and white checkered tiles and courtrooms leading off from it. Here on any day you would find people who had been involved in quarrels, drunks, prostitutes, a place with a smell all its own. This isn't, however, where he practises, being chiefly a company solicitor. Our case for him was quite unusual. He told us how barristers "take the silk," i.e., become Queen's Counsel, an office which entitles them not only to higher fees but also, I think, to practise in certain courts. The "silk" is what their robes are made from as contrasted with the coarser muslin of junior barristers; and their robes also have a different cut, being more like a cape. He admitted that solicitors sometimes feel envious of barristers on account of this uniform and wig they wear, but on the other hand a solicitor often has the more interesting job. He is the one the complainant deals with, or the defendant as the case may be, who interviews the witnesses; and although the barrister has the spotlight on him in court, the rest of his working hours are devoted to reading and researching previous cases. Barristers are never in partnership but always operate alone, except that they may pool their resources for secretarial staff, a library, and library clerk. The barrister never sees the client out-side of court except when the solicitor is present.

Montague is a country boy who came to Sydney to attend uni-versity after originally intending to train for the Army at Dun-troon. He would still prefer to live in the country or a small town if he could make a living there. But he wouldn't like to be a small-town lawyer as this would plunge him into the factional feud every small town is plagued with. The house he grew up in was without electricity or telephone, without even a gas refrigera-tor until a year before he left. Until then they used a cooler, an open box covered with flannel kept wet to evaporate. They operated a washing machine with a long hand lever and a heavy fly-wheel above it. And all this would be not much more than ten years ago.

We got over to my theory that Englishmen and Australians are two peas in a pod—which he challenged. England with its welfare state, its military and diplomatic decline, was worn out—like Rome of old. This was reflected in the character of the people, discouraged, unadventurous, content to let the State take care of them. He saw no future for England. There had been a time when it was producing the best military aircraft but even this supremacy had passed to the U.S., and it had been many years since Australia bought its last Viscount. Australians, he thought, in their optimism and spirit of gamble were more like Americans than Englishmen. He chuckled at my asking why, then, they rose to their feet so loyally when God Save the Queen *was played. This, he said, was the pressure of the establishment. Englishmen rarely stand, yet the Queen is to England what the flag is to the U.S. Australians stand, not to honour the Queen, but because they lack anything else to stand for. "We're a young country—rather I should say, a young nation...."*

One of the surprising things he said about the English was that they didn't like hard work.

JANUARY 8: I wonder if there might be a certain special charac-ter about an Australian cruise, how it snowballs into a rapidly growing circle of acquaintants. Australians are so quick and at the same time so fleeting in their friendships that a cruise is the ideal climate for them. I'm already beginning to grow confused over names and faces. I remember the names as well as the faces, but am not always clear as to which goes with which. Yesterday one of the passengers came to me on deck and asked, "Do you know who the Saviour of the world is?" I thought long and hard over this, wondering what I might be getting myself into, and finally answered, "Well, I've heard of Him." He then flashed a copy of *Newsweek* with President Johnson's picture on the cover. Here was the Saviour of the world. This retired British Army captain, who owns a 1,000-acre sheep station in western Victoria, was delighted with *Newsweek*'s sales promotion. When his subscription was about to expire he received a letter written in gold ink assuring him that as an old and valued subscriber he was worth more than gold. While he pondered over this and delayed sending his seven-dollar cheque for renewal, he received a second letter telling him that as a new subscriber he could have a year of *Newsweek* for seven dollars and forty additional weeks free. He shook his head in wonder over this sample of American business enterprise. He's a slight, craggy-faced fellow with a dazzling smile and a sparkle in his eye.

He doesn't look at all like Newt Baldock, also from Victoria, but a younger man with a round face and build and with whom I had a long conversation on deck this morning. Nevertheless I get their names confused. Baldock is among the few Australians, if this ship is at all representative—apart, I understand, from Parliamentarians—who have done much travelling in the United States. He is a steel merchant and contradicts the widely held view that the Australian workingman is lazy and inefficient. On the contrary he says he is more efficient than the American or British worker, especially on tools and dies which require a high proportion of manual labour to machine. Australia even exports these to Detroit. The big problem Australian manufacturers have to contend with is overseas ownership, both British and American, which restricts Australian production to keep the market for their locally owned plants. He's highly optimistic over Australia's natural resources, especially the iron ore reserves in Western Australia and two iron mountains in South Australia which have the purest content of iron anywhere in the world except one small deposit in Sweden. The country's most severe shortage is oil but Newt thinks even this is about to be overcome; in ten or fifteen years' time oil imports may no longer be necessary. I asked him about the immigration programme and its purpose. He said it sometimes looks as though its only purpose is to fill a certain quota which the bureaucrats set for themselves; and that as long as they can get a specified number of whatever quality into the country and induce them to stay, the blokes in Canberra are happy. He thinks special inducements should be made for highly skilled people including teachers. These inducements would be mainly in the form of housing.

"Yesterday the ministers of State Parliament came to tea at college. It was really a big deal. Notices were put up all over about how we were to behave and how we were supposed to address them "Mr Minister" and never speak to them without addressing them thus. They might have been royalty for all the formalities we were cautioned to follow. Each group of about six girls had one at a table. We were awaiting ours rather worried and going through in our mind all the polite things we had to do like being sure to tip the soup plate away from us instead of towards us when you get towards the bottom. We were mostly scared stiff and expected some austere, tight-lipped old man that would probably make a motion in Parliament to close the college if we once spoke to him omitting the 'Mr Minister.'

"Finally he came. We all sat down in stony silence and looked at our laps. Lee Wah, whose duty it was, introduced us. I looked at him then and he didn't somehow look the stiff austere sort. He had wispy white hair and bright little eyes and then when he spoke I was sure of it. He spoke just like the father in One Day of the Year! After that it was really marvellous. He talked to us just like old friends and no one said 'Mr Minister.' You felt he would have been offended if you had, that he would almost have wanted us to call him Alf, or whatever his first name was.

"Almost as soon as he sat down I could tell he had been to the U.S. He noticed the glasses of water on the table and remarked on it as a quaint American custom, with that particular half-patronizing tone of voice of someone who has been there and observed the natives at first hand. As soon as he heard I came from California he was overjoyed. Disneyland was the highlight of his whole trip around the world. He made a speech like the ones he must make in Parliament about how he spent three dollars and fourteen cents and stayed from 10.00 a.m. to 1.00 a.m. next morning; and had I been on the submarine and didn't it seem like you were really under water. The words just flowed from his tongue. He was such a simple, friendly chap you couldn't help liking him. The hay was still sticking to his hair. He was so impressed with everyone in the U.S.'s hospitality as soon as they heard he was a member of an Australian parliament.

"Then after soup Miss Petunia got up—a signal for silence. He was telling me how he used to evade organized tours and see the real America and he wanted to finish his sentence. Miss Petunia couldn't help giving him that cold look of disapproval she quells us students with. He shut up, abashed.

"After Miss Petunia's speech there was a bit of a shuffle and our *minister tried to resume his anecdote. This time the minister at high table, the Premier or the Minister of Education, stood up to answer Miss Petunia. He gave a speech like in Parliament, continually poking fun at the Leader of the Opposition, who was at high too. He would say something like, 'I guess the Leader of the Opposition missed that. Too busy trying to translate the grace' (it is in Latin). You almost expected the Leader of the Opposition to ask the chair to speak on a point of privilege. But finally the speaker sat down and our minister stretched, sighed and murmured, 'Well, that looks like all the speeches.'*

"He went to the U.S. at the height of the Berlin crisis and everyone there was absolutely frantic, buying air-raid shelters and fallout pills, and he was rather scared because he was coming part of the way back in a Russian plane. Then when he got to England he met a young M.P. and sort of asked him what about this Berlin business. The young M.P. put an arm across his shoulders and said, 'Don't worry about it, old man. While they're fightin' among themselves they're too busy to worry about us.' "

We have been passing some islands along the Queensland coast. They're mostly rather small and stand up high in the water, and show every ridge and gully with extreme clarity in this brilliant sunshine. They seem to be great barren rocks. Tomorrow we put in at Townsville for our first port since leaving Melbourne, four days and nearly 2,000 miles ago.

JANUARY 10: Mrs Thorne and her daughter Sylvia invited us to a cabin party last evening. There were a dozen or more crowded into the tiny stateroom and one of them, a Welshman, was as big as three normal people. But we had a gay time learning about the American neighbour of a young Melbourne couple, Steph and Julie Gilroy.

This American—Hank by name—came over to take a job in an advertising agency at the fabulous salary by Australian standards of $10,000 a year. The Australian Government paid $460 of his family's passage money to come here. He was reasonably happy with, in addition to his salary, a car supplied by his agency until he received his first electric bill. He'd been keeping warm without the central heating he was accustomed to by the simple expedient of burning electric heaters in every room of the house day and night. That first bill floored him and convinced him he couldn't afford to live in Australia any longer, so he's going home when his two years are up.

Hank turns out to be a perfect example of the Australian image of an American. He is boastful, claims to be an authority on any subject under the sun, and talks at great length. He does a hundred push-ups a day, criticizes Australia and Australians, is a real loud-mouthed American. His only sign of weakness is in the face of the Australian motorist, and he cites statistics on the Australian road toll per head, car, and miles driven that are twice as high as in the U.S. He came home one afternoon trembling over the near escape he had with an Aussie driver who accelerated whenever Hank tried to pass him. Yet with all his failings Steph is convinced there is some good in Hank. He loves dogs. Steph thinks no man can be wholly bad if he is fond of animals, and he has entrusted their dog to his care while they are away.

Steph's father has more or less retired from active participation in the meat packing plant he owns, but though Steph fills his shoes his father still considers $4,000 a year enough for Steph to live on. The father's favourite is his second son who had his face disfigured by fire when he was a boy. But he has become an avowed Communist, was even gaoled once for addressing an illegal meeting in Fitzroy Gardens. He lives in a poor part of town, in a house he threw together himself, and—most surprising to Hank—has a job with some firm producing munitions used in Vietnam. Hank thinks the American State Department ought to be told about this.

Mrs Kennedy of the Macquarie Peace Council had a brother who for many years was editor of one of the Washington newspapers. During his last illness she was denied a U.S. visa to see him before he died. No reason was given for the refusal. Instead she was asked, "What meetings have you attended?" and at the vice-consul's request a heavy file was brought out to demonstrate the thickness of her dossier. The most incriminating meeting she could think of having attended was one calling on the U.S. to stop the bombing, at which she was asked to be chairman. She had always been a pacifist, even during the second World War. She had previously spent ten months in the U.S., including three months in Washington where she accompanied her brother at dinners with notable people such as ambassadors and oil men—and had generally been a model guest. It was a shock therefore to be told on her subsequent application that she was "an undesirable person" to visit the U.S. To add to her perplexity, partly on account of her first visit which left her with a favourable impression of the country, partly owing to her brother's eminence and her admiration for him, and partly because like so many Aussies she saved her sharpest criticism for her own country, for all these

reasons she had tended to be pro-American in assessing the blame
for the Vietnam war. She was anything but anti-American now but
the blow to her self-esteem of keeping a file on her as "an undesir-
able person" would never be forgiven. It was the first thing she
told Peggy when they met. What a wastage there must in what
Wendell Willkie called "our reservoir of good will" if there are
many Mrs Kennedys! What better spokesman could we find for
American principles and point of view than the intelligent, critical
visitor from abroad whose opinions about the America he has seen
are the more highly respected by his countrymen just because he is
critical? After Mrs Kennedy's brother died she plunged with greater
enthusiasm into peace work and gradually relaxed her pacifism
to make an exception for the "just war" Vietnam was fighting. She
was invited to a peace conference in Hiroshima and later visited
China itself. There the consideration extended her reached the
point where she was given the option of a visa on a separate sheet
of paper so that her passport would be unsullied for any future
visit she might contemplate to the U.S. She declined the offer.

10

The Armstrongs had rain practically the whole time they were in Cairns and less than happy recollections of their hotel, which was supposed to be a very posh establishment. One evening before dinner they heard a woman screaming as if she were being clubbed to death, just a few doors away from them. Stella asked Ian to investigate. He said, "If she wants to get herself murdered it's her affair." Later they learned it was no murder attempt, just an argument between a woman and her daughter over the daughter's recent bedtime escapades. The woman's own bedroom was the hotel lounge—the one overnight guests used. A larger and more handsome lounge—without a bed in it—was reserved for drinkers. It was warm in Cairns despite the rain—never below 75 degrees—but the shops were stocked with winter things, warm bedding and clothing including kangaroo skin jackets. They asked a clerk wearing a heavy cardigan, who bought these things. "We do," she said. "It's so cold now that I wear flannelette pajamas to bed, with a thick eiderdown quilt over me, and a hottie for my feet."

JANUARY 11: We have now seen both Townsville and Cairns, the two principal cities of Queensland's tropical north. Both are hot, humid, and green. Both are on the ocean. But each is quite different. As a city apart from its environs Townsville is the prettier of the two, although some of its footpaths could stand improving. It is surrounded by mountains except on the ocean side, and has a number of very charming buildings—mostly hotels—with lacy ironwork balconies. I seem to recall it having had more drinking hotels per capita than any other Australian city. But now it is growing rapidly and the population is catching up, brought in by a large meat packing industry and a copper refinery that serves the busy Mt Isa mines in western Queensland. An Olympic pool, where Australia's swimmers train, is set in a handsome waterfront park, which is also equipped with some excellent bowling greens. Lawn bowls are to Australia what golf is to America, a solace to the elderly and retired; and there are many of these in Townsville where the year has only one bad season. Its ring of mountains traps the summer heat. Hence Townsville is sultrier than Cairns which, though 200 miles farther north, gets a sea breeze. Palms and flowers adorn the main streets. Residences climb the hills as they do in San Francisco, old and weather worn, built mainly of wood, and rising to a great height on tall stilts which allow cars to park and air to circulate underneath. Two rivers run through the town, one called Ross River, the other Ross Creek, with launches and cruisers docked and at anchor. A ferry makes regular trips to Magnetic Island, one of the Great Barrier Reef chain of coral islands.

In one large department store we witnessed a small corroboree, danced and sung by three full-blood Aboriginals from Palm Island. The singing was very much like the sound of a low-pitched flute and seemed hardly to have words. The dancing was done in bare feet but only the right leg was moved as the foot stamped the time. The men had painted their torsos, arms, legs, and faces with thin white stripes; and for their second dance, called the Mosquito Dance, they slapped themselves on the neck, back, and chest. This was a labour of love and sales promotion for some Palm Island craft work on display at the store, at the behest of the Queensland Welfare Department. The men were not paid. For several of our Australian cruise passengers these were the first true Aboriginals they had ever seen. They were to see many more at Cairns however.

An almost imperceptible odour of mothballs accompanied Mr Ungas, so faint I could detect it only after he had gone. He was the living image of Lionel Barrymore and sounded like him too, so un-Australian I guessed he must be from England. No, New Zealand, but he had left in his early twenties at the time of the first World War, and had been back only once. This was for a two-week stay with a sister in Auckland at the close of the second World War. He didn't notice any change in the country. He preferred Australia, especially Sydney, though he thought Perth was prettier. The State with the future was—

"Western Australia?"

"Queensland—if the Government ever manages to persuade the foreign owners of its natural resources to develop them. Queensland is floating on oil!"

"But I thought oil was the one vital mineral Australia lacked. You import all you use."

Mr Barry—er, Mr Ungas shook his head and muttered, "Floating on oil!"

Saturday night he had gone to the trotting races for the first time and was scandalized at the eagerness of people trying to get rid of their money. One tall man clutching a fistful of ten dollar bills reached over the heads of people in front of him to shove them at a bookmaker.

"You're an unusual Australian not to gamble. Don't you even buy a lottery ticket?"

No; his only gambling had been in oil stocks and these weren't supposed to be a gamble—not for him. His son-in-law and his son-in-law's brother were both oil geologists and actually witnessed some of the Queensland oil finds. Nevertheless the stock he bought fifteen or more years ago for 75 cents a share was now selling for 13 cents and in all that time had never paid a dividend. The oil was there, he knew. There never had been a gamble on that question; his own son-in-law had seen it, but the British and American oil companies wouldn't let it be taken out of the ground until they were ready for it, which would be in about twenty years, when their reserves in south-east Asia were used up. His son-in-law *finally gave it away and went down to the Amazon where he didn't have to watch wells being cemented over as soon as oil was struck. His son-in-law's brother went to the States to lecture or do research at Harvard. He soon lost a pack of money in Canadian oil.*

"Oil! If a gusher shot up in my own backyard I wouldn't buy into it."

The dynamism of Townsville is completely lacking in Cairns. A dirt road, wet and miry on this rainy morning, connects the wharf with the town, and the other streets, though wide enough, have had little attention. Their outstanding feature is a large wide-spreading evergreen tree pruned in a perfect circle, flat underneath and across the top, looking like a column of giant green toadstools down the middle of a street, with cars parked in their shade. But the harbour, surrounded by green hills and mangrove trees, is a sleeping beauty. Gliding into it is like it must be to arrive at an uninhabited tropical island. No one could possibly make his way between the closely massed trees, which stop so abruptly at the water's edge that a giant knife seems to have sliced down through them.

The most popular excursion from Cairns is by launch to Green Island, one of a 1,250-mile chain that marks the Great Barrier Reef. During low tide at the right season of the year—which unfortunately is not now—the coral of the reef is exposed in all its varied pastel colours: a remarkable thing to see, I'm told, against the intense tropical blue of the surrounding water. But Green Island at any season is a rewarding sight in itself: palm trees on a white sand beach, ferns, vines, flowering trees, all concentrated on a dot of ground—the desert island of one's dreams. And all around the island, visible from a glass-bottom boat or from an ingenious underwater observatory, are millions of tropical fish of all colours, shapes, and sizes, not to mention four-foot 250-pound clams, Moray Eels, Loggerhead Turtles, Pistol Prawns, and Great Anemones amid the teeming multitude of strange marine creatures that inhabit these seas.

The next most popular trip is by train up into the mountains to Kuranda Station. Your journey begins among stilt-raised wooden cottages and flaming poinciana trees, their blossoms the reddest red you'll ever see; the white blossoms of frangipani; verandahs enclosed with wooden louvres; the green lawns of caravan parks; past Red Lynch and its picture-post-card hotel, and into the tropical rain forest at the start of the climb. There are great trees, mottled with fungus and festooned with creepers, as the train makes ascending semi-circles around two gorges, Stony Creek and Barron River. Every so often through a break in the dense foliage you can see the flat plains reaching to the sea and covered with a patchwork of sugar cane plantings and fallow land, and the numerous houses that bespeak that rarity in Australia: the small farmer.

Math Francis owned two stations in Queensland, one of 20,000 acres between Bundaberg and Gladstone, carrying 2,000 head of cattle, on which the family lived; and the other under managership near Mackay. Math Francis had no cowboys working for him, just a man and a dog to drive the beasts from one fenced pasture to another. When they were shipped to market they went by truck, 200 or so at a time, though a really large mob might go by rail. Not everybody used a dog; he just happened to like dogs. Because the stock was hybrid, specially bred for early meat and for heat endurance, he couldn't use his own bulls but depended on a bull breeding farm. A bull was good for three years after which it was sold to slaughter. The stock too was ready for slaughter in three years, whereas before hybridization it required five. A great advance, he felt, but still far behind southern Texas which he'd visited recently and where, by sending them off to feed lots, the beasts were butchered at the age of eighteen months.

He'd found quite a few Texans interested in settling in Queensland, surprised that good freehold land sold for $15 to $20 an acre. By contrast a Texas acre commanded $200. To be sure this was down in southern Texas where they grew rice as a rotating crop with the artificial pastures the stock fed on. And yes, the Texas land carried more cattle. Still, if an American farmer sold, say, 20,000 acres at $200 and bought 20,000 Queensland acres at $20 he'd show a nice profit wouldn't he?

But the most dramatic thing that was happening in northern Queensland was the leasing of land by big American corporations who were then introducing artificial pastures. This, Math said, had never been done before in Australia and the land would otherwise never be opened. Not if the Government loaned the money and leased the machinery to individual Australian farmers? He was afraid not; the loan would never get paid off. Something of the sort had been tried in Western Australia with indifferent success. The State Government offered to loan $48,000 to any individual who would put up $24,000 of his own to clear, prepare, and fence the new land for artificial pastures, and there were few takers. Only the big American corporations were willing to take the gamble. Australians were not as agriculturally minded as

67

they used to be, and the isolation of northern Queensland made it particularly unattractive to individual settlers. The big corporations overcame this drawback by establishing settlements having maybe forty or fifty families—all working on the one big enterprise. This gave them a social life of their own.

The question of isolation had recently come home to the Francises as the elder of their two daughters turned eighteen and received her Leaving Certificate from boarding school. Not being scholastically inclined she didn't want to go to university; her ambition was to be an air hostess. She would now have to leave home just to find people of her own age to associate with. Meanwhile her sister was still at the school in Toowoomba, some 300 miles away—not a great distance in Queensland. They often drove there. The younger children in these remote areas study by correspondence until they reach secondary school, and the mother in the family acts as the teacher.

I could appreciate the disadvantages of living a lonely life in the outback but why, if the corporations could overcome them, couldn't the State or Federal Government? Even the settlements that the corporations founded doubtless had many of their social services paid for by the Government. Why didn't the Government found the settlements and encourage more private enterprise in agriculture? Wasn't decentralization the great aim of Australian planning?

Math Francis shrugged.

Space for the narrow-gauge track has been carved out of the rock, and as you look across the gorge you can see the hairline ledge above an almost sheer drop of several hundred feet. When you look down into the great round basin filled with trees you can't see the bottom, and when you look across the car through the windows on the other side all you see is the mountain wall. Our guard wore a floppy felt hat, unbuttoned vest with pewter buttons, a blue shirt open at the collar, dark blue pants, and green socks. He said that formerly they used to run what they called a grandstand train. This had windows reaching along a whole side right down to the floor and up into the roof. On the other side the seats ran lengthwise in ascending tiers, with the people in back looking over the heads of those in front.

Seated now on the "good" side of a conventional train we saw sugar cane with mauve tassels rising like pampas grass or toe-toe, looking something like sweet corn, growing more thickly; morning glory vines on some of the trees; immense spreading mango trees with clusters of blossoms or fruit similar to those on sterile date palms; a double poinsettia near Stoney Creek Falls with deep maroon leaves. Down the river and across the gorge we could see the second section of our train, dense tropical bush above and below it, trees rising and spreading at the top like fountains. Barron Falls is dry now since the power development. Some passengers went over to check. They'd heard this was one of the sights not to miss. They returned to report the falls had indeed disappeared. We saw the dam however and the fine wide river behind it.

Kuranda Station is almost buried in flowers, flowers and plants in the ground, in pots on the platform, a section devoted to maiden-hair ferns, others to altheas, red-leaved rhododendrons, tiger lilies. Cut-off tree stumps, covered with fungus of a warm brown colour, hang from the platform roof, elks horn growing vigorously out of them, moistened I suppose by the air. Only a small clearing accommodates the station. Surrounding it is almost impenetrable forest growth. The beautification programme was begun by the station master. Others contributed as the word got around.

While we waited, the power-driven car of our two-car train was disconnected, made a circle of the station, and reconnected at the other end for the downhill trip. Meanwhile the passengers who were not taking the bus to the Atherton Tablelands walked around the station, eating. This notwithstanding that we were only one and a half hours out of Cairns and two hours since break-fast on the ship. They devoured cakes, giant scones, jelly sand-wiches, and what most of them vowed was the first good cup of tea they'd had since Melbourne, ours being an Italian ship where the tea is made by soaking two tea bags in a tall pewter coffee pot full of warm water. While they walked and ate they casually dropped paper sandwich wrappings, cups, and cigarettes packages on the flower-bedecked platform.

Our descent to Cairns is much faster than the climb. The train whips around curves and through innumerable tunnels. With the river on our left the bush-covered gorge drops down to grey rock in the mere trickle of a stream below. There are glimpses of settled plains between the hills at the far end of the gorge, and a highway bridge and tunnel several hundred feet straight down. The trees roll down the mountain sides like gobs of green lava, with an occasional green spear thrusting up. We leave the Barron and make a circuit of its wide flood plain, looking over red earth fields, clusters of farmhouses, the sea in the distance, and moun-tains beyond the sea on the other shore of a bay. We race into

Stoney Creek Gorge and clatter right over the top of Stoney Creek Falls. We see trees or shrubs with large fuchsia-like red flowers, serrated leaves. At Red Lynch passengers dismount for cold beer and hot dogs. The station is surrounded by cane fields and misty blue mountains. Along Kamerunga Street in Freshwater we see trees with bright red and yellow leaves. And back in Cairns, houses are set on posts, lattice work around the posts; long stairs lead up to their living areas, with cars parked and clothes drying underneath, or a child's swing, Dad's workshop, miscellaneous storage.

11

*I liked the tape recorder but regretfully turned it down, saying
the duty would be prohibitive when I took it back to the U.S.
"Not if you wore it over your shoulder?" Rick asked. "No. They
even charge duty on any mending we have done to our American-
made clothes." He marvelled at this, but the clerks in the store
said it was designed to compel Americans to do all their buying at
home. Australia should have the same kind of laws. "We'll see that
you have them," I said, "just as soon as we own all of your industries. It won't be long now." They agreed; but the first American
who came into their minds in this connection was Art Linkletter.
Most Australians I have met seemed convinced that he alone
already owned nearly half the country.*

*Iris said: "We're a country of slobs. Take General Motors-
Holden for instance. The Yanks are just pulling money out of the
country and then they even have the hide to lay men off every year
with just one week's pay. We're a lot of slobs to let it happen and
that's the main trouble."*

*"And another thing," one of the clerks piped up. "Look at all
our iron ore in West Australia being shipped off to Japan. By the
time we get around to using our own natural resources there
won't be a bloody spadeful left."*

*But Iris thought this was a minor detail. "If we let the Yanks
and Canadians"—she knew a big Canadian concern that she
ranked second to GM-H in exploiting Australia—"do it we might
just as well let the Japanese."*

*Rick was all for the Yanks and GM-H. He reckoned Australia
needed developing and this was the only way to get it done. "Also
it will help Australia to get defended if we keep friendly with
the Yanks."*

*Iris agreed with him there. "Yes, they've got that much bloody
dough in Australia, that's one thing—they'll probably do something*

71

about defending it. Or will they? England has a packet of money in Australia too, but who's been defending who? All the wars we ever fought were in defence of England."

JANUARY 12: There was great excitement last night when our ship became a floating bar for the people of Cairns and its hinterland. An estimated 5,000 came aboard, crowding the passengers out of the public rooms and into the corridors where they became grumbling groups. When they complained to the Captain he pretended he couldn't understand English, and the ship continued to serve drinks until 4.00 a.m. Police were called to remove the last stragglers.

I am now satisfied that, not Sydney, but Cairns has the loveliest harbour in Australia. It is shallow, like Melbourne's Port Phillip, and has to be entered and exited through a narrow channel between two lines of guide posts terminating in a pair of lighthouses. As you glide down this long channel, with the distant shore receding and the mountains behind it seeming to grow larger, and wisps of smoke rising from cane fires all across the plain in front of them, it's rather like coming out of a fiord. The mountains on either side are not directly above, to be sure, but they are there, together with the mangrove trees, and it's all very still, wild, and very natural. Then if the sky is overcast and if the late afternoon sun breaks through, as it did for us, to light up the little town and set the windows glistening, you will agree that the Sydney harbour may be more exciting, but the one at Cairns is the more majestic—quite the most beautiful thing I've seen or hope to see in Australia.

JANUARY 13: We are cruising through the famous Whitsunday Passage of the Great Barrier Reef. Mountainous islands are visible, one beyond the other, far into the distance and on both sides of the ship. Some are covered with grass, though evidently not grazed, others have little or no vegetation on them; some are almost bare rock. The day is warm, sunny, and pleasantly humid, the sea calm and deep blue. Australians say it is the bluest water in the world. Few of the islands have beaches. Out in the distance you occasionally see a long thin strip of white that looks like a beach, but is most likely the bare coral, submerged at high tide.

We've met a few Americans. One, a small, dark, rather intense woman whom everyone calls by her first name, Angela, finds—so she says—the trip tiresome. She boarded at Honolulu during the previous cruise in order to see Australia, a country she had pictured, thanks to recent books and *Holiday* articles, as an amazing

72

new frontier—a virgin country bursting with vitality, youth, and golden opportunity, fortunes won and lost in daring ventures, a re-creation of the American wild west. She intended to go into the interior at the end of this cruise, but now says she's seen all of Australia she wants to. She doesn't see it as a particularly lucky country or at all enterprising, but timid and unadventurous, and the people she has met, for all her evident popularity on the ship, she thinks boorish and crude. A man at a table next to her in a Cairns restaurant yesterday kept on burping loudly while his mate kept saying, "Excuse the pig."

Thurkow, another American, has lived in Australia several years, having married a Brisbane girl during the war. He was born in Boston, says "tink" for think and "dem" for them and, though securely settled in his new country, has an incurable nostalgia for home. This is his first Australian cruise but he recalls an American cruise when he had five stewards, including an Englishman whose only job was to draw his bath water and test the temperature with a thermometer. He also recalls visiting New Orleans in 1928 and getting "real beer" at five cents a schooner and oysters on the half shell at 15 cents a dozen. He ate three dozen.

The couple across the hall—he is a white Australian and she is a native of Australia's colony of New Guinea—had a meal outside their cabin for the first time at today's barbecue luncheon, having boarded at Townsville. He is extremely withdrawn and hardly ever shows himself; she is more open but still very quiet, and they have this little boy who is also dark. And he, by the way, is a very handsome young fellow—well, Candi doesn't agree that he's handsome—but she's quite beautiful. She is a teacher in New Guinea, speaks good English and is evidently well educated. As a native employee her salary was ten dollars a month. Immediately she got married she became an Australian and her salary moved up to 52 dollars a month.

JANUARY 14: Last evening was supposed to be the big one of the cruise, the Fancy Dress Ball, and when the ballroom opened at ten, people raced for seats, sat down in one and distributed scarves, cameras, purses, and knitting bags over four or five others. Early as we were, Peggy and I just managed to find two empty seats. After a long wait the Compere (master of ceremonies) arrived, a young Englishman dressed in a costume half-way between Mephistopheles and Dracula. Vociferous applause. The Compere regretted having to apologize for the Captain who couldn't attend, having a difficult job of navigating to do. I didn't much mind, recalling how he had brought half the population of northern Queensland aboard to make merry at our expense; nevertheless a dutiful sigh went up from the audience. After another long interval the judges arrived and were seated at a table behind the Compere. Then we settled down for a serious wait, while the Compere conferred in whispers with the judges, and the small ballroom, meant to hold half our number, became supersaturated with carbon dioxide. When, with a fanfare, the contestants in fancy dress entered the room, the air was so thick you could cut it in cubes and sell it for dry ice; and their additional presence didn't sweeten it. Yet it was such a change from sitting and doing nothing that they got a rousing reception as they paraded in a circle with funny signs on their backs:

Item, two gentlemen dressed as butlers carrying serving trays and wearing toilet seats for tails. The sign on one read, "1st sitting —cold buffet"; on the other, "2nd sitting—very warm." Item, a girl surrounded by balloons bearing a sign, "A bunch of grapes." Item, a girl surrounded by balloons bearing a sign, "Sour grapes." Item, a girl with a large pillow in front of her bearing a sign, "I should have danced all night." Item, ditto. Item, ditto. Item, a girl with a large pillow worn in front, a young fellow beside her, and a man behind him with a shotgun, bearing a sign, "Shotgun wedding." Item, a girl with a roll of toilet paper on her head, bearing a sign, "Night trots."

Everybody split their sides laughing. Meanwhile two fellows in Arabic costume had settled on the floor in front of the Compere and said they had no number. This number was a very important thing because, after all the contestants had made their grand tour around the ballroom and gone out again, each had to come back one at a time in numerical order, put on an act, be sized up by the judges and sit on the floor in front of us. The atmosphere got thicker and bluer. The two clowns in Arabic costume began cutting up. The Compere rebuked them. The contestants continued to come in. The Arabs continued to cut up. The Compere finally lost his patience, threatened to have them evicted, and—wonder of wonders—discovered who they were. None other than the Captain and First Officer! Wave after wave of applause swept through the audience. Only the other night they had been cursing this captain and his first mate up one stairway and down the other, and now just listen to them. When the applause began to die down the Compere, who evidently couldn't hear very well, said he thought the two officers deserved a good hand. Then the whole vessel shook with hands clapping and stamping feet. The judging went on, 169, 170, 171, . . .

"Everyone stood around swatting flies on their arms and cooking their feet as the heat from the footpath came up through their shoes. Finally the magnificent beginning of the procession came into view and everyone held their breath: a shiny red fire-truck crawled along followed by a schoolboy in armour on a horse covered with chain mail. He could hardly move. Then came the marching girls. I don't know how many troops of them there were altogether but they really made the procession. They were fitted in between floats, pony club members, Red Cross recruits, boy scouts . . . everywhere. And they really did their part. You couldn't imagine them enjoying it walking along in the heat and flies without even the emotional thrill of keeping in step with a band. There was a police band somewhere in the parade but nowhere near them. They just walked and they paid no attention to the crowds. Some of them must have recognized friends or relatives as they passed but they didn't even smile. I thought this odd but Milly, a veteran marching girl, said that was one of the rules. You have to concentrate on marching; that's what you're judged on. In fact Milly got a real bang out of it. She knew the names of all the

troops and which were good and which weren't. She recalled heroes, famous marching girls that all young marching girls admire for their deeds of great bravery. Like one girl that was bearing the standard of her troop. You aren't allowed to flake out. Every person that does makes the team lose eighteen marks or something. So this girl carried on until she crossed the judges' line, then whammo! she was out like a light.

"Milly was inspired by watching them I guess, so on the way back to the oval she marched. You just sort of walk with your knees stiff and swing your arms a bit."

The big thing in Brisbane is the river. It's a wonderful river, winding along past rather flat land, grassy and treeless, emptying into a large bay dotted with dune-covered islands. As we are sitting on deck, looking at the lights on a bridge in the distance, I recall our first night in Australia, docked at Pyrmont in Sydney harbour, New Year's Eve; how we sat on deck then and watched the moon rise; and how the delicately soft, velvet evening of Sydney's midsummer made an unforgettable impression on me. There is no moon tonight but the feel of the evening is just the same. Up the hill on this side of the river are the grey shapes of Queensland's characteristically tall wooden houses; atop the hill on the other side are blinking navigation lights. A small freighter or dredge has just sailed by. Another larger freighter is moored at the wharf just ahead of us. And beyond this freighter a string of orange coloured lights trails out to the left, throwing black shadows and brilliant orange reflections on the water. The air is warm, with a soft warm breeze blowing down from the north, and the sky is solid black with here and there a white pinpoint. Hardly anybody else is out, the first call for dinner having sounded. Many are planning to take the city lights tour to the top of the highest hill for a view of the city at night, and Peggy plans to go with them, but I think I'll stay and watch the river.

We taxied the four miles into town this morning, and the thing that strikes me most about Brisbane in comparison to other Australian cities is its Americanism. There were more American troops stationed here during the war than in any other part of Australia. Our cab driver pointed out to us the exact office, on an upper floor of an insurance building, where General Douglas MacArthur had his Pacific headquarters. All this has rubbed off on Brisbane, so that everywhere you look you see signs of America: American goods in the shops, the very word American incorporated into many business names, a daily newspaper column devoted

exclusively to news from America. By and large the feeling of almost everybody I've talked to, not only in Brisbane but among the cruise passengers, is in favour of closer and closer ties between America and Australia. There is less and less interest in Britain, ever since the war and the Coral Sea naval battle when the Japanese southward drive was halted. It's quite the normal thing for an Australian to say, "Well, Britain couldn't protect us, could she?"

For all that Brisbane is among the smaller Australian capital cities and its business centre is limited to a few blocks around Elizabeth and Queen Streets, it's extremely busy—partly, no doubt, because the big event of the year, the Show (comparable to an American State Fair) is about to open and many out-of-town visitors are here. The wide asphalt footpaths were jammed with shoppers; and the traffic police, colourfully garbed in khaki uniforms with white pith helmets, had their hands full. We took a ride on one of the peculiar looking trams, open on the sides and pointed at each end like a boat, and found it an exhilarating experience. Not all the trams carry passengers. Some are empty and have flamboyant advertising signs mounted on each side, veritable sandwichmen on wheels.

"I was just noticing on there the sort of Brisbane male. He's an absolute—you know you can see him a mile off. From the age of forty to about seventy, or perhaps from twenty to about seventy, he doesn't change. He's not fat, not really thin either, but sort of bony and really brown, brown as anything and muscular. His skin is all wrinkly, probably from the sun, and he wears a short sleeve, open neck shirt, and baggy pants, nondescript, none of those Adelaide-type pipe stems. No matter what his age is he has loose baggy pants with wide cuffs, and these awful looking socks that stop half way between the pant cuff and the foot, and sloppy shoes that look like they've been worn for ten years. Every male is just about the same, you know, there's no difference. And if you see one that isn't dressed like that or doesn't look like that, well, you can bet he must be up from the south."

Of our city tour I can form no easy impression. There are houses on stilts with skirts of lath to hide their legs, but the terrain is hilly enough that few are off the ground on all four sides. So they are not made to look interesting by their long staircases, merely ungainly; and they share with so many other Australian houses, on and off the ground, a lack of architectural distinction and a fatal propensity to roofiness. We saw an extraordinary number of monumental public buildings, including the University with a main building 600 or more feet long, and the reproduction of a Gothic cathedral said to rival the Sydney Opera House in cost. Many of these are faced with a yellow stone, probably of local origin. But my most memorable sight of the day was the railway station, or rather the roofed-over platforms behind it, into which switching locomotives emerged from a steep cut, pushing up clouds of white, old-fashioned steam.

12

Des says Brisbane is a dead town, no intellectual life here whatever. This he attributes in part to its remoteness, in part to its having been twenty-five years under a Labor government. Although Des doesn't appear to think much of the Australian Labor Party he isn't really anti-Labor, either in his thinking or his associates. Until it came under new management his favourite Sydney pub was St Crispin's where what he called a libertarian group used to meet. What did he mean by a libertarian group? Were there wharfies in it? There was one wharfie. Communists? Yes, and a Nazi too. And a Jewish girl used to come around also. Where else except in Australia would you find a Nazi and a Jew sitting down together and arguing things out? Yes, they sat at tables. The pub had a room at the back and discussions went on there all day. Bank employees and others would wander in for anything from a few minutes to a couple of hours. The group has continued to meet at one hotel after another, without Des. Beatniks are attracted to it, and when the beatnik element gets too strong the others move on.

Usually he prefers to drink standing up, moving from acquaintance to acquaintance, seldom joining one of the "schools" that are shouting one another. They don't talk about horse racing nearly as much as they used to back in the days when there was very little money. Then they would put sixpence on a horse with an illegal S.P. (starting price) bookmaker and this gave them an interest all week. Now "the bricklayers lay their bricks in the pub instead of on the job"; and, with Government-sponsored totalisator bookmaking, betting has shifted from the pub to a place of grilled windows looking very much like a bank—and just about as cheerful. Still the one meeting place continues to be the pub, and most Australians—unless they have heavy family obligations—spend one or two evenings a week there from just after tea time until closing.

This he contends is because Australians in general are unsociable people. They build their brick houses not to invite others in but to keep them out. Alcohol makes them loquacious.

After spear-fishing and argumentation Des's major hobby is running for office. He has little hope of winning because voters in Australia vote for the party rather than the man; the party caucus selects the man, and Des will never be selected, if only because of what he stands for. In election after election Des puts up a single poster, on light poles, hoardings, railway embankments: "STOP MIGRATION NOW; Vote for D. Rougham." He makes no speeches, calls no meetings, contentedly sits through the speeches of other candidates so that he may rise during the question period, introduce himself, and ask what his honourable opponent intends to do about the scandal of assisted migration. His honourable opponent invariably replies that he will work day and night to accelerate it, assisted migration being the single political issue on which all four Australian parties are in complete agreement.

As to how Australia would manage without a constantly widening stream of migrants to buy homes, expand the market for other consumer goods, and build up the labour force, Des says the only people who really benefit are land agents and those employers offering jobs which, because of low wages or poor working conditions, Australians won't accept. Greeks, Italians, and other Europeans have to take them until they learn English. Then they get out and into something else and the employers hire new migrants. But if the employers didn't have a virtually inexhaustible pool of cheap, unskilled labour to draw on, they would be compelled to modernize their operations—the steel mills particularly—and bring Australia up to the rest of the world industrially.

Could this be the reason so little effort was being made to attract American migrants, that their skills and wage demands are too high? Des doesn't think so. He thinks there must be plenty of unskilled Americans put out of work by automation and glad to get any job at all. As to a vigorous drive being made for them by the Australian Immigration Department, similar to those among Europeans, "They daren't. They're afraid Negroes would want to come in." So the best the Department can do is repay part of an American's passage after he arrives.

It costs Des $100 filing fee every time he runs for office, and his mates rib him about this. "What else could I do with $100? Buy a power mower and push it around the garden? Not me!" When there's no election campaign on he looks for jobs in the remoter parts of Australia, where the big new construction projects for

81

defence and the exploitation of minerals offer higher wages and almost unlimited overtime, and where temperatures in the shade often read 120 degrees or more. The weekly pay is $10 higher than in the cities, plus "found," and with no other distractions an additional thirty-two hours at overtime pay is easily managed. These are some of the privileges that convince Des the manual labourer in Australia is better off than the white collar employee, and a great deal better off than the small businessman. He often earns more money and has virtually no responsibility.

Most of the remote jobs are temporary. Thus Port Hedland and Goldsworthy are both busy now, building loading facilities for Japanese ships to take out the Western Australian iron ore; but when this construction work is finished there'll be work for only a few railwaymen. The ore will be loaded more or less automatically and the mines are mechanized; so with little or no employment for Australians, the profits going to American firms and the ore to Japan, Des says it's hard to see what's left for Australia.

Only about a fifth of the men working on the construction jobs are Australians. About one-third are British migrants, newly arrived, and the balance Europeans. The contractors get in touch with them before the ships bringing them to Australia arrive in Perth. They'd rather hire new migrants as this disposes of union troubles, and Australians are more apt to stand on their rights. Des at any rate.

When he arrived at Exmouth Gulf to work on the U.S. Navy headquarters building for transmission and reception of radio signals to atomic submarines—a structure twice the size of an average three-room flat, with a few large rooms lined with aluminium foil and liberally sprinkled with insulators—he found the job proceeding with a dispatch that made the Sydney Opera House dangerously hasty by comparison. Men either worked little or not at all —less from choice than for lack of direction. Small groups at one task or another were always on strike. Des asked about smoko and was told there was none and never had been. When Des left the project, after Parliament was dissolved and a new election was called for, in which he wished to run, there were two ten-minute smokos and he was starting the ball rolling for a third.

There was very little social life in these far-off places on the fringe of the emptiest part of the Australian continent. Talk, such as it was, was about different places the men had been to, never about Australia or current affairs. The migrants tended to keep to themselves, thinking about the families they had left in Perth and the size of the weekly paycheck they would send them. The others were mostly wanderers, stopping only long enough to earn the money to go somewhere else. For some, their only interest was the money. They earned it, banked it, and seemed never likely to spend it. Others drank all they earned; and those who didn't were in bed by seven or as soon as tea was over. Nobody read. There was nothing to read anyhow. The films were all old Westerns. Many of the men worked every day of the week.

Des took Sunday off because he could get a lift up to Broome with a truck convoy and he liked to go fishing. There were six drivers in the convoy. All were well paid, earned as much as $120 a week. When they stopped at a pub one of the drivers—an Aboriginal—had to have his beer brought out to him.

When he was a seaman on an Australian ship the best job Des could get was clearing tables. Merely to be an ordinary able-bodied seaman he would have had to be an apprentice fitter when he was eighteen years of age—or twenty-one at the very latest. Now well over twenty-one, he can't become an able-bodied seaman or a welder or a bricklayer or a carpenter—or any regular trades-man. All trades are forever closed to him. Australia meanwhile is so short of skilled men in such trades that she imports them by the tens of thousands from other countries. Most of the skills are of the sort that any reasonably intelligent person could master in weeks. Some Des has already mastered, but because he didn't take the six years' apprenticeship when he was young he can't work at them. If he works on a welding job his task is restricted to handing welding rods to the welder. Over an eight-hour day this involves about thirty minutes of actual work, and the irony of the situation is that he gets paid nearly as much as the welder, who has to work pretty steadily the whole eight hours.

Had he been apprenticed as a fitter and become an able-bodied seaman he could still never hope to become an engineer. For this he should have enrolled in a different apprenticeship when he was eighteen.

To get away from Exmouth Gulf, Des had to be sacked. If he quit voluntarily the plane fare back to Brisbane would come out of his own pocket. There happens to be on the books in Australia a so-called Master and Servant Law which specifically limits an employee's responsibility for goods and tools in his care. If these are lost, stolen, or damaged the master cannot make the servant pay for them. At Exmouth Gulf, however, when an employee took out tools the U.S. Navy required him to sign a responsibility contract "printed in America." This had evidently gone on from the time the project commenced, and Des was the first either to know *it was illegal or to make an issue of it. I suspect he was the first to know, because there is very little about Australia—except its history—that he doesn't know. So when he was ordered to sign for the tools he refused, declaring this was against Australian law and he was still on Australian soil. He was sacked the next day—without his return plane fare. Still he remained optimistic and full of plans for forcing the U.S. Navy to cough up.*

This carefree optimism is another trait he shares with his fellow Australians. Like them he thinks Australia is the best country in the world to live in, and he at least has been elsewhere, having served on ships for a number of years. He doesn't think Australia will go as far toward Americanization as Canada has, even though so much of her industry and natural resources are foreign owned. Australia wouldn't tolerate unemployment to the extent that the United States and Canada have; it would bring down the Government and put a Socialist government in its place, one that would nationalize the overseas concerns and pay them off in instalments. "Australians are more Socialist-minded than you people think. We'll do without it as long as we can, because we're easy-going and fond of the good life, but we're not afraid of Socialism the way you are."

Australians, he says, lack the American passion for money-making. Give them a house, a car, and a television set and their wants are filled. Beyond that their only interest is to keep wages in line with higher prices. They'll take whatever else they can win from the industrial Arbitration Court in the form of increased annual leave: four, five, or six weeks at Christmas time and a chance to spend it at the beach. The Greek and Italian migrants are more ambitious. They work long hours and make their children work, while Aussie youngsters are out surfboard riding, and they make a lot of money. Some they send back home and the rest they'll leave to their grandchildren who will, of course, spend it on surfboards. "So it will all come back to us in the end."

One of the most interesting things he had to tell me was of the changes that have come over Australia since the war. Before the war people had almost no material possessions. None of the youngsters going to school in Darlinghurst wore shoes, and not more than two in the whole school owned a pair. Few had a change of clothing, hence the first thing a young man did when he went to work and earned some money was buy two or three suits of clothes —to impress the girls that he was a person of wealth. They had no cars at that age of course.

The war changed everything. Australia had to defend herself

84

*against Japan and this woke the Government up and put every-
body to work, and labour-saving machinery was brought in for the
first time. In 1942 when the American forces arrived, there was
only one mobile crane in the whole country. The gates at Woolloomooloo were too narrow to allow the American equipment to
pass through, so they bulldozed the fence down. This for him was
symbolic of the suddenness of the change.*

    *I suggested to Des that he must be the Australians' idea of an
Australian because he lives just for the moment and has no
encumbrances, neither family, house, nor car. He buys books,
mainly fiction, and reads a lot, but gives the books away so he
won't have anything to carry around. He said he'd met an
American woman once who had a complete set of* Esquire *from
the first issue but he couldn't imagine what good it did her. But
he doesn't see himself as a typical Australian. Far from it. An Australian would marry and have a family, pay off his house, own a
car and television set, and never read a book.*

13

JANUARY 15: The State lottery of Queensland is called the Golden Casket and every block in Brisbane's main business section has at least one, and as many as four, sales agents. Lest the buyer think one lottery ticket has the same winning potential as any other, each agent—like each manufacturer of identical cigarettes—gives to the tickets he sells his own brand name. Thus I saw Lucky Casket, Lucky Black Casket (with a Black Sambo figure trademark), Golden Casket, Duncan's Casket, Mac's Casket (with a Scotsman), Crackerjack Casket, etc. They all endeavour to create the impression that theirs are somehow luckier than the others. If they've had a winner recently they post the number in chalk on a blackboard in front of the shop. All the agents make a big feature of the raffle being just about to close, and the signs asserting this are so tattered and worn they've obviously been up continuously for months or years. One sign, very old, said: "Definitely LAST of tickets." One enterprising agent had a recorded sales talk which he played over and over on a loudspeaker:

"Try a winning share or full ticket today. EXCELLENT numbers are selling now. So why not avail yourself? Why not buy a ticket, a *winning* number? Remember that you too could be FIRST, right here at Mac's."

Besides the Government lottery there are also a number of private lotteries with salesmen hawking their tickets like newsboys selling extras. One offered a $20,000 home on a 20-cent ticket; another had a whole assortment of household gadgets and appliances spread out on display on the footpath.

There was a spirit of gamble in the jewellery auction on George Street, held in a store with an open wall and only a large red banner saying "AUCTION" across the front. Inside, the prospects pressed close back to the banner lest they be suckered into buying, while the auctioneer's assistant carried the merchandise around the room, giving everyone a close though brief look. This was a real American watch and the starting price was £7. Around the room it went but there was no action. Another watch, and then another, had the same fate. "These people aren't interested in watches," said the auctioneer. "Put the watches away and let me have that brooch." He held it up and described its virtues. The young assistant carried it around: a silver-winged affair with a large green round stone. "How much am I offered?" No response. "Make me *any* offer. Three pounds, two pounds, one pound. Come, come now. Don't just stand there. Make an offer." "Two bob," murmured a young man across from me. Crack! went the gavel and "Sold for two bob!" before anyone had time to raise the ante. The auctioneer stared belligerently around the room. Nobody could stop him making a sale even if he had to *give* the stuff away. "Let me have that necklace." It was a string of large flat blue beads that looked like plastic. Around the room it went in its box on a velvet tray. "How much?" "Two bob," with more confidence. Crack! "Sold! Do we have any more of these? We'll sell them for what was bid—two bob." There were half a dozen and all were taken. "We'll try the watches again." Another beauty in its case went round the room on its velvet cushion. This time the minimum £7 was bid and followed by £7/10. Without drawing it out the auctioneer let it go for £7/10 and said another just like it could be bought for the same price. It was.

In the play Three Men on a Horse *a meek little man who writes verses for greeting cards has a hobby of picking winning horses. He never bets though, fearing it will spoil his system. He falls into the hands of some professional gamblers who persuade him to tell them the names of horses he has already picked. They win. So do the gamblers; and all goes well until, when the time comes to pick a new list, he can't. Much the same fate befell Cecil, who had never heard of the play. For nearly a year he had been operating a system of betting on the dogs but without actually placing any bets, just recording wins and losses. In that time, having started with $40, he won—on paper—nearly $8,000. He explained the whole system to Millicent and together they decided to put it into operation, going to the track every Saturday night and investing real money. The first night they won two dollars and then there were three successive Saturdays of nothing but losses—something which had never happened when the system was on paper. So they quit going to the track until Cecil worked the kinks out of the system and they got up the nerve to try again.*

Cecil said the three kinds of racing—gallop, trots, and dog—all have their peculiar features. In the gallop or regular horse racing, run in the afternoon, there are four areas for spectators. Lowest in price, order of social prestige, and bookmakers' odds is the paddock. Next comes the leger, then the grandstand, and finally the members' stand to which only people wearing a special armband are admitted. These are the owners of horses (always respectfully called "Mr" in the newspapers) and their families; and the women especially are elegantly dressed in furs and large floppy hats. The trots, run at night, have just two areas—the paddock and the grandstand—and are attended by just two kinds of punters. One consists of punters who made a killing at the races that afternoon and feel this to be their lucky day. The other consists of punters who lost nearly everything at the races that afternoon and hope to win some of it back. The trots don't have the excitement of afternoon racing. One horse sets the pace and the others follow, keeping their positions, until just before the finish when the race picks up.

The dogs are strictly proletarian. You don't have to be wealthy to be an owner. A pup can be bought for as little as $100 and you do your own training, and the crowd in attendance is very chummy and democratic. However nobody will ever admit attending the dog races.

The only apparent rival to the lottery in Brisbane is beer. Eagerly consumed throughout Australia, beer is said to run its freest and coldest in Queensland. At the same time Australia's largest and best patronized temperance hotel is Brisbane's Canberra where, if a bottle of brandy is found in your room, you'll be politely asked to leave. We called here at Christian Tourism which sponsors tours of Australia and overseas under the direction of a pastor. Prayer services are held every morning during these tours and inter-denominational services on Sunday, and the tours themselves have an aura of Christian fellowship about them. A Brisbane Methodist minister started them informally a dozen years ago, and now has officers visiting other cities to recruit tourists. The agency also sells general passage on a Mediterranean line which they favour because it has been "more co-operative." "By more co-operative do you mean they offer you lower fares?" "Well, that, and also they provide better facilities for morning devotionals and Sunday services." Many people take these tours who would otherwise never travel, finding in them a source of confidence other tours lack.

"Are you right?" an all-purpose Australian inquiry, is so often heard in Brisbane it may well have originated here. From a shop assistant it means, "Are you being waited on?" From a well-meaning stranger, "Can you manage without assistance?" From your waitress, "Have you finished with your plate?" From a motorist, "Do you want a lift?" People are on the whole extremely friendly in Brisbane, but as one of the passengers remarked, nearly everybody you meet came here from somewhere else. So it isn't so much the people of Brisbane who are hospitable as the folk from the south who have moved up here.

Martha, a lady of uncertain age—fortyish, Peggy thought; much younger, I'd say—said the Australia-wide belief that people are friendlier the farther north you go is purest myth. She came here with a girl friend on a working holiday, intending to spend no more than six months in any one place. They avoided the cities, thinking they stood a better chance of getting to know the real Australia in the small town and rural areas. They started in New South Wales and moved on up to Cairns, and at first found it difficult adapting themselves to the easy-does-it, she'll-be-right, mañana type of thought and behaviour there. They found themselves reacting to every outlandish thing with a "it could only happen in Cairns" attitude. Insensibly the Cairns spirit overtook and absorbed them so that after six months they were unable to rally the spirit to move. Cairns seemed so far from everything it was a problem deciding where to move to. Even after the girl friend got married Martha stayed on, and only managed to pull herself away at the end of two years. After that she kept pretty well to the six months schedule. Thus she had lived and worked in Darwin, Broome in the far northwest, Mt Isa, Broken Hill, and Alice Springs—all, save Broken Hill, north to a great or less extent. The friendliest faces she saw were those of tourists, up from the south.
Of Mt Isa, the American-owned copper-mining model company town in north-western Queensland, she said everybody who lived there hated it, and the two main classes—blue collar and white collar—hated each other. The wholly Australian silver-lead mining town of Broken Hill, nearly 1,000 miles south of Mt Isa in New South Wales, was run by the union. The union even controlled its police force. But, apart from its two-up school and beer on Sundays, it was more law-abiding than the average Sydney or Melbourne suburb. The people there never went to Sydney on holiday, but always to Adelaide where it was quiet and respectable.

89

Now, after five years, Martha was determined to go home. She had avoided the cities and wondered if she had been wise; thought nevertheless it would be pleasant for a while to have absolutely nothing to do. She knew two girls who had precisely that experience waiting five days on the Nullarbor for a hitch. When I guessed aloud she must be wondering how she'd find her place again at home, how after five years they'd have accustomed themselves to doing without her, and who would move over to make room for her?—she shivered and said I must have read her mind. She'd be a nine-days wonder until she had told everything and then. . . .

Though the day was warm and sunny Brisbane residents complained of the cold summer and went around in cardigans. Some of the women wore winter coats and the coffee shop of David Jones department store was dotted with felt hats.

JANUARY 16: Peggy and I have decided not to attend tonight's Farewell Ball, as the ship will dock early tomorrow morning and we plan to go ashore at Sydney. Better say I have decided. Peggy will wait and see how she feels. Candi of course will go, though she angrily vows she won't. There's a dearth of male youth on board.

This has been a quiet day after a certain amount of difficulty last night getting the Brisbane visitors off the ship. We have been sailing for the most part out of sight of land, but ever so faintly in the distance we could sometimes see what appeared to be mountainous islands. After lunch, while Peggy and Candi were getting their hair done—and the queue outside the hairdressers' never seems to shorten—I finally settled down to reading W. H. C. Eddy's *Orr*, the account of Australia's own Dreyfus case, which I've carried all the way from Sydney. It's a thick documentary, published originally at 59/6. I found it on a table of publishers' close-outs where it was being "flogged," to quote one of the Angus & Robertson sales clerks, at a dollar. It is a shocking book, not alone because a professor was framed by the oldest trick on the campus—the charge of a student that he seduced her—but that the courts and his university were happily unconcerned about making it look like anything else than a frame-up.

Sydney Sparkes Orr died on Friday, and with him the last embers of the Orr Case which had been kept smouldering for ten years by that frail little man. Saturday's Australian *covered it briefly in about a sixth of a column on an inside page. He had*

90

finally accepted the University of Tasmania's offer of $32,000—
only a tacit admission of its guilt; and for him this must have constituted surrender. Last December when I talked to him in Hobart
he was still fighting but already close to the point of discouragement. Most of the issues represented by his case had been won for
every academic who might trip over them in future; and now he
was urged on every side to give up altogether, call off his suit
against the University's vice-chancellor, and leave himself without
any personal clearance, just a general assurance that his future
would be provided for somehow. His last forlorn hope was that an
Emile Zola might appear to dramatize his case as symbolic of the
struggle for academic freedom—but if he did appear it would have
to be out of England or the United States, not Australia. Someone
had told him Arthur Miller was interested; well, a J'accuse won't
do him much good now.

Sydney Sparkes Orr, professor of philosophy, was an Irish
migrant and a trouble-maker. He agitated for reforms in the University administration to take it out of the hands of local politicians.
When he seemed to be succeeding he was called to answer a series
of charges, all more or less to the effect that he was mis-using his
position in the Department of Philosophy to extort special favours
from subordinates. Orr managed without much difficulty to
answer most of them, whereupon new or amended ones would
crop up until, losing patience, he retaliated by taking out writs
against his persecutors, spreading his net wide enough to include a
Hobart businessman whose daughter had been one of Orr's
warmest defenders in the overwhelmingly sympathetic student
body. Their effect was electric. The businessman appeared before
the University Council to read a list of some twelve alleged sexual
acts between his daughter and the professor, performed with Mrs
Orr's knowledge and consent! In the course of Orr's suit against the
University for wrongful dismissal and the progress of the case
through the Tasmanian and Australian Supreme Courts, these
charges were altered in time and place, but never for one moment
disbelieved by the Tasmanian, or the bulk of the Australian,
public. There was one unassailable proof: no girl would publicly
confirm them unless they were true. Orr was shot at through the
window of his home, the rifle bullet creasing his temple. The
Tasmanian police shrugged and said he probably shot himself. Orr
went out on the streets of Hobart and distributed printed throw-
aways accusing the girl and her father of perjury and inviting suit
for libel, a more serious offence under British than American law.
Tasmania's jurists saw no compelling reason why she should sue:

91

they were satisfied she was truthful. Orr's friends compared his case to the famous Tennessee "monkey trial," and evidently felt no charge could be more scathing; for at this trial in British eyes, American ignorance plumbed its uttermost depths. But the trial of Scopes for teaching evolution back in the 1920s was no true comparison. Scopes had one of the world's great lawyers to defend him; Orr had to depend on the slim pickings available to him in Tasmania. No Clarence Darrow from Sydney or Melbourne, or even London, offered to take his case. Scopes was not actually on trial although he had manifestly broken a Tennessee law; the real defendants were the rural State of Tennessee and its Bible-banging advocate William Jennings Bryan. With Orr it was quite the other way around: what was supposed to be a trial of the University for wrongful dismissal became a trial of Orr, and his own dreams as reported to his psychiatrist were admitted as evidence! A weak counsel even allowed him to be cross-examined on the University's reasons for dismissing him before he or the court was told precisely what the reasons were. The University witnesses then easily tailored their stories to fit Orr's answers. One resemblance that it bore to the Tennessee anti-evolution circus was that it was all right out of Hickville.

Australia didn't much care what went on in Tasmania. The Australian tacitly reaffirmed this in a brief obituary which showed that nobody on the paper had bothered to study the case. Like the man in the street, who smirks and says "he did it all right but he oughtn't to have been sacked for it," the obituary referred only to Orr's "alleged misconduct." It quoted friends as saying he died a broken man, but made no effort to get statements from his biographer, or from the heads of the Anglican and Lutheran Churches in Tasmania who had investigated and cleared him, or the Australian Federal Council of University Staff Associations which had also cleared him.

14

"For some reason," wrote D. H. Lawrence in Kangaroo, *"he felt absolutely wretched and dismal on that Saturday morning when the ship came into Sydney Harbour. He had an unspeakable desire not to go down to the Quay and into that town. The having to do it was a violation of himself. . . . The morning was very rainy, and Sydney, big city as it is, a real metropolis in Pitt Street and George Street, seemed again like a settlement in the wilderness, without any core. One of the great cities of the world. But without a core. . . . Everybody very friendly and nice. The friendliest country in the world: in some ways, the gentlest. But without a core. There was no heart in it all, it seemed hollow."*

JANUARY 17: Coming back to Sydney was almost like coming home: the Heads, the wooden lighthouse and its seagulls, the cubist harbour shores, the destroyers moored off Taronga Park point. We berthed at Woolloomooloo, about as far east of Pitt and George Streets as Pyrmont is west, but close to King's Cross where we were going when we got off the ship. Too close, as it turned out, to please our cabbie who said he'd been waiting an hour for the ship to dock. He was a Greek and an angry one—over here fourteen years—though he turned friendly as we conversed. He says Aussie's a good place to make a living, but if he could support his family in Greece he would go back. "You don't really live here. You just work." When we got to King's Cross—the centre of Sydney's if not all Australia's night life—and saw how tawdry it was, I asked him to wait while we photographed its celebrated El Alamein fountain. From the footpath King's Cross looked better, a picturesque neighbourhood of Greenwich Village type residents in the coffee shops, their laundry strung out on balconies of three-storey flats in gingerbread architecture. I took a picture of Candi and Peggy by the fountain, a tricky thing of pipes sticking out like a porcupine and forming a translucent ball of water. Few cities can have the passion for fountains Sydney does. The Village Arcade at the Cross has a squarish structure which sends streams of water down terraces; and another new building in the Circular Quay district has water churning about in its base—x-ray of the drains.

Our cabbie had earned in waiting time enough to compensate him for the short trip, especially as he was able to pick up another fare on the way to Central Station. It was an elderly couple whose lives revolve around the faith healer Oral Roberts. They hoped fervently that "the Americans get here" and described miraculous cures of Roberts's which they had seen with their own eyes. The woman, a German migrant of twelve years, said she likes Australia but the Australians have no—and she put her hand to her heart. The man was Australian, however, and he thought of almost nothing but her, and Roberts.

Our trip by suburban railway south to Cronulla went through one suburb after another with names like Wooloware, Gymea, and Kogarah—three whose pronunciation I had to ask and have since forgotten. Close in, the residences were row houses, blackened by smoke. The farther out we went the wider the space between them grew; and, with their empty treeless and shrubless yards, seemed more widely separated than they need be, like scattered gums on Australia's savannah.

Cronulla is a bustling little city on the ocean just south of Botany Bay, where Captain Cook made his first landing. It has a fine beach with a park behind it, resort hotels, restaurants, fruit stores, milk bars, and innumerable real estate agents. All save the restaurants and milk bars were closed, of course, but there was surf riding along the beach and boating on the river bay at Cronulla's back door. Swimming seems almost a thing of the past in New South Wales. Cronulla has constructed some pools along the shore for swimmers but these were hardly used on this beautiful Sunday morning. Youngsters who lacked the skill to ride surfboards sat or lay on them and paddled, and had more fun with less effort than they could swimming. Others paddled out and rose to their feet on the way in. Others tried to rise and failed. Such is the appeal of surfing: a skill to be acquired by patient effort and a chance to perform before an audience; an aquatic ballet without women. I saw only one girl enter the water and this was in one of the pools. Our return train took us around past Circular Quay to Hyde Park.

Cronulla

Bennett accepted a cup of tea, was tongue-tied at first but gradually opened out, particularly on his hobby surfing. Not board
riding. I had them confused. But rescue work with a boat, four
men on oars and one on sweep, and with reel and line. During the
season the club members contribute a day every two to four weeks
as volunteer life-guards, ready to help distressed swimmers and go
after sharks spotted by the beach patrol plane. Bennett thinks the
shark hunting futile if not foolish. Only rarely do they see something worth throwing a spear at. Once one of the men was standing in the boat "with a fresh pack of cigs in his shirt pocket."
They saw this shark, swimming lamely. "It was crook." And quite
small. Bennett held his hands not far apart. The man with the
cigarettes hurled a spear, got caught in the rope, and fell in. "He
was out of the water and back in the boat before the cigarettes got
wet."

Their chief pastime when not on life-guard duty is practice for
surfing contests in which different boat crews start at the water's
edge with the helmsman in the water. At the gun he jumps in and
the oarsmen row to a line some 200 yards out, turn around and
row back over a line close to shore. Winners in local and regional
contests compete Statewide and ultimately for national honours.

95

Any club may send a crew whether it won a previous contest or not, and luck plays such a large role in a particular wave a crew must buck, that sometimes one of the inferior crews will win.

In the winter when there are no contests the members work on their boats and on fund-raising campaigns. Funds are also voted by the various councils. The board riders began cutting into their membership five or six years ago, especially among the young recruits who don't fancy the life-guard weekend stint. But board riders have begun to join some of the surf clubs which are involving them in rescue and patrol work on their boards.

Even on Sunday, with virtually everything closed as it is throughout Australia, Sydney is anything but quiet. Our two local taxi rides had seemed a succession of hair-breadth escapes from collision. Hence Hyde Park, the Domain, and the Botanic Gardens were a delightful anachronism—all very formal, English, and Kewish. We followed Mrs Macquarie's Road along the harbour shore—the one she sketched out when her husband succeeded Captain Bligh of the famous *Bounty* mutiny as governor of the colony of New South Wales. This was in 1816 and little has been done to the road since. Not that I would have it any different. In a city as rumbustious and growing-out-of-its-clothes as Sydney, a shoreline drive a modern car wouldn't trust itself to venture on and a couple of severely formal gardens can be quite relaxing. You have only to lift your eyes from the lawns, benches, trees, and fountains to see cranes piercing the sky in every direction as new structures go up.

We found three-fifths of the wall space inside the handsome National Art Gallery given over to the sort of thing usually displayed in a framing shop window—slickly painted portraits and landscapes with pink clouds and golden barked gums. The other two-fifths was divided between a retrospective of William Dobell, Australia's leading portrait painter, and some very interesting work by her younger contemporary artists. All the same, the exhibit which most captivated me was a thickly clustered collection of Aboriginal tree sculptures—grave markers from Melville Island off the far north coast, across from Darwin. Though none of the individual sculptures was meant to be figurative the whole cluster resembles in a striking way Rodin's *Burghers of Calais*. This, my first sight of Aboriginal art, was sheer revelation.

We emerged into the bright sunlight again to find the Domain thronged with people. I took them at first for picnickers and, from the great size of some of the groups, Sunday School picnics and family reunions. But they were listening to preachers and soap-box orators, to the Salvation Army and a skiffle group singing religious songs. We joined the largest crowd, a thousand or more seated on the grass and standing several rows deep behind the sitters. The speaker, a spare man growing grey and neatly dressed in a shabby brown suit, was extremely clever. Where the others were dull and earnest he was witty and entertaining. His theme today was Vietnam, in opposition to a Labor Party protest meeting near by which attracted only a tenth as many people. But a bearded man I talked to later said Finn always drew a great crowd, whatever his topic. He had been a lieutenant of Oswald Mosley, the British fascist, and came to the Domain every Sunday, bringing his own stage to lecture from and six husky men to carry it.

Today the stage was decorated with Australian and American flags. We arrived just after he had yielded it to an admitted Communist, who proceeded to make an utter fool of himself, besides being quite drunk. The crowd howled him down and Finn sent him off in a flood of scatological abuse. He had no sooner resumed his speech when a man seated on the ground behind him started to heckle him. Finn at once offered his platform, but this heckler was coy. Finn taunted him and called him a bludger. He would stand up and be booed by the crowd but he wouldn't take the stage. He was a red too, of course. With the last heckler presumably disposed of Finn began reading from a mimeographed bulletin which he offered to sell for 20 cents. He took jabs at Catholics, causing several people to walk away with set faces, and at Protestantism which he described as sexual something or other. But he had a pat on the back for the Jews, who make jokes at their own expense.

At another meeting a man standing very low on a wooden box was being mercilessly taunted by youths who crowded close around him and shouted in his face. He had some sort of message for his fellow workers and spoke for some unnamed organization. He was snapped at from so many sides that he managed to say very little. We left him to listen to a guitar, accordion, and girl gospel singer followed by a most fiery Torres Islander, one of the Polynesian people under French rule. The music would attract a crowd, which maintained the respectful distance people invariably do from religious meetings, and the preacher would drive it away. On our way out of the park we passed a Communist answering questions from his dwindling audience. One drunken man asked what the Communist Party position was on pubs and clubs, and the speaker gave an answer meant to offend neither—for about half the male population of Sydney belongs to a club which is

97

licensed for gambling and selling beer after the pubs are closed, and about half does not. By a series of transitions the speaker worked his way from pubs and clubs back to Vietnam. Then he noted it was a quarter to five, so were there any more questions?

In Hordern's I bought a small electric heater. The clerk then knocked 60 cents off the price after the sale was made. He belonged to a Catholic club, joined it a few months before, dues $4.50 a year. He had just had a nice win on a poker machine there when three queens turned up paying, I think, $20. He also hit the jackpot once, working a machine another man had played repeatedly with no success. He recalled each play and what winning hands showed up—a pair of tens, two pairs, threes and sevens, etc., and what he put back out of each win. He thought he was ahead but knew the machines must win in the end. He said you don't have to be a member to eat at a club, only to drink and gamble; that members take their wives and some clubs have women's auxiliaries. Some of the largest and most handsome buildings overlooking the harbour and along the north shore are Returned Servicemen's League (comparable to our American Legion) clubs which charge an annual membership fee cf $3.00 and sell beer cheaper than the hotels, as well as better and cheaper meals than restaurants—all on the mighty poker machine.

A police patrol wagon was drawing up to gather in the constables. I asked a sergeant named Bill Koenig when curfew was. Five in winter, 5.30 in summer, with no set starting time. He said the police were there only to keep order and, while they sometimes made arrests for fighting or trying to break up a meeting, they didn't bother either the speaker or the hecklers. He said the hecklers helped the speaker by keeping the meeting lively and interesting to listen to. Except that no speaker may set his stand up within 30 feet of another, thereby cutting in on the other's audience, there are no restrictions either on subject matter or point of view.

The Domain meetings have been going on for a long time, possibly as long as fifty years. "In a young country like Australia, where nearly everything is new, they're one of the oldest institutions." The sergeant thought all of the speakers must be unbalanced because, as he said, "I have things I could say but I would no sooner stand up in a public place like this and say them than have my head chopped off. You no doubt have opinions but you wouldn't go into a public park in the Southern States and speak them because if you did you'd give yourself away, you'd let

98

everybody know what side you were on." "Australians must be a pretty serious lot though, to come here in such numbers to listen?" He grinned. "What else is there to do on Sunday If the pubs and picture theatres were open the Domain would be empty."

Johnson talked so fast and so incessantly I was unable to make out the names of the politicians he was talking about. They all seemed to be Irish however, so if I give them Irish names it should do. As he talked he would fish out and hand me newspaper cuttings, and finally one long article in the Herald *about himself. While I tried to read this he continued to talk. He bubbled over with words. I would stop reading to ask, in hopes of a shorter answer than the article seemed to supply, "But why does the* Herald *have such a big article about you? What did you do to deserve it?" This would release a new torrent of words. He had once briefly held "the acting Lord Morality." He had represented Goonoo Goonoo for seven years in the State Parliament. He had been an active trade union officer for donkey's years. He and one Reilly, another union official, had been bitter enemies. . . . "Who was Reilly?" I started to ask, and thought better of it. No telling where this would lead and I still hadn't a glimmer of an idea why the* Herald *had such a long feature article on him. The article itself didn't say. It merely said he was a big talker, a prodigious talker, and a man from whom words bubbled as water from the El Alamein fountain in Sydney's King's Cross. This I well knew.*

He has a little shop that must be seen to be believed, handwritten slogans everywhere, the window almost completely covered with manufacturers' advertising stickers. The plastic cover of his freezer compartment is broken, and on it stands a little bell you tinkle when you want service. Besides ice-cream, bread, cookies (called biscuits), and other standard milk-bar products he also deals in coins. Without the coin business, he said, he couldn't make ends meet. Behind the store, which has room for about four customers to stand, is the miniature living apartment of his wife and himself.

Bit by bit, as his flood of talk rushed on, interrupted from time to time when he waited on a customer or went back to his flat to bring out one or another large scrapbook filled with newspaper articles about the Johnsons, I pieced part of his biography together. After thirty-five years as a union secretary he, or rather his wife, bought this store, which had been allowed to run down, was overstocked with unsaleable goods, and had lost most of its custom. They had proceeded to build it back up again, and were

in sight of a secure living for their old age when it happened.
"What happened?" I started to ask, and again bit my tongue. In
one form or another I had been asking the same question all
evening.

In a nutshell Herbert Johnson was the man who almost single-
handed turned out the Government which had ruled his State for
a generation. The Reilly he spoke of was a leading figure in that
government and Reilly's chief lieutenant was a man named
O'Halloran, whose job it was to police the shopkeepers in their
hours of business. Reilly had once held the "Lord Morality" for a
term or two but his hopes of re-election were dashed when John-
son spoke in favour of his opponent. Soon after the Johnsons
acquired their little shop the State Government, spurred on by
Reilly, revised the law regarding trading hours. This law, which
went back to the 19th century, was so old it was no longer enforce-
able.

Theoretically the revised law was in the interest of the retail
clerks, giving them their evenings and weekends free, but actually,
according to Johnson, it was drafted in consultation with the big
chain and department stores. While appearing to legalize late-
hours trading in necessities like frozen peas and sliced ham, it
made it impossible for the small mixed store, which also handled
ordinary groceries, to stay open after the big stores closed. Those
who chose to were required to lock up out of sight such staple
items as canned milk, tuna fish and salmon, canned fruits and
vegetables, soap—things, in short, a housewife could have purchased
during regular shopping hours had she known the unexpected
weekend guests were coming. Soon after the new law was on the
books O'Halloran sent inspectors around to arrest shopkeepers
who were open on Saturday afternoon and who had any of
the prohibited items in sight. And by a curious coincidence the
drive began in the very block where the Johnsons did business.
Reilly had never forgiven the man who cost him the "Lord
Morality."

Mrs Johnson was arrested and announced she would plead
guilty but would go to gaol rather than pay a fine. Just before her
trial O'Halloran dropped the case against her on the grounds that
her husband was putting her up to it "for its propaganda value."
Mrs Johnson replied that she had a mind of her own, that she had
only been trying to help the public. "I probably wouldn't have
done anything more anti-social than sell a jar of pickles."

O'Halloran retorted that "a jar of pickles was perfectly legal to
sell after hours." "Well then," said Mrs Johnson, "I'm going to

sell my razor blades, baby bottles, and toilet paper tonight just as I always have done."

Now other women refused to pay fines and dared the Government to send them to gaol. Men followed. Reilly and O'Halloran were in a bind. They had to enforce the new law or it, too, would become unenforceable, yet popular feeling was all against them. Men did run short of razor blades and women did break baby bottles after Coles and Woolworths had closed. Gingerly the Government began gaoling the shopkeepers, each to banner headlines and irate communications to public letter boxes. The men were no better suited to prison life than the women. Most were elderly, hoping like Johnson to provide themselves security in extreme old age. When, predictably, one of them died in gaol, the Government fell.

Not at once, to be sure. It needed an election to certify the result. But there was never any doubt.

It was now late afternoon. We decided to walk to Woolloomooloo instead of hunting a cab and were back on the ship by six. Still too early to eat but, as we had eaten practically nothing all day and dinner was on open sitting, we cleaned up in a hurry and got down to the head of the queue. There was the usual wild scramble for seats when the doors opened.

15

I asked a little girl on the ferry whether she was going in to see the President. She said no, they were going in for fun and games. Her daddy wouldn't let them see the President. "Maybe he's seen too many presidents." She didn't think he'd seen any. Despite the magnificent efforts of the State Government to drum up a sizeable crowd—even to granting free railway passage from anywhere in the whole of New South Wales—this seemed to be the prevailing attitude. Horse racing went on as usual and there was no falling off in the size of the Saturday picnic crowds going to Manly. Manly had put up but a single Australian flag and this inevitably was in the fashionable area of Fairlight. Over Sydney's office buildings, to be sure, American flags outnumbered the Australian, and trucks moved along the route in advance of the procession throwing out American and Australian pennants to be picked off the street by anyone who wanted them. Some clever characters picked them up by the armload and hawked them for a shilling apiece. One woman protested she'd got hers for nothing. The hawker cried, "You're lucky! You have a flag! Who else wants to buy one?"

What the onlookers lacked in numbers they made up for in persistence. They greeted the President on his route as he drove from the airport into the place of speeches at the Art Gallery. Then, while the speechmaking was going on, they carried their trannies to new vantage places along the route he would take from the Art Gallery to Circular Quay for a cruise on the harbour. The hour-long cruise gave them time to make still another move to the route of march coming back from the Quay.

A priest and a ferryman joined us on the second leg of his journey. They'd both seen him go by on the first, but too fast for their motion picture cameras. The ferryman said he'd been in New Zealand recently and wherever you turned you saw a twenty-year-

old Australian youth hiding out from conscription. "But won't they be tried and sentenced for draft evasion when they come back to Australia? They would in the United States." The priest said Australian law didn't work that way. The ferryman compared the handful of diggers dead in Vietnam with the thousand or more Australians killed each year on the roads of one State alone. The priest said there were more conscripts killed in motor accidents than by enemy fire. I interrupted to warn them that the speeches had stopped on the transistor radios around us and the procession ought to be arriving soon. I'd hardly got this said and they their cameras to their eyes when it went by like a jet rocket or—as one other spectator said—"like a Bondi tram." We saw a dim shadow that might have been the President waving lazily behind bullet-proof glass, followed by another car with six men on the running boards like firemen going to a fire.

Coming back on the ferry I overheard a dignified elderly lady speak disapprovingly of the paint bombs some Melbourne students had thrown on the Johnson windshield the previous day. Her escort replied, with just the suspicion of a chuckle, "It was rather rude."

JANUARY 18: If I lived in Manly and commuted by ferry to Sydney as thousands do, the time might come I suppose when I too could close my eyes to the harbour's magic and bury my head in a newspaper. But not this morning in the mist and the ferry's own smoke drifting low over the water. The water was calm, the sky blue with wisps of white. And the colours changed. As we looked back toward our wake, the sun gave everything a yellow glow. Forward, almost into the sun itself, the water and the dim shapes on the shore were in gunmetal.

We passed close to the unfinished opera house and to Wool-loomooloo, where I just managed to discern our ship amidst a tangle of masts, ropes, and booms. We overtook a working launch of some kind, fishing probably, with three men divesting themselves of T-shirts. Some small boys whistled at them and waved but they disdained to notice us. Two youths curved by in a motor-powered sailboat. One waved negligently, the other turned his back. The Manly ferry is as common as whitecaps on Sydney harbour. Women at work on their picture-window balconies had as little interest in our passage as the fishermen.

Now we turned to bring the sun slightly on to our side as we rocked and pitched in the roll of the sea from between the high vertical heads. An apartment house in the shape of twin cylinders

The Manly Pier

caught the sun in its floor-to-ceiling glass walls and bounced it back from the heavy curtains draped over them. Thorstein Veblen could have imagined nothing more conspicuous in the way of consumption: a view worth a king's ransom conspicuously disdained. At the fun-fair carnival on the Manly pier a ferris wheel rotated, rubber-cushioned cars collided, and speedboats took off for their all too short rides while we groaned and trembled to a standstill. A wedding at the big church on the Corso, Manly's typically suburban main street, was just coming out as we passed on our way to the ocean beach. There were scores of surboard riders on the water. The beach curves here to afford good surf, just as it does all the way up the coast in a succession of coves and promontories.

One of the desirable views from Manly is the string of coves up the Pacific Coast as far as any land is visible. It was along this coast we went. The sea was high, the highest Edgar and Philippa Twopenny could remember seeing. Some of the waves could have measured twenty feet when they broke. A heavily loaded freighter steaming toward the Heads was pitching visibly. So, while there

were plenty of cars parked along the beach between Queenscliff
and Dee Why, they still had their surfboards tied securely on; and
at Bilgola the waves were so high there were not even any parked
cars. When we passed Curl Curl, Narrabeen, and Avalon, however,
we found Whale Beach sheltered by being in the lee of a hill.
Here there were surfboards and riders bobbing up and down all
over the water. Then again beyond Whale Beach up to Palm
Beach, which straddles the peninsula at its narrowest place just
before it ends at Barrenjoey Lighthouse, the water was either too
rough or too flat. Surfers who hadn't been able to find parking
space at Whale Beach were driving back down along the bay, or
Pittwater, side of the peninsula and again up the coast, hoping for
a change of wind. We turned off to go through Bayview and
Church Point into Kuring-gai Chase, and north beside Coal and
Candle Creek to West Head, where we stopped to look out over
the estuary of the Hawkesbury River. Edgar said he considered
this the finest view around Sydney. It was indeed lovely, a circle of
sea, islands, and hilly shoreline covered with bush.

Back at the ferry end of the Corso we turned west and followed
a winding asphalt footpath up and down hill round Manly Cove
to a small boat marina. Boats sailed and skimmed over the smooth
water. Men fished and hunted for mussels on the rocky shore and a
small boy tried to net something in one of the tidal pools. The
rock itself was fascinating, mostly creamy tan, reaching out to and
under the water, with no sandy beach except immediately alongside the ferry wharf. Even higher up on the footpath where there
was enough soil for flowers, shrubs, and trees, you could still see
shelves of bare rock outcroppings.

Half way back to the ferry I felt a large warm drop splash on my
forehead and looked up to see a heavy cloud about to screen the
sun. Sydney's weather had been so perfect I couldn't believe it
would actually rain. We made a dash for it all the same and got
under the roof of the ferry dock just as the storm broke.

In the heavy rain the buildings, rocks, and trees on shore were
merely grey shapes, though the sky above them was quite distinct
—not at all like at night. Close to the boat the rain hit the water
with such force that it bounced up again in small white drops
which looked like marbles bouncing on the dull green water. The
drops grew less distinct with distance and so did the greenness of
the water until the whole became a white band on which the grey
shapes on shore merely floated. The rain decreased as we moved
past the Heads and little by little, first white then other colours

came out of the grey and the drops didn't bounce any more. A rainbow spanned the Heads, separating the dark upper sky from the much lighter sky just below it. By the time we glided into the wharf the sun was fully out. On our walk back to the ship for lunch it was bright and hot and the bush flies were taking full advantage of it.

Only yesterday I was asking Perc Monk, the newsagent, whether Sydney ever had any winter. Was it always dry like this and would it be this way through the winter, clear skies, warm days and cool nights, bright sunshine all day long? Or was there something in store for us I hadn't seen? Well ...

You start with a thunderstorm, with rain coming down in buckets and thunder cracking before the flash is finished, and it goes on from there to get worse. Next comes the wind. Well, no, not next. The wind comes first. It also comes next. There's never a lack of wind in Sydney and never a reason not to be aware of it, indoors or out. Windows that can't keep out flies and mosquitoes in summer make no pretence of resisting the Sydney wind. They rattle, bang, whine, but the wind cuts through them contemptuously. Last evening it blew down a main power line, and all the house lights and most of the street lights were out for nearly an hour. Today it's been driving rain all day, with clouds sweeping across the sky from two or more directions. The rain has now stopped temporarily and people are hurrying to get their Commonwealth Day fireworks shot off before it sets in again.

Perc said yes, when it rained it really rained, sometimes for days or even weeks, dropping on the city in a single 24-hour day enough water to fill two-thirds of Sydney Harbour. This brought to mind an event when trams still ran on Elizabeth Street. It was during one of these torrential storms which struck almost without warning, causing a large crowd to gather under the awning in front of his shop. In the midst of the storm a car trying to make a U-turn rammed into another car parked alongside the awning, pushing it right up on to the kerb and almost into the laps of the crowd. The driver, a tall thin man with a small black moustache, got out into the pouring rain and, with all the people looking at him, attempted to pull the two cars apart. Not succeeding he got back in behind the wheel and tried to pull away, but the other car stayed right with him, following him out into the roadway. Now his car, with the parked car at right angles to it, completely blocked the half of the street between the tram tracks and the kerb. The driver got out again, took his hat and coat from inside

*and, without a word to anyone, walked away down the street. Perc
assumed he was going for the police, but an hour went by and he
didn't return. After another half hour the owner of the parked car
arrived, asked what had happened, and went himself to summon
the police. He came back with a young constable and together
they prised the cars apart. Seeing little damage had been done the
owner of the parked car went on his way, leaving the abandoned
car still in the street.*

*As Perc told this story he would break into laughter every so
often, and then say he shouldn't be laughing as it really was quite
tragic.*

*The constable busied himself getting an eye-witness report on
the accident, and another half hour went by. Perc asked him if he
didn't think it might be a stolen car; otherwise the driver would
certainly have returned by now. The constable said the Department would already be checking on this. More time passed and the
evening rush-hour traffic began to back up behind the stranded
car. Perc asked if they ought to move it and break the traffic jam,
and the constable said he's just been thinking that very thing; so
together they pushed it into the space the parked car had
occupied. After another hour the constable said it was time for him
to quit and go home, which he did, leaving the empty car still
unexplained.*

*Perc laughed again and said he really shouldn't be laughing this
way; it was a tragedy really.*

*What happened was the owner walked straight down to Circular
Quay and threw himself in the water. He was a new migrant. He
hadn't a driver's licence although he did have a learner's permit.
He had just bought the car and was driving it home. The accident,
his fear of the consequences, the silent crowd watching him, and
above all the rain had driven him to desperation. Perc felt a bit
guilty about it too. He had thought of offering the man the use of
his phone to call the police; and if only someone had spoken to
him and reassured him the tragedy might have been prevented.*

We stopped on the way for a closer look at the rising Opera
House from a special viewing platform in the Botanic Gardens. It
is a building created out of sound shells, hoisted into place by
cranes, and bolted together. Men were building forms and filling
them with concrete for the huge pre-cast members that constitute
the sound shells. Close at hand we could watch the concrete mix
being poured out of a large funnel, then raised by a fork-lift which
roared and groaned with the effort, and packed into the forms by

men and boys with spades. The sheer size of the building, measured against the tiny men working about on it, and the massiveness of the concrete made me think of Egyptian overseers whipping their Hebrew slaves over the construction of one of Pharaoh's tombs. The concrete, the tremendous thickness of it, and its use everywhere, walls, roof, seats, this is what makes the Opera House the spectacular thing it is. Yet I don't believe it will be nearly as impressive finished as unfinished, the way it is now, hedged about by cranes, crisscrossed by catwalks, tiny workmen dangling from ropes and walking about on the immense forms.

We were half way through lunch when Barry and Elaine Forrester, who left the ship yesterday, called around with a station wagon and three small children. I gawked at the kids; they had said nothing about them. But both they and the station wagon belonged to Barry's brother whom he wanted us to meet. We took a circuitous tour, with the aim of crossing bridges—a particular love of theirs—over the Harbour Bridge, across Middle Harbour on the old Roseville Bridge and back on the Spit Bridge, back again over the Harbour Bridge, then Pyrmont and Iron Cove Bridges, returning to the North Shore over the toll-free Gladesville Bridge, which they like best of all. And justifiably so, for it is simple and structural, a rise and fall of pre-stressed concrete ribbon across an immense circle, 1,000 feet in diameter. It is light, strong, as elegant and as structurally well designed as a cobweb. We went through a number of suburbs whose names I'd heard on the ship: Leichhardt, Glebe, Hunter's Hill, Lane Cove—all with their streets of shops with wooden awnings. The Forresters said these awnings are not British, and Barry's brother Athol agreed; yet Athol's first view of New York disappointed him. He could not think it a proper city without them.

In our discussion at Athol's house I found many of the attitudes I have encountered on the ship confirmed: a firm belief that Australian politicians take bribes as a matter of course (I still doubt this) and that a certain tycoon is the leading bribe-giver; approval of lower pay to women on the grounds that all working women are merely supplementing their husbands' income; opposition, with as much emotion as an Australian can bring to any social or political issue, to subsidized immigration, coupled with a fatalistic acceptance of it (the only alternative—a really substantial baby bonus —would fail to satisfy immediate labour needs) ; opposition to the spiralling defence budget on the grounds that any conceivable sum Australia could afford for arms is insufficient to wage a modern war.

Still, like all the others whose words I've read or listened to, the Forresters can see no alternative to the Government's "all the way with LBJ" foreign policy. They don't like it. They'd rather Australia had a foreign policy and—if she must arm—an arms industry of her own, instead of being dependent on America for both. But the same problem of time that rules out the baby bonus rules out this as well. Faced therefore, on all the big issues, with having voluntarily to agree to policies they vigorously dislike the Forresters' reaction is one of apathy. They were apathetic even about their apathy, which they accepted with a smile and shrug.

Of Australia's seven major capital cities only Hobart has fewer clear days a year than Melbourne's 51 and more rainy days than Melbourne's 156. Only Brisbane has more foggy days than Melbourne's 29; no capital city has fewer daily sunshine hours than Melbourne's 5·6; only Canberra and Hobart have lower mean winter temperatures than Melbourne's 42·6 degrees. However Sydney, Brisbane, and Perth all have more total rainfall than Melbourne's 26 inches, and Adelaide, Brisbane, Perth, Canberra, and Sydney have higher mean summer temperatures than Melbourne's 78·6 degrees.

Nowhere is it possible to find comparative information on the single factor most relevant to living comfort in Australia: flies and mosquitoes. Yet when I told a South Australian I was thinking of spending a year in Canberra he replied at once, "The flies and mosquitoes are a lot worse than they are here." For a long time the blame for this was put on man-made Lake Burley Griffin (named in honour of the American architect who laid out the capital) which took years to fill up. Now the cause is said to be the great herds of cattle and sheep surrounding the city.

JANUARY 20: In Melbourne again after a tempestuous twenty-four hours. At every meal yesterday there were almost as many stewards as diners, and we ate in groups of two and three at scattered tables. All day long the ship pitched, its stern rising and falling I should say thirty feet. In the evening the stabilizers were disconnected and she rolled as well. The lifts refused to work. After the Sydney cruisers had left the ship and their places had been taken by disillusioned migrants returning to Europe the scene on the stair landings outside the dining rooms resembled Ellis Island. We knew the cruise was over when we sat down at the table. The little bottles of Chianti were no longer at each place. The menu from which we had been able to pick and choose an incredible variety of dishes was gone. In its stead was a single card which said in effect, "This is what we have to offer. Take it or leave it."

The ship was full of Sharpies and Stylists, and girls in black tights and pullover sweaters. After dinner we old-timers gathered in morose little groups. The prevailing theme of our remarks was, "It was good while it lasted." Though it was a cruise which had been billed as starting and ending in Melbourne, the hard facts of life had come home to the Victorians when the Farewell Ball was given the night before docking in Sydney. And I mustn't forget the two elderly ladies on the wild passage to Melbourne who got up, put on their life jackets over their nightdresses, and got fearfully back into bed.

We lost all our table companions in Sydney, the two venerable kiwis, Ralph and Sam, and the retired paper merchant whom everyone called by his first name Arthur, notwithstanding he was the oldest man on the ship. It was a congenial table, often nearly three o'clock when we got up from lunch and nearly ten when we finished dinner. Ralph and Sam, who considered themselves cobbers though they had just met, shared a four-berth cabin with two others, known to them only as the Greek and the Yugoslav. They also shared it with the clothes of the Yugoslav's wife, which filled the entire wardrobe, and the suitcases of the Greek which were so huge that Ralph had to sleep with his own case on his bunk. The Greek stayed in the cabin all day, pleading illness; and Sam, who was the picture of health during the Tasman crossing before the Greek got on, took to staying in with him. Each meal he ate less and less, each day he grew more and more like a wraith.

The Greek was no wraith; in the evening he got dressed, ate a good meal, and haunted the bar; but in the cabin he couldn't keep warm. On the second or third morning after he joined the ship he persuaded the Chief Electrician to shut off the air conditioning. Drafts were killing him. The four men slept that night in an air-tight room—smoky too, for sick as the Greek was, he smoked incessantly. Ralph, who loved fresh air so much he was hardly off the deck from early morning till bedtime, complained to the Chief Steward and got the porthole opened. The Greek countered by closing it when he went to bed. Ralph then took to leaving the cabin door open; the Greek insisted it be kept closed. Too drafty.

When Ralph appealed to the stewardess she, who had discussed it in her own tongue with the Greek, said, "Door open—no good. Door closed—good." Ralph got the Chief Steward to check on the air conditioning. The Greek counter-attacked on the open door.

111

Finally Ralph, who had been bringing hot broth each morning and afternoon to Sam—by now the only nourishment he would take—brought a cup also to the Greek, and the feud was over. The Greek accused the Yugoslav of stirring up trouble. More and more it became clear that he had no wife. He had bought the wardrobe full of women's clothes in Hawaii. Rather than take them through Customs he stayed on the ship for the second cruise which, being all-Australian, had no Customs inspection. The huge suitcases which Ralph thought belonged to the Greek were also his. He carried the clothes ashore in them.

One out of four adult Australians was born overseas. Among doctors, university staff members, shopkeepers, and the office personnel of foreign-owned concerns the proportion is closer to one in two. In Melbourne, Sydney, Adelaide, and Perth one-fourth of all the people, children included, are post-war migrants. They came, if from Britain, with an average per family savings of over $1,100, of which $700 was cash; they found after settling in that they had moved substantially up on the economic ladder if they were of the working class, and slightly down if not. Like the Dutch, who had also moved up, they came with every intention of staying permanently. Australia's appeal for them was in its climate, space, greater opportunities for their children, and most of all the promise of a home of their own in a small town. They had to settle for a suburb instead of the small town, but the British in particular stayed in the hostels—at four dollars a day for a family of four—until they got the home.

The south Europeans were undecided about how long they'd stay; one-third of the Italians meant to stay only a few years. They came frankly to improve their economic lot and did so; left the hostels as quickly as they could and clubbed together, four or five families to a flat, in an urban slum. Four out of five Greeks and Italians paid their full passage to Australia and, given a free choice, 53 per cent of the Greeks and 79 per cent of the Italians would go home. In actuality, judged by their behaviour, Greeks and Italians are among the most dependable of migrants; more than 88 per cent of them are still in Australia five years after their arrival.

Only three out of ten Dutch and four out of twenty-five British migrants paid their way to Australia. Given a free choice, three Britons in ten and four Dutch in seven would go home. But this of course would be among those who have elected to stay, for according to one survey, half of Australia's Dutch migrants have already gone home. Among Britons in particular the ratio of departures and arrivals varies from year to year and depends as much on conditions back home as in Australia.

A British travel agency advertises in Australian papers:

"Amazing offer!!! RETURN TO BRITAIN. TRAVEL NOW —PAY LATER! For a minimum deposit of $30 per adult ($16 for children) and the balance payable over a period of 12, 18, or 24 months arrangements can be made for your repatriation. Quotes from letters from Australia: 'If you only knew what your help means to us. We are all very grateful for all you have done. Please accept our very great thanks.' 'Thanking you very much for giving us this opportunity to return to England, for without this service you are giving it would take years of hard work and saving to achieve what you are doing for us in a matter of months.' Send NOW 35 cent Postal Order for U.K. REPATRIATION BROCHURE."

Notwithstanding such appeals eighty-six Britons out of a hundred stay on after five years; and of the fourteen who leave four will come back to give Australia "another go."

113

Americans are the least reliable migrants, and almost the fewest —although their numbers are increasing now at an average rate of nearly 25 per cent a year. About half are assisted and many come frankly with the hope of making a lot of money, only to discover that in Australia no less than the United States, it takes money to make money. "If you come to Australia with less than $20,000, have a round-trip ticket. But if you have money, this can be a commercial paradise." "You can barely move in this country without money, but if you have enough and know what to do with it there's plenty more to be made. I don't care where I become a millionaire as long as I do."

Not every American migrant can bring with him $20,000 or more to invest in one-piece bathtubs, attic fans, all-meat hot dogs, twin-basin sinks, double-glazed windows, electric door chimes, his and hers towels, central heating, or the dozen and one other things he sees a crying need for in Australia. Yet even among Americans eighty-one out of every hundred stay on.

A taxi took us to Victoria Market which turned out to be closed. I asked the driver to let us out there anyhow. We had talked the weather out, this being a subject which, he said, never got boring in Melbourne: it was always so changeable. He liked Melbourne for its weather and because it was the prettiest of Australian cities barring perhaps Perth which he hadn't seen. The marvel to him about Australia was that you could go anywhere and find the same kind of people speaking exactly the same language. "You hear a lot about different dialects but it's rubbish. Up in Queensland the people are supposed to drawl in their speech, and if you call their attention to it they do drawl because that's what they're supposed to do."

"How about Sydney people? I've heard they're quite different from Melbourne."

"Nothing but rubbish. They're no different. They all speak the same language."

"I have the impression of Australians being really quite like the English, a lot more so than you care to admit."

"Rubbish! I'm no bloody pom. My father and mother were both Australian."

"No. I didn't mean you were poms, but you have to be like some people and to me you seem very British. Both my father and mother were English but I feel I'm much less British than you are."

"In England everyone speaks a different language. You go just a

few miles away and you can't understand what they're saying. Here over the whole continent, or whole country if you like, we're all the same. I reckon we speak the best English that's spoken anywhere because everybody can understand it."

It was the Olympic Games he thought that changed lots of people's ideas about Australia. "People came here for the games and right away they asked, 'Where are your kangaroos? Where are your bloody blackfellows?' Surprised to find us living in cities and no kangaroos or blacks to be seen outside the zoo."

"I spent most of yesterday afternoon in the Uni library where I found a really good book called The American Language *by Mencken. They have a queer system where you have to present all your books to a man at the door so he can make sure you're not trying to pinch them I guess, when you are taking them out, that is. I have done it millions of times and usually he just sits there like a statue and never even smiles, let alone says anything. But my* American Language *really rocked him. It is a very big book, about three inches thick, and first he thumbed through it and said something about 'they haven't got that many swear words over there, have they?' Then he had another look at the title and said, 'They've got a cheek. They haven't got any language in America. They've just mucked up ours—English!' "*

Walking back into the city we saw a large procession tramping along on William Street toward Flagstaff Gardens. They were carrying placards reading: "Negotiations Now," "A Man's Life but a Boy's Pay," "Go Slow for More Dough," and "Demand a Decent Wage. Raise Wages not Prices." They paraded into the park and held a meeting. It was short and snappy. The main speaker declared they were getting the runaround from the Arbitration Court on their claim for a wage increase to match the increase in production efficiency. So now they were taking the matter to the rank and file. This drew applause. Then he said that when the court made its new award they would demand it be made retrospective to the end of the year. This drew more applause. Then he called for a motion to hold regular weekly one-hour stop-work meetings at lunchtime and this was voted unanimously.

I asked one of the men about this stop-work business. It seems that under Australia's arbitration system a union is fined thousands of dollars if it calls a strike, but a stop-work meeting doesn't count if it lasts no more than four hours. Wages are not determined by collective bargaining between the union and employer, but by court decree in the form of awards that apply to different classifications of worker over the whole country. Theoretically each award incorporates a minimum weekly sum that every working man requires to support a family, together with an additional amount meant to reward him for his skill. The man I talked to, a union officer evidently, said the system had its advantages in promoting industrial harmony, but the court awards never managed to keep pace with the rise in the cost of living. The minimum wage for a skilled workingman amounted to 93 cents an hour (U.S. $1.04) in Victoria; and for women doing identical work it was considerably less.

"Still you do have strikes," I said. He agreed but said these were mostly in the public service, places like the railways, the post office, and city transport. "Why on earth should that be?" I asked. He didn't know. That was the way it was.

Day after day the postman wheeled by, stopping at no more than one mailbox in the block. I could imagine his going to the striking sorters and saying, "Look, mates, I have to make the run anyhow. Can't you let loose of just a few letters?"

In their widely different reactions to an event like a postal strike I found the greatest contrast between Americans and Australians. In the United States, long before such a strike had gone on this long the President would have appeared on a nationwide television hook-up to mobilize public opinion against it. Newspapers would have printed headlines two inches high; columnists would be assessing the strike's cost to the nation. Wall Street would have reacted sharply downward, and new Congressional investigations would have been launched to ferret out the Communists behind it. Here the Prime Minister didn't, until the strike was a week old, appear to know it was going on; and all he did then was issue a mild statement deploring it: which statement was dutifully paragraphed in the press.

Otherwise there was virtually nothing about the strike either in print or over the air. The stock market was blithely unaffected; no parliamentarian saw fit to denounce the Communists responsible; nobody had the least idea what the cost might be to the Nation or how the strike would affect the morale of the troops fighting communist subversion. As for the people, they trotted out to their mail boxes, came back empty-handed, and shrugged.

When at last the strike ended and the postman arrived on his bicycle, carring a full bag of mail for the first time in weeks, I said, "I bet even the dogs were glad to see you." "Yes," he said, "they all gathered around along with the people." I said if there was a postal strike in the United States, the newspapers and Government would be up in arms; there'd be demands to call out the National Guard. How did Australians feel about it? He said 90 per cent of them didn't even think about it. The union made special arrangements for pensioners to get their cheques and nobody else minded the mail being held up.

He said the strike was for equal pay for women which he thought they should have, although it was not in their best interest. Only fifteen years ago an Australian would have been ashamed to have his wife work, whereas today the wife who didn't work was the exception. And nobody was really any better off. Prices and rents were set at a level the average family could afford to pay, and now they had simply gone up to take what the wife earned as well. It was no longer possible for a man to support his family on his earnings alone—or, if possible, not as easy as it used to be—but, he said, "When women get equal pay they'll simply put themselves in tighter bondage because of the higher rents and prices."

I asked how the dispute was likely to be settled and he said, by arbitration as they always were. The problem the Australian unions had with the arbitration system was that it was a battle of lawyers, and litigation costs were steep. The Government and big employers had unlimited funds and could keep a case in court until the union went bankrupt. That was why the postal sorters went on strike. I told him it was a good thing Australians were so easy-going. "In the U.S. you'd have been lynched." He said he knew it.

17

Dr Dunhill said Melbourne and Sydney were comparable to San Francisco and Los Angeles. Melbourne it was true didn't look much like San Francisco but in temperament they were similar. In both cities, for example, people entertained in their homes; in Sydney it was rare even to get inside a person's home. The club was the centre of Sydney's social life. When he was last in Sydney a friend told him he was planning to open a chess club.

"Nothing unusual about a chess club," I said.

"True," said Dr Dunhill. His friend's first move had been to apply for a licence. "To play chess?" "To open a club." A club licence was like money in the bank, and to get one you needed a worthy charity for the club profits to go to. I said his friend must be dreaming if he hoped for any profits from a chess club. Dr Dunhill said the profits weren't to come from chess; they were to go to chess. Chess was the worthy charity. Everything depended on getting that licence. Once he got it his friend would finance the building and fittings with monthly payments of $600 for five years, and by then the club would have earned enough extra to pay off the rest. It would be located at Mascot Airport, an area Dr Dunhill knew to be more crowded with factory hands than chess-players. He asked his friend: "Will you find enough who play chess in Sydney to fill out your club?" The friend replied: "We hope they don't play chess. Then they'll play the poker machines."

Not all of Sydney's shop windows are decorated like shoestores; so that if you don't see what you want in the window you know the store hasn't got it. Nor all of Melbourne's tasteful and chaste, featuring a single model or a single colour; but the trend is in these directions. Sydney's arcades are bustling affairs; Melbourne's have, many of them, the spaciousness of a cathedral and are almost as quiet. The shops themselves, with their equally quiet windows, appear almost incidental.

The contrast between the cities begins at the moment of arrival. If you come by sea you meet Sydney at its best and Melbourne at its worst; the reverse is true by rail. Sydney's Central Station is a big draughty barn overflowing with people and heaps of luggage, with no place to sit and long baggage trains and tractors barging through what amounts to the waiting room. Melbourne's Spencer Street Station, where interstate and interurban trains arrive, is clean, bright, new; clocks everywhere you turn, trolleys available for passengers' luggage, and a large waiting room and restaurant on the first floor (first off the ground, that is). In the late afternoon we watched the changing sky above industrial Melbourne from this waiting room—smears of smoke over thin pink clouds, the blue smoke turning purple as it went up. Below was the complex of tracks, signals, and trolleys of Victoria's remarkable railway system, and beyond them the Yarra River and Victoria Dock crowded with ships.

As long ago as 1883 a traveller could write of the two cities: "The natural beauties of Sydney are worth coming all the way to see; but . . . there is more Society in Melbourne, more balls and parties, more intellectual life, more books and men of education and intellect, more and better theatrical performances, more racing and cricket, football and athletic clubs. There is a better leisured class than in Sydney; . . . here is the best development of Australian civilization—in commerce or education, wealth or intellect, manners or customs. . . . Coming up the harbour, Sydney is charming and picturesque, while Melbourne is commonplace and repellent. But the crooked and narrow Sydney streets look like old friends, and so are forgiven. . . . Melbourne has always its dress clothes on. Sydney is perennially en deshabillé."

Neither of Melbourne's two railways stations has put a blight on its part of the city the way Sydney's Central Station has—a veritable hole in the city: empty and abandoned hotels and department stores, a plethora of pawnshops, auctions, surplus stores, and second-hand book stores; and in the evening, female evangelists singing and preaching to down-and-outers. Busy and attractive shops, on the other hand, line the streets leading up to Flinders Station; and Collins Street near Spencer Station must be Australia's architectural showpiece—an entrancing row of 19th-century baroque palaces in stone, crowned by the splendid Federal

Hotel, proud and well-kept and sporting a cupola at the very top, with windows all round for a haughty panoramic view of the city.

There are several attractive restaurants in Collins Street, but before we could all agree on one we were at the other side of town coming back on Bourke—or was it Little Bourke? Anyhow we ended up in a Chinese café owned by a young man from Hong Kong named Jimmy Young. He came to Australia to study industrial chemistry at the University of Melbourne. After graduation he got a job at General Motors-Holden but something came up about his being Chinese and he was not permitted to work as an industrial chemist under the white Australia policy. However a loophole in the law allowed him to stay in the country as a businessman if he owned his business. So he started a café and has been here thirteen years. He'd like to have gone back after getting his degree, but the trouble was Hong Kong didn't have any industries where they'd need industrial chemists. They were all quite small—button making and things like that. He wouldn't consider going to Taiwan, and Red China, well, he didn't know what to expect.

Almost the first thing the Australian colonies did after forming their federation was to adopt an Immigration Act. The second thing was to levy a tax on sugar. The second law was designed to put coloured people out of the country, the first to keep them out. Queensland sugar was being harvested by "Kanakas," or Pacific Islanders. The tax was three pounds on each ton of raw sugar, with a rebate of two pounds if only white labour was used in producing it. In almost no time at all the kanakas were gone and new white workers, specially imported from Italy, had taken their places in the canefields. The Immigration Act—sometimes called Australia's Natal act—did not specifically exclude migrants because of colour or race. Joseph Chamberlain, Britain's colonial secretary, recommended instead as a model a law recently adopted by Natal. This prescribed an education test for each would-be immigrant by requiring him to write his application in a European language. It seemed fair enough. Such a test would protect Australia from hordes of unlettered Indians and Chinese while leaving the door open to the educated Japanese or Siamese, who could usually read and write at least one European language. But there was a catch to it. The choice of language was up to the Immigration examiner and there was no limit to the number of different languages he might require of any one applicant. Thus a Filipino might know Spanish and English and the examiner select Italian; and, finding the

121

applicant also knew Italian, go on to Greek, Russian, Swedish, or Icelandic. The depth of absurdity was reached in 1934 when the left-wing writer Egon Kisch was given the test in Gaelic. Technically Gaelic was the official language of Eire but not one native Irishman in 10,000 could have passed the test. Kisch, who was later to become Czechoslovakia's Minister of Education, had no intention of migrating in the first place. He had been chosen as a delegate and speaker to an Australian anti-war conference; but when his ship reached Perth he was locked in his cabin and forbidden to go ashore. Four days later in Melbourne he leapt ashore and broke his leg. He failed to pass his test in Gaelic. He was arrested in the hospital and charged with being a prohibited immigrant. He was convicted and sentenced to six months in jail. Pending appeal Kisch and another fugitive, a New Zealander, addressed public meetings in different parts of the country. As almost always happens in Australia's immigration cases public sympathy was on the side of the lawbreaker and Kisch's sentence was suspended on condition that he leave the country.

JANUARY 21: Melbourne's widely hoped-for heat wave arrived in the form of "a dirty day," as a salesgirl in Treadway's described it to Peggy. It had been building up to it. There's a high pressure area more or less stationary over Tasmania. This has caused the air to move very slowly across the hot continent and a north wind has been pushing the super-heated air into the city. On Tuesday, when we were battling the seas of Bass Strait, Melbourne's highest temperature was around 70. Yesterday it moved up into the 90s and today it went over 100. Everybody was cheerful on account of the weather having "warmed up at last" but even more cheerful, I thought, over the prospect of "a cool change."

Once or twice in Sydney I overheard a casual reference to the cool change, and I suspect Perth's "Fremantle doctor" is just another name for it, so it's evidently something all Australia counts on: but to Melbourne the cool change is an article of faith. As the thermometer climbed in the afternoon I saw people looking anxiously to the west for the clouding over that would augur a south wind. And well they might. Going out from any building, and in particular an air-cooled department store, was like going into an oven. The nearest thing to it in my experience was a 115-degree day in Las Vegas, Nevada.

The only real difference was that in Melbourne you knew it wouldn't last. The cool change would come. So everybody kept assuring us. When it finally did come it was quite dramatic. We were in the railway station at Moonee Ponds. It set up a whirl-wind, blowing dust and leaves and old tickets around. People said, "Ah, the cool change!" and through the clouds of dust you could see their dispositions change. By the time we got back to Flinders it was hard to believe it had ever been hot; and in Port Melbourne my teeth were chattering.

Our train going in had been filled up with shoppers so quickly that seats grew scarce. The same must have been true on the other lines because the wide footpath up Swanston Street from the station was filled from shop window to kerb with women and prams. And all were heading for the same place we were: Myer's Emporium. When we got to the entrance on Bourke Street there were other streams of women and prams funnelling into it from three directions.

The city has installed special traffic lights in the middle of the block, giving a passage across Bourke Street somewhat wider than the street itself. While the red lights were on against the cars and trams the pavement was almost hidden from sight by the steadily moving stream of women and prams. The aisles in the big store were choked by the sluggish stream but somehow it all got dispersed: up the escalators prams and all, and up the elevators. The operators were old hands at arranging the prams to take full use of the floor space. It was a miracle what a long line of prams a single car could swallow up.

The pram or pusher is the single most identifiable feature of the Australian street scene—next to the dog and the bag. Everybody carries a bag, men, women, children, all save pram-pushers. Men's bags are brown leather, or leather-plastic, long, narrow, and low, and clasping together at the top where the handle is. They look like tool kits but are called tucker bags. Children's are briefcases and as heavy as lead, ideal for warding off dogs—a handy weapon to have in Australia. Women's bags are of string or canvas, some-times so large they must be propelled on wheels.

Myer's is much like an American department store but with certain major differences. There is less emphasis on seeds, plants, fertilizer, cans of paint, and home workshop tools—suggesting that Australian males don't do a lot of work around the house; and more emphasis on patterns, yard goods, and yarns and knitting materials—indicating that Australian women do. A large part of the ground floor of one building (there are two) is a grocery supermarket where I saw pickles from Poland, dried shrimp (for *nasi goreng*) from Holland, mushrooms from France, *saké* from Japan, tinned spiced duck from China, tinned enchiladas from the U.S., and pure maple syrup from Canada. An even larger area is devoted to hot and cold take-out foods, and here I discovered Melbourne's answer to Sydney's lunch in the park.

Before noon the counters were lined with purchasing agents, each with a cardboard box at his or her feet into which were packed dishes of steak and onions, steak and kidney, lamb stew, creamed crayfish, braised lamb with rice, curried chicken, and macaroni with cheese for the mates in the office or on the construction job. By noon there were queues reaching out from the most popular items on sale: hamburger with fried egg, fish and chips, barbecued chicken, and that great Australian staple, meat pie.

Candi proposed we buy something ourselves and take it up to the cafeteria where we could get a drink and dessert to go with it. I felt very conspiratorial off in a corner of the large restaurant when I surreptitiously unwrapped my fried breast of chicken. But as I looked around I saw that about half the people there had anticipated us by bringing their lunches from home. And one, disdaining Myer's tea, had her own can of pineapple juice and a can opener in her purse. All that Myer's supplied, besides the table, was a drinking straw and it was free.

We caught a cab near Myer's entrance. The driver was just back from a two-week vacation at Surfer's Paradise. The climate is ideal —80 degrees all year round—with just one off-season month when most of the annual fifty inches of rain falls. It was costly, $400, but worth it; and what's money for if not to spend? He was born in western Victoria, a descendant of one of the squatters, and some of these squatter families, he says, are far wealthier than a city executive ever gets. He'd rather live in Sydney than Melbourne, partly because there's more cab business but mainly because it's a livelier town. The clubs are open to everyone, not just a select few as in Melbourne. "More democratic," I said, "That's it!" he replied eagerly. "More democratic!" And from then on it was his touchstone. He didn't consider the climate any better, or job opportunities. Just that Sydney is more democratic.

A large arrow atop a ten-story building greeted us in Moonee Ponds, urging us to "shop on Puckle Street." Moonee Ponds and Puckle Street are as undistinguished as anything can be, but they are undistinguished in an altogether distinctive Australian way. The coin laundry and supermarket have still to invade them. Not all the women and prams were streaming in and out of Myer's; there were hundreds on Puckle Street, bustling into the little shops and along the footpaths, stopping for long conversations, strolling two or three abreast with mounds of newspaper-wrapped meat, vegetables, and fruit heaped precariously on the hoods. We have still to see the outback, the interior, the bush where the real Australia is supposed to be, but until we see it Moonee Ponds and Puckle Street will do me.

18

"There were crowds of people in Port Wakefield and we were bumper to bumper for about two miles approaching it. There were caravans and boats and little trailers full of camping gear and motorcycle convoys with teenagers in black leather jackets and long hair. The B.P. service station where we picked up the caravan was alive with people. Everyone seemed to be leaving to go on Easter holiday. On the way down Grandpa talked non-stop about herding sheep down the peninsula before the days of the motorcar, and fox hunting, and the big year in 1928 when the crabs were so thick they fetched out piles of them, as high as a man, along the beach at Clinton.

"We finally got to Bullamakanka and the camping ground. It was already jam-packed with caravans. We had fish and chips for tea cooked in the two electric frypans. On Saturday the boy scouts had a cake sale opposite the old hotel where Grandpa had his first teeth pulled. The guy that pulled them was half sozzled and took him upstairs and yanked them out all eight of them, and then took him down to the bar and gave him two glasses of brandy, one to wash his mouth out with and one to get into him. The cakes were pretty awful but we bought two. Then we went cockling which means digging for clams and got a kerosene tin full. Then we went back to the town.

"The whole town is old. Every building is made of stone and mud, with a galvanized iron or wooden roof. There is a big general store with a great high roof and you can see the kitchen with an old wood stove in the living quarters behind. The town used to be a thriving wheat market and ships pulled into the jetty and were loaded by the townspeople. Grandpa once carried fifty bags of wheat with only four horses from one of the farms down to the town. But now the whole town is silent as a tomb. There

126

didn't seem to be any motor-cars and Grandpa said all they did for
entertainment was sleep with each others' wives.

"On Sunday we went to visit Auntie Laura who lives in Wook
Wook, a small town like Susanburg but kept alive by the salt
works there. The house is big and old. The kitchen, where we
stayed mostly, has a wooden stove that she uses when the power is
off, and also an electric one. The kitchen table is in the middle
and there are cupboards around with fancy canisters on top for
everything. The whole place is old-fashioned and dark because she
keeps the blinds down. She cooked while she talked, first making a
huge trifle out of custard and jelly and old cake and pears. Then
she put enough meat to feed a battalion into her electric frypan
and enough grease to deep-fry it. Her main topics of conversation
were her hysterectomy operation and her children and grand-
children. Then she sprung the news on us that we were to stay for
lunch because she had cooked for us. It must get very lonely in
such an isolated spot, though, and they thirst for visitors. It would
be awfully boring really but it does have an atmosphere.

"We went for a drive down to the jetty and Grandpa got abused
by the driver of this other car because it was a one-car-at-a-time
road and he reckoned we started after him. All along on either
side were mangrove swamps, and the creek where the jetty was
meandered through the mangroves."

JANUARY 23: It must have been all of 11 o'clock this morning,
after docking at Outer Harbour last evening, before our car was
freed, cleared by Customs, and allowed to travel over South Australian roads. We had just enough time to get into Port Adelaide
for our weekend necessities before the shops closed. There were
lots of other last minute shoppers as well however: hatless women
in coloured cardigans and high heels pulling shopping carts or
pushing prams; long-haired youths in black or bright red cardigans emerging from cars with matching two-colour cushions
propped in the rear window; sailors in soiled khaki pants, dark
blue pea-jackets, pullovers, battered felt hats—almost the only hats
worn; workingmen in overalls with the snap-closing brown leather
bags from which they will apparently never let themselves be
separated; farmers with red faces and grey, wide-strapped overalls.
A few Customs officers wore white shirts and black ties; all others
had open collars and loose fitting pants that drooped over their
shoe heels. Except for the wide main street with statues at the
intersections, and the crinoline and lacework public buildings of

this old port town, I could easily have mistaken it for Moonee Ponds. Another State but still Australia.

We headed south along St Vincent Bay. It was like driving through the desert beside the Salton Sea. There were almost no trees; the few growing there were Norfolk pines which cast no shade. Houses faced the water and the blazing afternoon sun. Amusement park succeeded amusement park, but eating in any other form than from a bag and bottle seemed impossible. We stopped to do this at Glenelg, the largest of the seaside resorts, with a two-car electric tram on the main street. The beaches were covered with people and canvas shades; the flies were everywhere —small flies which liked nothing better than a face on which to land and stick. Men's hats were sprinkled all over with them, and once settled they wouldn't move. The grass-covered hills were tinder-dry. A cigarette stub could set the entire country-side ablaze.

When we reached the campground recommended by Austin of the Automobile Association it was crammed full. But Fred, the cheerful superintendent, found us a space at the far end and he warned, "You aren't going to like it," but we do. Neighbours offered to help us as soon as we started to stake down the tent. One group of youths, with half an eye on Candi, came over and stayed for a long conversation about Sydney where they hale from, about hunting roos, America as they see it in the movies and TV, their jobs as fitters or assemblers in a road machinery plant where they earn $42 for a 40-hour week; about abos and corroborees and their skill with the boomerang and their unfamiliarity with clothing. They see a bleak future for the Aborigines because, as they explain it, they're lazy. All Australians are lazy, they added. Life comes too easy for them.

In 1950 at the age of seventy-eight Bertrand Russell spent two months in Australia on a lecture tour of Sydney, Brisbane, Canberra, Melbourne, Adelaide, Perth, and Alice Springs. Whereas he had always thought Australians were "rather like Americans, only more so," at the close of his tour he had come to believe Australians to be the happier, without "the same restless itch to be always doing something else, or being somewhere else." He conceded "American restlessness is bound up with American energy and enterprise, and it is possible that if Australia were inhabited by Americans its resources would be developed more rapidly. But, if so, this result would be surely purchased at the price of universal discontent." Had he the choice of being born again it would be in Australia rather than in western Europe. "The greatness of Australia lies ahead—the greatness of Europe lies behind. . . . To live with a vision of the future brings hope and vigour and happiness. . . . If the old culture of Europe can be transplanted into the environment of an expansive economy, a new vigour and a new renaissance are to be expected."

By now I've become accustomed to the Australian lingo: the invariable "me" for my, and the diphthonged *a*. Nevertheless the boys completely fooled me on one word. I said something about the experimental rocket launching base up north in the South Australian desert at Woomera. "My word!" said Dennis, one of the lads, "we've got a proper big spice industry!" For the life of me I couldn't grasp what the subject of spices was doing in the conversation.

They talked about bushrangers, and of Ned Kelly in particular, Australia's Jesse James; of the boys' very real pride in their country, its great size and surprising growth in the less than 200 years since settlement; its mineral and manufacturing potential, and withal its Aborigines still hunting and fighting with spears; how a new tribe was recently rediscovered after being thought extinct.

When they learned we meant to tour the country they cautioned against the coast road to Melbourne, a narrow cliff-hanger, and said the best surfing beaches were in New South Wales, just out of Sydney.

Why, I asked, didn't I see a streak of bleached hair on their heads? Aw, this was out. There were surfers and surfies. Surfies bleached their hair, carried boards on their trucks, and lay on the beach—but did no actual surfing. Then there were those who drove around in wooden station wagons: they were woodies. And there was another group whose name escapes me who do nothing but lie on the beach: it might be sandies. There are also bodgies and widgies—native Aussie words—as well as sorts and she-las; but a girl doesn't fancy being called one. The most common expression of all is, "I haven't a clue," sometimes shortened to "I'm clueless."

The greatest Australian literary success of all time was Nino Culotta's They're a Weird Mob, *the purported impressions of an Italian immigrant trying to "sort things out" in the "lucky country." First published in 1957 it had gone into innumerable printings by 1966 when it was made into a film; and the film in turn played for months to packed houses all over the country. The book, which by then had sold nearly half a million copies, all in Australia—comparable on a* per capita *basis to eight million in the United States—is almost entirely in dialogue with the words spelled in a way calculated to show peculiarities of the Australian dialect: a dialect given the name of Strine from the way the word "Australian" is supposed to be pronounced in it. Thus in* Weird Mob *the word "it" is written "ut" and "what" is written "wot."*

At the other end of the critical spectrum Patrick White, unanimously acclaimed by the literary quarterlies as Australia's foremost contemporary author (and by some the foremost author writing today in the English language), has the same strong predilection as Nino Culotta for short punchy paragraphs and for words misspelt to symbolize dialect. Some examples: waddaya, ter (for "to"), yer (for "your"), anythun, waddaboutut, mornun, gunna, evenun, inter (for "into"), yairs (for "yes"), pomes (for "poems"), waddayaknow, cryun, waddayaget.

There is nothing distinctively Australian about these, or about most of the words given peculiar misspellings in the various Strine dictionaries. Josh Billings used the identical spellings a century ago in an equally forlorn attempt to reproduce American speech.

130

Australians don't, as a matter of fact, mangle their words nearly as much as the speaker of what is called cultured English. A word like "again," for example, is so carefully uttered in Australian that it becomes two words: "a gain," with heavy emphasis on "gain." "Stupid" becomes "stchupid" and "duke," "juke."

Australian differs from English on the one hand and American on the other, first of all, in where the sound seems to originate. In English it is the head, in American the chest, and in Australian the throat, with characteristically a slight rasp. Australians give a distinctive twist to vowels, a trait said to be borrowed from the English cockney dialect, though this is doubtful. The most noticeable instance, and the one invariably stressed by all who endeavour to imitate Australian speech, is the turning of long a into the diphthong ah-ee. "Today" becomes "to die," "tape" becomes "type," and lace, "lice."

There is a story in this connection of the diner who, having finished his meal, thought he'd top it off with a piece of pie. He told the waitress and, growing impatient when he didn't get it, called out, "How about the pie?" "Pie," shouted the waitress. "You pie the cashier." Tales of such misunderstandings abound in Australian folklore.

The chief characteristic the Australian shares with American language is a colourful slang. Perhaps not a great deal of it actually originated in Australia; much seems to have had its beginning in England, then to have been forgotten there, and lately to have been borrowed back from Australia. "Mate," the universal Australian form of male address, has now been taken over wholly by Britain. Other terms Australia shares with Britain are "bloke," "blighter," and "joker," meaning guy or fellow, "bird" meaning girl, and "bod" meaning person; the oaths "bloody," "bastard," "bugger," and "my word," all used with much more zest in Australia; "laid on" for installed or prepared, "bung up" for to install or prepare, "flat out" for all the way, and —curiously—"reckon," presumably borrowed from America but now almost never heard there outside the cowboy films.

Some of the more native Australian words and expressions are: "I gave it away," "sling off," "barrack," "rubbish," "shout," and "send her down, Hughie," meaning respectively: I quit, open one's big mouth, root or cheer, denigrate, offer a drink, and pray give us rain, oh Lord. Then there's a welter of mainly occupational words ending in o or ie like smoko (coffee break), garbo (garbage collector), milko (milkman), postie (postman), Commo (Communist), Woolies (Woolworth's), Presbo (Presbyterian),

131

Salvo (Salvation Army soldier), hottie (hot water bottle), arvo (afternoon), drongo (a dope), pommie or pom (English migrant), reffo (refugee or other European migrant), Aussie (pronounced awzie or ozzie: Australian or Australia), mozzie (mosquito), pozzie (position or spot), cuie (cucumber), and dinkie die or dinkum (genuine or native to Australia.)

And finally, though not by any means exhaustively, there are: offsider (partner or helper), cobber (buddy or friend), ratbag (a creep), shickered (drunk), lurk (an angle or scheme), stickybeak (nosey), bonzer (swell), skite (boast), bowser (gas pump), crook (sick), lolly (candy), paddock (field or yard), wowser (bluenose), dicey (chancy), souvenir (steal or pilfer), hoop (jockey), blue (a fight), nohoper (a deadbeat), mob (flock of sheep or herd of cattle) and outback (the rural interior).

When the tent was up we thanked the boys and took off for Adelaide—set well in from the sea coast, as are all Australia's capitals except Sydney. It's very like Melbourne, though only about a quarter as large, its streets carefully laid out on a square flat piece of ground—the initial attraction of the site, I should imagine—and the whole surrounded by parkland, with sheep nibbling on some of the dry grass! The central avenue, King William Street, is banked with commodious old buildings. It is crossed at what was originally the northern limit of the town by North Terrace, with the railway station and platforms reaching along it west of King William, and the Governor's residence and grounds, succeeded by the Public Library, National Art Gallery, and Adelaide University along on the east. Facing them, east and west, are more commodious old buildings, while to the north, through what remains of the original parkland, runs the Torrens River, a miniature Yarra that further points up Adelaide's resemblance to Melbourne.

We ate a second lunch in Elder Park beside the river, amidst every kind of tree except the native eucalypt and in the company of other picnickers, sleepers, and courting couples stretched out on the grass. Hired paddle-boats were being blown into the spray of a large fountain rising from the surface of the water; several dark ducks and a black swan swam about; but a few oared sculls which ventured out had to turn back because of the wind. A motor launch named *Popeye* dawdled at the bank, hoping to attract enough passengers to justify a cruise to the Adelaide Zoo and back. After our light lunch we walked down King William Street under colourful retaining walls of native stone, and on to North Terrace, wider even than King William and bordered by stately shade trees.

These were the more noticeable because of the almost total absence of trees on our drive through the suburbs coming in.

More and more I find a surprising similarity between urban Australia—South Australia in particular—and California. The climate is similar, even to some extent the architecture, and the way of life—well, in the park it was baseball the small boys were playing, not cricket. They wore regular uniforms, had a regulation bat and ball, everything the same except the umpire consistently referred to each inning as an "innings"—"innings" being the cricket term. I told a young policeman I really missed only one thing from home: the beautiful gum trees waving gracefully above the houses and low buildings, their feathery foliage letting the sun filter through to lawns and gardens beneath them. He agreed it would be a good thing to have native Australian trees in Australian cities, something besides Lombardy poplars, weeping willows, and Norfolk pines. He said, though, that trees in general and eucalypts in particular are viewed with a kind of horror by the different councils—light and power, telephone, highway, and water—who suspect them all of white ant infestation. In Marion, South Australia, a fight by residents to preserve some centuries-old gums against a council's chain saw got national attention, but the gums were cut down nevertheless. However, the policeman assured me I could see gum trees any time I wanted by following a narrow dirt track for several miles off the Main North Road to a reserve called Humbug Scrub; and there were special parks in Brisbane and Perth where the eucalyptus was preserved, together with the nearly extinct koala bear.

19

Ray Lawler's Summer of the Seventeenth Doll *is an apparently simple and not too remarkable play about two sugarcane-cutters, Roo and Barney, who come to Melbourne during their five-months' layoff to spend the holiday with their girl-friends, Olive and Nancy. They have been doing this for sixteen years, keeping alive a custom that in its youth and freedom has been superior to marriage—a constantly renewing honeymoon. Then in the seventeenth summer of the idyll, age overtakes it. Barney, who has always been a phenomenal lady-killer, finds at forty that the girls laugh at him. Roo, head man in a gang of cutters, is beaten on the job by a young recruit. This on the surface is what* Doll *is about—not the sturdiest peg it would seem for Australia to hang her own native theatre on.*

But behind the simple plot is something else, something of very special significance to Australia. What gives the play its peculiar pathos is that it is not merely an idyllic existence which comes to an end in the doll-decorated room shown on the stage. Dying with it is the great Australian myth. Roo and Barney personify the myth. "They'd walk into the pub as if they owned it—even just in the way they walked you could spot it. All round would be the regulars—soft city blokes having their drinks and their little arguments, and then in would come Roo and Barney. They wouldn't say anything—they didn't have to—there'd be just the two of them walkin' in, then a kind of wait for a second or two, and quiet. After that, without a word, the regulars'd stand aside to let 'em through, just as if they was—a coupla kings."

The play revealed to its first audience in the mid-1950s an Australia no longer free enough or young enough to support such a myth. The myth, the very myth—let alone whatever reality it may or may not once have had—had been outgrown. It had survived briefly and most uncertainly in this room decorated with kewpie

134

*dolls. The room was in an old house in the Melbourne suburb of
Carlton; and Carlton—once the epitome of Australian middle-class
respectability, now overcrowded with "Balts" and "reffos"—
typified the tremendous changes that had overtaken Australia in the
past seventeen years. Under the impact of the war and of the post-
war immigration, from being an agricultural supplier of Britain,
Australia had become an industrial nation in her own right. Factories and factory hands had doubled; manufactures had tripled;
labour-saving machinery had gone up four times. A million European migrants, with their strange tongues and customs, with myths
and traditions of their own, had been suddenly received into a
total population of ten million.*

*What chance had the Australian myth, the unlikely myth of the
swagman, shearer, bushranger, of the free Australian of the outback, to survive in such an environment? It couldn't—any more
than the doll-decorated room of Ray Lawler's play. One girl lost
faith in it and got herself married. One outsider, representing the
new aggressive younger generation of Australians, walked into the
precious room and withered its pretences. And one woman, with a
mother's grasp of reality concerning her own daughter, proved by
her scepticism that there had never been any such myth: the free
life symbolized by the doll-decorated room had never existed
either. "But," even she seems to say, "if it had. If it only had."*

In Adelaide later today, to shop and borrow some books, we
were able to park comfortably close to North Terrace where most
of the city's cultural and business interests are centred. Here
amidst trees and monumental statuary we briefly visited the
National Art Gallery and I liked it better than the one in Sydney,
if only because the old portraits and landscapes done in yellow
varnish, which every public gallery must own, seemed mercifully
screened from public view. In the succession of large rooms there
were English and Australian watercolours, Aboriginal bark paintings, and oils by contemporary Australians including one by Nolan
which caught Candi's eye, and another by a South Australian
Jacqueline Hick which interested me. Nolan paints with the
self-assurance born of success as the recognized leader of contemporary Australian painters. His painting is brilliant, brittle, professional, and entirely international. Hick, apparently unrecognized
outside her own State, still seems to be finding things out. To
some extent she may be influenced by the Aboriginal bark painters
but evidently no one in Australia really is.

I find I had an entirely false impression of bark painting, either

135

because of some bad reproductions or the name given it. It is not bark painting at all, any more than oil painters produce canvas painting or masonite painting. Bark is not the medium; it is the ground. The medium appears to be vegetable dyes for the most part and white clay, perhaps, which produces a slight tactile effect. The paintings do not, as a rule, make an effort to retain and incorporate in them the essential nature of the bark. The bark was used to paint on because it was handy and portable. I wished they had been grouped by district of origin. It would have been easier to observe regional similarities and differences and understand the artists' aims.

With some effort, due to their not being grouped, Candi and I worked out certain regional traits. Yirrkala painters for example have a passion for covering every inch of space. Groote Islanders on the other hand set their objects boldly and with consummate economy and precision on dramatic black backgrounds. Oenpelli artists like to tell a story: how the shark devoured the porpoise; how I speared the kangaroo; how we paddled our canoes, etc. Another group—possibly Arnhem Land—used the texture of the bark as part of the picture.

All have a narrow palette of brown, black, and liberal use of white in the form of brushed lines, never massed. Decoration takes the place of light and dark, bringing out the form; and the decoration is flat, consisting of diagonal lines with horizontal bands for divisions. Functions of structure are also shown schematically. A kangaroo, for instance, reveals its backbone and its trachea leading to a cross-hatched stomach (cross-hatching I suspect implies volume), with a wavy intestine below it down to a more carefully drawn anal region. Likewise people wearing clothes reveal their cross-hatched arms, torsos, and legs under the clothes. White, as I say, is liberally used in this cross-hatching.

I learned from Miss Peach who comes from Adelaide that there's a geographical library with a lot of Australiana I never knew about. And how I used to comb over the shelves in search of the smallest scrap! She said they'd had difficulty getting their new building. They'd planned a six-storey structure capable of shelving a million books, got all the materials for it stored in various places, and then had the building cut down for budgetary reasons to three storeys. She also said that under a former librarian, Huntington somebody or other, the library was much better handled, being purely a reference library. But in his decline and illness a decision was taken to create a lending library. Instead of insisting that this

be separate and that books be purchased especially for lending he
let them go ahead lending the reference books, and this has played
hob with the library. I can imagine that. I rather think much the
same thing may have happened to the other city and State libraries,
notably Sydney and Victoria. Both are dark, dingy places in
their lending sections, ill-suited to reading, with a yawning dearth
in some fields and an unnecessary over-supply in others.

I looked at a number of domestic periodicals: *The Bulletin*, a
weekly news magazine; *Walkabout*, an Australian version of
Arizona Highways; *Meanjin*, a literary quarterly; the *Australian
Quarterly*, devoted to political and economic matters, and several
different newspapers. I was looking in general for something up-to-
date on the Aborigines because nobody I've talked to seems to know
anything about the present day status of their reserves or whether
any land at all has been left inviolate to them. There wasn't a
great deal about Aborigines, except of an anthropological nature,
in either books or periodicals; but one thing I noted was that everybody spelled Aborigines with a lower case *a*, just as we used to
spell Negro with a lower case *n*. I got in a wrangle about this with
one of the librarians, a young Englishwoman. I asked why there
seemed to be such a shortage of upper case *A*'s in Australian type
fonts: surely they weren't all used up writing Australia. "It's not
what you do to the Aborigines that matters so much," I said in
a fierce hoarse whisper. "They may not read, or if they read, may
not be enlightened enough to see the insult in it. It's what you are
doing to yourselves, to your own hearts and minds." "But I've only
been here three months!" she protested. "Very well. But look how
you treated the Jamaicans in England." "I have no feeling one
way or another about the Jamaicans," she maintained. "They
couldn't get good housing but this was because they were black. *I*
had nothing to do with it."

Parallel to and just south of North Terrace are two narrow
streets—Rundle and Hindley—on which is compressed virtually
all of Adelaide's commercial life. There is scarcely room in the
streets for cars to travel one way and scarcely room on the footpaths for people to walk more than two abreast, but travel and
walk they do constantly, in a sluggish thick procession, laden with
bags and jostled by prams. Here I caught up with my wife and
daughter.

The plight of the pedestrian, relatively good in Sydney and
Melbourne if he jay-walked, is miserable in Adelaide. What it is
like in Perth, capital of Western Australia, I have still to discover,

but an item in Saturday's *Advertiser* gave me some inkling. It told how the traffic authorities had experimented with marked crosswalks on which pedestrians were given right of way. This idea was abandoned because cars were unable to move fast enough. Now they have so-called "refuges" in the centre of a street and this is good, the writer of the news item says. "Traffic flows much more easily and once you have conjured up the courage you can find it exhilarating to rush for the refuge and make it before the motorist hits you."

And don't think he wouldn't. In Adelaide it's not even safe to cross at an intersection with the green light. Left-turning cars grab the road ahead of the pedestrians. One foolish man tried crossing on the red. A car crashed through at 50 m.p.h. and brushed his whiskers as the pedestrian leapt back. The car didn't swerve an inch to avoid hitting him. Yet intersections without lights are still worse on account of the right hand rule. The smallest side streets are the least safe to cross, because drivers whipping out of them into the main street have their heads cocked way over their right shoulders, this being the only quarter from which they need legally expect to be hit. With so much right hand watching and such incentive to get to an intersection ahead of the other fellow, on wheels or on foot, cars tend to move even short distances at high speed. A screech of rubber around corners is a common noise.

Peggy spotted the young fellow for a Yank as soon as he opened his mouth. Curiously, I didn't. Yet there have been times when I've blushed on hearing an accent from home—the slow cowboy drawl, the heavy, deliberate pronunciation of each separate syllable over the Voice of America: "Lu- ci is a Cath- o- lic." No doubt I've been specially sensitized to these particular models by their having been emulated by every actor playing an American part on the Australasian stage. This Yank, a migrant of little more than a week, spoke more slowly than the average Australian, but not to the point of caricature.

He was born and raised in a little town in Michigan's upper peninsula before moving to St Paul, Minnesota. I naturally asked him why he came to Australia and it boiled down to wanting to get out of the United States. He considered and rejected Canada, England, and South America. And how did he hear about Australia? The American newspapers and magazines have been full of nothing else but. What was there about the United States that made him want to leave? Oh, this, that, and the other thing. The war? No, he was 100 per cent behind the war and wanted it prosecuted with all possible vigour. There'd been a great moral decline in the United States in the last few years. Mob violence had been taking over. The individual no longer counted. Australia seemed a rather conservative country but this didn't worry him, not even the lack of movies and shopping on Sunday. He also believed his children would get a better education and would be more disciplined, as he had been at their age. Young people in the United States were now their own bosses; they had their own money to spend, and this didn't worry him, but then maybe it did.

It had cost his family $2,000 in air fares to come here, of which the Australian Immigration Department would refund about one-quarter—on the understanding that they would stay for two years. They had sold their St Paul house, their car, and their furniture; and he was sure they'd done the right thing burning their bridges. Almost the first thing he did on arrival, though, was to buy another car. Why do that, when the railway station was a mere two blocks away? He needed it to drive the wife to the store. Yes, and bless him, he would—being an American. He was a very pleasant fellow, typically American in speech and manner and, if I may say so, in self assurance. Although he had neither job nor promise of one he was unworried. He had talents he was sure Australia could use. Somewhere in this great country there would be some managerial post to suit him.

He said his wife was afraid to drive in Australia. "Oh, you mean on account of the right hand rule," said Peggy. "Sh!" I said. "All he means is driving on the left side of the road. He's never heard of the right hand rule"; and he hadn't.

There are few stop-and-go lights in Australia outside the business section of a big city, and almost no signs requiring vehicles to stop before entering or crossing a main thoroughfare. Yet there are such thoroughfares carrying many times the traffic of the streets and roads running into them. A motorist from overseas, tooling along on one of these busy arteries, is apt to feel fairly secure in his right of way until he is brought up sharply by a crash in his right side. Another car, charging out of an obscure and little-used lane or residential driveway, has ploughed into him. "Didn't you see me?" he splutters to the driver of the car that did the hitting. "Of course not!" says the other driver indignantly. "It was your business to look out for me. I was on the right." And on the right is in the right in Australia. The second driver may be drunk. He may have been grossly exceeding the speed limit. His licence may have been revoked. For all these offences he may have to answer in court; but sole responsibility for the collision rests with the first driver, who failed to stop when a vehicle was moving or about to move across his path from the right. This is the right hand rule.

In Victoria, last of the States to adopt it, a motorist is at fault if, proceeding through a green traffic signal, his car collides with one coming through the red from the right. Police in other States are less strict. Their policy is not to prosecute the driver who was hit while going through a green light, although "from the strictly legal viewpoint, a driver who fails to give way under such circumstances is technically in breach of the regulations." But I knew it would be futile to try to explain the right hand rule to the new American migrant. In the first place he wouldn't believe me. In the second place he wouldn't understand me. I doubt whether words alone are adequate to explain it. It needs a collision, even for a native Australian.

Driving back to camp from Adelaide on a three-lane highway almost choked with cars in the evening rush hour, we were stopped behind a long line. When it was finally our turn to move up I saw why. A traffic officer on a motorcycle directly ahead came to a complete stop to allow a boy on a bicycle, pedalling in from a residential street on the right, to cross in front of him.

20

*Sixth among the nations of the world in area, and forty-third in population, Australia ranks first in numbers of sheep, in production and export of wool, and production of lead and zirconium. She ranks second in export of beef, lamb, and mutton and—on the word of her Prime Minister—*per capita *ownership of automobiles; third in export of wheat, butter, apples, and lead; fourth in production of zinc and raisins and in tea consumption and number of telephones* per capita; *fifth in production of gold, copper, sulphur, and titanium, and export of sugar; sixth in production of silver and butter; seventh in production of wheat; eighth in production of oats, export of zinc, and* per capita *consumption of fat; ninth in export of copper and production of beer, and among lowest female death rates* per capita *(equal to New Zealand, Czechoslovakia, U.S.S.R., Israel, and Canada); tenth in* per capita *wealth; eleventh in numbers of cattle and* per capita *suicides; and thirteenth among lowest male death rates (equal to Puerto Rico, France, and Spain), not of course counting the Aborigines whose infant mortality alone in the area under Commonwealth supervision is 176 in 1,000. Australia's population density of less than 4 persons per square mile compares with 22 for South America, 23 for Africa, 26 for U.S.S.R. and Siberia, 30 for North and Central America, 166 for Asia, and 227 for western Europe.*

JANUARY 26: Today or yesterday was Australia Day, the anniversary of English settlement at Sydney. We celebrated it yesterday anyhow, at the invitation of Harold Austin, our patient Lancashire liaison with the Royal Automobile Association and the man chiefly responsible for getting our car through Customs. We joined in an RAA picnic 50 or 60 miles north of here in the Barossa Valley, at some town's oval. "Oval" and "picnic ground" are synonymous in Aussie Rules States because to picnic implies games,

141

games require a playing field, and the Rules football field is oval-shaped. Austin called for us at camp just before noon. We followed his jeep, blazoned with "RAA" on the outside, and his wife, three small sons, and a picnic hamper inside, up Anzac Highway, through Adelaide past the cricket ground—where a test match with England was under way—and out the Main North Road. We passed a large cluster of quonset huts (called nissen huts here) and clothes lines, surrounded by dried mud, which the Austins later told us was the hostel they stayed at on their arrival from Lancashire. Just beyond were the sheds, paddocks, slaughter-houses, and smells of a large abbatoir; and the whole area—bleak, ugly, and depressing—was the last place I should have chosen to try to make a newcomer feel at home in his adopted land.

Mr and Mrs Creaghan, both short, stocky, and slightly pugna-cious, came from Birmingham, sailing on the Arcadia, and enjoyed the trip, the food especially. On arrival they were separated from their closest shipboard friends and taken on a bus through dreary rain (it was April, the middle of the Australian autumn) to Smith-field Hostel. "Where is Smithfield?" Creaghan asked their official greeter. "I can't find it on this map of Adelaide." "It's up here," said the greeter, holding his hand several feet above the map.

At Smithfield they were herded into a large community hall, sat down at a long table with tea, bread, and butter, with the manager at one end. With little or no preamble he read them the rules of the hostel. Then they were shown to the domiciles, tiny rooms, as many as a family required—each with two beds and vir-tually no other furniture—with small windows, and a long corri-dor down the length of the building to get to them. They felt like prisoners.

They lined up for their food and it was tasteless. The menu was varied each day, and the kitchen was spotless as Mrs Creaghan dis-covered when she got a job working there, but everything was steamed. Each family had its own table, however, unlike another hostel in Adelaide where grabbing tables was a free-for-all—the aim being to get one less dirty than the others. With a table of one's own a family could keep it reasonably clean. Because Mr Creaghan was a "worker" (he got a job at Holden almost at once) his breakfast was supplemented with two hard-boiled eggs; but the lunch he took to work was often made from spoiled meat. The ordinary breakfast consisted of packaged cereal, an occasional scrap of fat bacon (which the breakfaster put in the toaster if he liked it cooked), tea, and bread for toasting. Many lived mainly on toast,

the other food was so unappetizing, especially after their shipboard meals. At the hostel toast was the staple for every meal. Dinner was at 5.00, and no supper afterwards unless they took bread from the kitchen, which was forbidden but everybody did. Mrs Creaghan and her neighbour in the next apartment would sup on bread, tea, and Creaghan's hard-boiled eggs. It was the only meal they really enjoyed.

Hepatitis and dysentery were rampant, from the public toilets they thought, although these were kept clean. One dance a month and housie-housie were the only social activities. A manager and one assistant tried to keep order among as many as 350 persons; but no particular effort was made either to welcome newcomers or to bring people together. The Creaghans stayed five months, and made up their minds to go to New Zealand, only needing reassurance on employment and housing.

However, some 15 miles farther on, we came upon a sight which caused me to rub my eyes. It looked like something out of San Fernando Valley, a myriad of new bungalows, green lawns, and bright modern shopping centres surrounded by extensive fields of tall billowing grass, with sere golden mountains in the distance. I later asked Harold what it was and he said, "Elizabeth," as if that explained everything, and I guess it would—to an Englishman.

Recently when Harold's wife Dierdre wrote some friends at home to tell them she was in Adelaide, they'd never heard of the place. Trying to locate it for them she said it was 400 miles northwest of Melbourne on St Vincent's Gulf, but still this didn't help. What was nearby? Nothing of much consequence actually. Like the other Australian capitals Adelaide is almost the only thing in its state of any great size, apart from the farms. Dierdre in one of her letters happened casually to speak of Elizabeth, having been there and seen how fast it had grown in the ten years since it was vacant farm land. "But why didn't you mention Elizabeth before?" they asked. "We may not be too sure about Canberra, or even Sydney, but everyone in England knows where Elizabeth is!"

Elizabeth, it seems, is a little England. It was created by the South Australian Housing Trust, a Government agency, as a step —and just about the only step, according to Austin—in the direction of decentralization of industry away from the capital cities. It has a well landscaped factory area, including a splendid new General Motors plant, large residential lots on curving streets, numerous churches and schools, and several shopping malls so distributed as to bring shopping within walking distance of every resident. This was done, Harold said, because the majority of residents are new English migrants and don't, as yet, own cars. He and his wife came to Australia before Elizabeth was dreamt of. Their children were all born here.

The sun was scorching, hotter inland than on the water. Wise picnickers had brought tents which they erected on the edge of the oval, side by side, cars parked on the higher ground behind them. Some of the tents were elaborately furnished with padded stools, tables, ice boxes and picnic hampers, and blankets—which Australians call rugs. Their occupants could sit or recline out of the sun, a pitcher of beer at the elbow, and watch the games in comfort. One farseeing tenter brought two glass pitchers and used one —half full of cold beer—to cool a bottle of milk.

Some of the picnickers also brought their dogs, who frolicked and gambolled on the oval—unless they were chained. But Mrs Austin said dogs in England are better liked than in Australia. The availability of roo meat and roo mince in cans and in butcher shops had not turned Australia into a nation of dog lovers; the dog lovers had created the market, and the shops I see everywhere specializing in roo had sprung up to fill an existing need. After New Zealand, where dogs are kept strictly for work on the farm, the packs which roam Australian cities and suburbs and the barking which goes on make Australia seem the doggiest country I've ever known. If England is even doggier . . . Mrs Austin's complaint about Aussies is they pen their dogs up in their yards and forget about them. She thought it might be the English migrants who were still considerate enough to bring theirs along on picnics.

"Grandest dog I've seen for years," he remarked, as he set the table. "Do you get many kangaroos with him?"

"Oh, no," I replied; "I never get one, and don't intend to. I never let him go after anything. It's quite enough, and sometimes more than enough, for him to do his regular travelling. The hot weather comes very severe on him; in fact, some days I have to give him a drink every hour, or oftener. Then he has the hard ground to contend with; and when the rain comes, the dirt sticks between his toes, and annoys him. Windy weather is bad for him, too; and frost puts a set on him altogether. Then he's always swarming with fleas, and in addition to that, the flies have a particular fancy for him. And, seeing that one half of the population is always plotting to steal him, and the other half is trying to poison him, while, for his own part, he has a confirmed habit of getting lost, you may be sure we have plenty to occupy our minds, without thinking about kangaroos. He's considerably more trouble to me than all my money, but he's worth it."

So it was in Australia seventy-odd years ago when Tom Collins wrote Such is Life—Australia's *Tristram Shandy, Moby Dick, and* Ulysses, *all in one.*

After the bag and three-legged races, the tug of war, and the egg tossing—where competitors vied to receive raw eggs at the greatest distance without breaking them—we lunched; and after lunch Candi and Peggy signed up for the men versus ladies cricket match . The match ended when the men, batting left-handed and coming out at last to help the ladies with the fielding, went two runs into the lead. The game might have gone on all night if they hadn't, for neither the men nor the ladies would have looked kindly on the men actually losing.

As the afternoon drew to a close the beer and ice-cream cups were dispensed with greater abandon. Hitherto a ticket had been required to get them. Actual sale of beer being forbidden on Sunday, some hocus pocus of tickets and quasi-membership was used to get over that hump. But at the end both beer and ice-cream were given away free and the kids gorged themselves on ice-cream. The beer didn't want for takers though either.

The cricket match was still on when we got back to Adelaide so, while Peggy and Candi were having afternoon tea with the Austins, I ducked into the oval to see how much championship cricket differed from the amateur games I used to watch in the Auckland Domain. I couldn't see a great deal of difference. Fieldsmen still clustered in a tight knot around the wicket and then ran in vain pursuit of the balls that were regularly batted over their heads. Except in the grandstand, where people sat and applauded politely whenever this happened, the crowd had evidently thinned since mid-afternoon. They sprawled on the grass, stood on steps, or occupied benches behind the picket fence. Some stood under the roof of a small refreshment stand where beer was dispensed in tiny fragile glasses. There was no marked gregariousness even among them. When I asked a pensioner, standing alone, "Could you tell me, does anything happen at this game?" he shied away and mumbled something about being a stranger himself.

On the way out I asked the gateman: "Was this an exciting session?"

"Very exciting," he said with glowing eyes. "England's four best batsmen had fallen on Saturday and these men weren't expected to do much of anything. But they put up a gallant stand. Fletcher batted 96 before they got him out."

"Is that what happened to Fletcher?" I asked. "I heard some shouting out on the field and a lot of scurrying around."

"Yes. He was run out. England doesn't stand much of a chance. They'd have to play all day tomorrow even to force a draw."

146

21

JANUARY 27: I heard a low whistle just at dawn and thought it must be a camper up early; but there was none stirring about. All I could see were some large black and white birds, or black and light grey with white or grey beaks, about the size of bantam hens. Fred later identified them as magpies. Fred is a small man with a rich Australian accent, even to pronouncing "bloke" rather like "blawk." He talks rapidly, uses the possessive "me," talking about his illness, the job of camp superintendent, and the birds. He hopes his sons, one four, the other two-and-a-half, will continue in his career: he can put the elder into his own job when he retires.

He was in his forties and still unmarried when he met this Austrian girl, a friend of a German girl who used to stop overnight at the camp with her motor bike and a tiny tent. He invited them to have coffee. They accepted, cooked some bacon and eggs, and they all ate together. In the evening a wind came up and the Austrian girl wanted to get back to the tuberculosis sanatorium where the girls worked. Fred offered to drive her. She was afraid at first but then accepted. In the car Fred was silent for a while. Finally he asked if she liked Australia. She said yes. He asked a couple more questions and she said no. Pretty soon he reckoned she was getting her yesses and noes mixed up. They were the only words she knew, plus "thank you."

He asked if she'd like to go to the drive-in to see the pitchers, and his hands framed a rectangle as he said "pitchers." She couldn't understand and looked to be afraid. Would she have coffee? She agreed eagerly. So they stopped and had coffee. Again he formed the rectangle and asked, "Pitchers?" but she still couldn't understand. Then by driving around he was able to show her the screen and she agreed to go. She was delighted when he pulled the loud-speaker into the car. At intermission he asked her to have coffee and she eagerly agreed. She was the greatest one for coffee he'd ever met.

He saw her to the sanatorium and left her with a note to her German girl-friend, who met him the next day and said the Austrian girl was delighted. The only fly in the ointment was she hadn't understood the pitchers. She went out with him again and —"I was hooked." She gradually picked up English from him. She thought he wasn't taking good enough care of himself, would taxi to the camp to cook his meals, clean up his house, wash his clothes.

"Did you wean her away from coffee?" He didn't, but the doctor did. She got off colour once and the doctor said she had to quit drinking coffee altogether. She used to smoke a lot but without coffee she smoked twice as much. Which was worse, he asked the doctor, the cigarettes or coffee? Keep her off coffee, the doctor said.

He'd had a time getting her to cook the Australian way. The Austrian food was too rich, although some things he liked, goulash and such. The boys took after her, eating metwurst and Polish sausage filled with garlic, and when he had all three of them together in a car—! But it was good she got off coffee because the boys lapped up tea. They were drinking it all the time. People would invite them into their caravans to have a cuppa.

Logging was Fred's father's occupation in Perth and Fred took it up, against his father's advice, felling logs at 50 cents a ton. Looking around he saw haulers getting $1.95 a ton and believed this was where the money was made. He bought a truck on time and carried, first one, then two, three, and finally four loads a day —leaving scarcely four hours for sleep. One night he saw a man on the road waving him down. "In that country you never fail to stop for anybody." He managed with some effort to bring his 18-ton load to a halt, waited for the man, hunted for him, couldn't find him. He called, sounded his hooter, finally drove on. After awhile a tram car ("You'd call it a trolley car") came out of the bush and crossed the road in front of him. He screeched the brakes and, after stopping, realized he was having hallucinations. He doused his head with cold water, took aspirins, drank tea. At the top of a long hill he checked his load, tightening the chains which held the logs, dropped into low with brakes half on, and descended. A man stepped out in front of him. He veered off the road, tearing down saplings, and just managed to reach the bottom safely. Then he went in search of a doctor, stopped in front of the surgery, and blacked out, starting at his feet and the pain moving up to his head. As he fell on the seat his hand caught the door latch and he

148

slipped half out of the truck unconscious. There the doctor found him, put him to bed for three weeks, and ordered him to get away. He sold everything and came to Adelaide. That was twelve years ago.

I said I understood Western Australians were the friendliest of all. Fred had been so put off by the coldness he found in South Australians he was ready to go back after two days. He still finds them cold and self-centred. "They come here, take a blanket and a transistor radio, and sit out in the sun all by themselves. In Perth you'll meet a bloke one morning going to work and you both say hello. Next morning you exchange remarks about the weather. The third morning you're walking along together. Here nobody has time for anybody else. Whenever I meet someone friendly I ask them 'Where are you from? Victoria or Western Australia?' It's always either one or the other."

He still sees himself as the odd man out in his family. The other day his four-year-old, looking at pictures of the Austrian Alps, told his father, "This is our country." "What's the matter? Isn't

Australia your country?" "No. Our country is beautiful like this, with snow."

Dennis, Rob, and Ken, the three lads from Sydney, dropped over after Fred left, to say good-bye. They have a late date this evening with some girls they've met, staying at a near-by motel. They'll pick them up at 9.00 when the girls come out from the pictures. "It's cheaper that way," said Ken. They're leaving tomorrow, camping overnight alongside the road, to be back at work at the end of two of the three weeks paid annual vacation all Australian employees are entitled to. The third week will come later on. Only those with six years' service may take all three weeks together. Winter vacations are not popular except with executives, who go up to Queensland and into the "Never-Never" (so called, according to Rob, because it never rains).

But now a South Australian Parks inspector I've just talked to says the Never-Never is a name applied to the whole of unoccupied Australia, and comes from a popular book titled *We of the Never-Never*. He often travels this country to and beyond the State line between South Australia and North Territory, and gave me a few pointers about driving up there. It's a thousand miles of dirt road to Alice Springs, covered with a six-inch layer of dust as fine as pumice. "You can't keep it out. You can close the windows of your car and seal the doors with masking tape; it will still get in. But it's a safe road to travel on, nothing to compare with the Birdsville Track. If you take along plenty of water and fill your tank with petrol whenever you can you'll be right; and if you break down there'll be someone come along to take you in. It's not like the Birdsville Track where the postman goes by only once a week."

All the while the Inspector talked a fly played over his face and on the ends of his lips. It didn't disturb him; he didn't disturb it unless it was absolutely necessary. Then, just as the fly was about to enter his mouth, his hand would come up casually and lightly touch his face. He didn't brush the fly away or wave his hand around. He let his hand drop back when the fly had moved from the danger zone. Long experience had schooled his hand to the minimum effective response: a conditioned reflex. I doubt that he even knew the fly was there.

By 1942 We of the Never-Never, *by Mrs Aeneas Gunn, first published in 1908 after rejection by six other publishers, had sold nearly a quarter million copies; 25,000 copies were sold by 1915 when the type metal was melted down for bullets. The original* manuscript is in the National Library at Canberra. By 1942, also, several of the characters in the book had passed on, in addition to Mrs Gunn's husband whose death brings the story to a close. The manner of their passing contributed to the legendary quality of the book: one of malaria in 1907, one of thirst on the Tamami route in 1909, one of exhaustion in 1910 on the Willeroo-to-Katherine route while staggering back to a fallen companion with a full water-bag, one by drowning in 1911 while crossing the Victoria River with the mails, one by falling from a horse in 1911, another by drowning while crossing the King River with pack horses in 1924, one of heart failure while in camp in 1912, one of unknown cause "about 1916," and seven in the natural way of illness and old age in the '30s and early '40s.

The story concerns the experiences of a new wife of the manager of a large cattle station called the Elsey south of the Katherine (to rhyme with wine). She arrives in 1912 during the Wet, travels 150 miles from Darwin by rail, zigzagging "through jungle and forest and river-valley—stopping now and then to drink deeply at magnificent rivers ablaze with water-lilies . . . Here and there, kangaroos and other wild creatures of the bush loped out of our way . . . again and again little groups of blacks hailed us, and scrambled after water-melon and tobacco, with shouts of delight . . . for travelling in the Territory has not yet passed that ideal stage where the travelling itself—the actual going—is all pleasantness."

Taking to horseback she has to cross the flooded Fergusson River by flying fox to reach Katherine Settlement consisting almost solely of a pub which "seemed to be hanging on to its own verandah posts for support." Here begins the story proper, consisting as it does of a struggle by one bushman after another to overcome his shyness in the presence of a woman. (The Aboriginal women, invariably called lubras, don't count.) They call her "missus" and, little by little, grow reconciled to her because she is a "little 'un" who proves to be "the right sort, the sort you tell things to." She is not a "goer."

Meanwhile she herself is learning how to live in the Australian outback, putting up with a bed-spring sans mattress, a one-room house, a temporary shortage of tea, and the trials and tribulations of managing native servants. I should imagine a virtually identical story could be set in South Africa, or pre-war India, or in any of the colonies. For the truth is, the Never-Never in this book is just that: an English colony.

Among her several adventures is a "nigger hunt"—not for real of course, the boss is too kind-hearted. "It was a foregone conclusion that our 'nigger hunt' would only involve the captured with general discomfiture; but . . . emergencies were apt to occur 'down the river', and we rode out of camp with rifles unslung and revolvers at hand." Failing to find any "niggers" in the river beds they are given a night of unease by being told, "Big mob bad fellow sit down longa island." The leader of this mob is a man named Monkey, "a reputed murderer many times over; and when he and his followers were about, white men saw to their rifles; and as we turned in we also agreed that this wasn't exactly the kind of nigger hunt we had set out for. It makes a difference when the other chap's doing the hunting." But they escape with nothing worse than a nagging thirst from a three or four-day diet of anchovy paste.

A young petrol attendant I talked to yesterday wants to go back to England after some years here. He can't stand the climate—too hot and too dry; but neither did he like Queensland. It was "too tropical." On the other hand two other discontented English migrants I've met here declare the only thing that keeps them is the climate.

However a clerk in Roy's delly has her percolater packed and is headed back after only six months. She and her husband are so dissatisfied they can't wait for their two-year probationary period to end, after which the debt for their assisted passage would be considered paid. They have already repaid it, the sum of $1,000. Their decision is based on a calculation of wages loss over the remaining 18 months, and they've concluded they'll be ahead cutting their losses now. As a carpenter Fred earned $70 a week in England and he earns only $40 here. Thus in less than ten months they can pay their $1,000 passage home and be a bit ahead. They brought another $1,000 of savings with them and this is gone; so their six-months' sojourn in Australia cost, in out-of-pocket expense and lost wages, more than $20 a day, or the price of a holiday. But it was no holiday. They worked or looked for work the whole time.

Sheila, who also works at Roy's and came over on the same boat, hasn't made up her mind. She and her husband were sponsored by an Australian home builder, one of many active in England who promote migration on the strength of the migrant's promise to buy a house. They sold the bungalow on which they had a $1,600 mortgage in England at a nice profit, and deposited $1,200 on a similar bungalow in Australia. This carries an $8,000-mortgage and she isn't optimistic about the profit when they sell. She sees

152

grocery prices a shilling or so higher on every item and feels aggrieved over the difference between the Australia that is and the one they were told about. Evening after evening, before deciding to migrate, they used to meet in an organization called the Cobbers' Club, founded by a returned migrant who was saving to come back to Australia. There they saw films and colour slides presented by tourists, industrial sponsors of various kinds, State government tourist bureaus, and numerous real estate promoters.

Why, I asked, did they commit themselves to buy a house which might be a millstone? Couldn't they have waited a bit longer and done without the real estate promoter's sponsorship? They were young enough. They'd have got here eventually under Commonwealth nomination and then they could simply rent. She said it was a six-months' wait for rentals at anything less than half her husband's pay; and while they waited they'd have to live in a hostel. Was that so bad? She said it was. One family they got to know stayed in Australia only three weeks. The hostel life did for them.

A working man came into the milk bar and said it was a mistake to let your mates know you were going out to dinner as you had to shop for all of them. I asked Sheila about this use of the word "dinner" for lunch, especially when—as for a workingman—it really was lunch. This she said was a British habit. Australians said "lunch." "Still this man was an Australian, wasn't he?" "Yes." "He wouldn't have picked up the expression from you English. Didn't his use of it surprise you?" "I have never ceased to be surprised at the way Australians behave," she said wearily.

"I believe you do want to go home." "Yes I do. Only I'm afraid when I've been there awhile I'll want to come back. I'll stick it for two years and see how I feel then. My mother and all my sisters want to come out if I decide to stay." "I presume they have no reservations at all. This is the land of sunshine for them." "Yes. We send them pictures and everything always looks so good. But," with a sigh, "I expect there are drawbacks to every place."

Sheila gets up at 6.30 and does a complete house-cleaning job before making breakfast for her family and sending them off to school and work. She herself works in the delly only till 2.30 in order to be home for her children, has no time to look at TV in the evening, works Saturday morning, has her hair done Saturday afternoon, entertains another English couple when they call on Sunday; hasn't read a newspaper since she came to Australia. What spare time she has she writes to her mother, who sends her nine-and ten-page letters and expects detailed answers. I said it didn't seem much of a life, hardly worthwhile coming out for. She said

153

they'd had the trip, seen Port Said, something they'd otherwise never have done. She is working not just to make ends meet but for the passage home in case they do decide to leave after their two-year sentence is served. Couldn't she, by working two years in England, have saved enough for a cruise and seen Port Said that way? Perhaps. But they'd never have done it.

22

JANUARY 28: The weather was cool and clear and the skies cloudless as we returned to Elizabeth for a closer look at Australia's "city of the future." I also hoped we might find, among all those new houses and flats, one for rent before Candi goes back to school. The day, the terrain, even the city had a familiar look about them: tract houses going up next door to other tract houses which had been lived in long enough to reflect their owners' idiosyncrasies; ant trails running across white concrete sidewalks, reddish-brown barren lots (called blocks here) criss-crossed by paths, soaking wet lawns of Bermuda grass kept green only by constant sprinkling, flowers and pomegranates, and a nearby neat, trimly built shopping centre. The sun was bright but not hot; the air when it wasn't poisoned by diesel fumes from buses and delivery vans was light and odourless. If I had seen a few eucalyptus trees and if there weren't so many flies and furiously barking dogs I could easily have imagined myself in southern California.

Jess, a friendly carpenter-contractor working on one of the new Housing Trust bungalows, said the only place in the world the flies were worse was Egypt. They dove into my face, aiming at eyes, nostrils, ears, into my mouth if I were incautious enough to speak without waving a hand before me. But Jess talked a blue streak—admittedly in the Australian manner with scarcely opened lips—and seldom had to wave one away. He said you could tell how long a person had been in the country by the amount of waving he did. He himself was now almost completely Australianized; had lost most of his original Yorkshire accent and used an oath with every few words—cocking an apologetic eye now and then at Peggy and Candi who were off inspecting another part of the house.

He bubbled over with enthusiasm for the South Australian Housing Trust which had built all this—with a sweep of the arm

155

to embrace the 10,000 or more cottages around us—on empty farm land. The actual construction work was done by private contractors like himself, under Housing Trust supervision. The Trust leased out the shops and factory buildings, and sold or rented the houses, many to newly arrived migrants.

On our way home in the car, which Little drove expertly despite the beer he'd consumed, I learnt he had recently brought his family here from Manchester. They'd needed a sponsor to qualify for free passage to Australia on account of his lacking any of the specific skills the country required. They wrote to Australia House in London, where the Department of Immigration maintains a large staff, and did this regularly over a five-year period. At last they were told that the South Australian Government itself would sponsor them if they had $2,000 for a deposit on a Trust house. They had the money and said so, and got the free passage without anyone taking the trouble to check on whether they were telling the truth.

"The Australian way," said Little. He knew of some families that were brought over on this basis, only to show empty pockets when they arrived. It was then too late; they couldn't be deported. One of the family heads said he'd still like to buy a house if the Trust would trust him for the deposit, and they did, letting him pay it off by the week. Many of the migrants were sponsored by employers who claimed to have jobs for them but didn't. "For a fee, probably," said Little, with a shrug. Even bona fide *employers could sack a migrant after a week, and their obligations as sponsors were discharged.*

Little was quite content with Australia, said he lived better than he would in U.K., was promoted more rapidly, had money for leisure time pursuits. He was a roly-poly fellow, fairly short, with wispy grey hair, a toboggan nose, wide-set eyes in a rather Slavic face. My impression of the typical Britisher is a long face, with a long thin nose (jib sail) and a slightly pointed, slightly receding chin. Seeing a news picture of Aussie and South African cricket captains together—both fitting this description—I could have believed they were twins, most certainly brothers.

Mrs Little was an inconspicuous, quiet wife of an extrovert husband. They picked out their house in a two-hour period which Little took off from his job, and Little did the deciding. As Little's fortunes steadily improved (he had never dreamt of owning a car in England) they built a carport in front of the house to accommodate a second car, and a glassed-in passageway between lounge and

*kitchen to let in more light. The Housing Trust, like many
another developer, paid scant attention to the orientation of windows in relation to the sun.*

Much as he admired the Housing Trust, Jess declared he
wouldn't live in Elizabeth. "Too many poms." "You're not a
pom?" "Not bloody likely. I've been out here 16 years." Australia
itself, he reminded me, wasn't a great deal older: a young country
with a splendid future and more untapped resources than any
other. When the vast north was developed Australia would
become the greatest country in the world. It wouldn't be long
either. Take the Housing Trust, far ahead of anything of its kind
in the world, "even in America." I said it wouldn't be tolerated in
America because it infringed on private enterprise.

"This encourages private enterprise," he said, tapping his
white-overalled chest. "I'm private enterprise."

"You're little private enterprise," I said. "I mean big private
enterprise."

"I don't want to hurt your feelings," he said confidentially, "but that's the trouble with America. You're too much for the big *fye-nan*-cier." No 51st State for him.

It was a 21st birthday celebration—a big event in all British Commonwealth countries apparently—held in the backyard of Piermont House, with perhaps forty or fifty other guests and plenty of sausages, lamb chops, potato salad, and drinks. Our host was an English migrant of fourteen years, who had worked with MI5 in postwar Germany smuggling scientists and engineers out of the Russian zone. Eight of his men, experts in geodesy, were hired for Australia's big Snowy River irrigation and power project, and Crawford—no expert but eager to go to Australia—got himself hired number nine, working as a welfare officer. The welfare consisted exclusively of a club with liquor and dart board, which he ran, and if any man came to him with personal troubles that was strictly out of his department.

He moved on to Perth with a soft drink concern—having been with Coca Cola before the war—and rose to a top job. His company advertised its new cola as a "real American cola," and to prove it they had an American flag as part of the advertising. Crawford studied the flag they were to use, found only forty-eight stars, and told the boss there should be fifty. The boss disputed this and to settle the argument he called the U.S. Consul. The Consul was outraged at the thought of their using any U.S. flag with any number of stars and said he'd take steps to stop them from doing it. "Bugger the stars!" said the boss. "Put up as many of these as you can and get them around before he finds out about it!"

Jess was browned off by the British Government giving him a few paltry pounds when he came out of the Army in 1947, and resolved to go to South Africa. But in 1948 he married a girl from Perth on a working holiday and his wife wouldn't leave England, least of all for South Africa. She later agreed when he switched his affections to Australia. They were bound for Perth, but she took one look at it and got back on the ship again; she hadn't realized it was so small and out of the way. This was before Western Australia's great mining boom, Jess explained. They were talked into Adelaide on the ship, stayed three months at Smithfield, then a couple of years up bush on a farm.

"Europe and England have had it," said Jess; America was shouldering them aside. He wasn't happy about this, nor the way Australia was ditching England to ride on America's coat tails. It wasn't right. "You go over to the American consulate and you hear the Americans talk big. Me, I'm for everybody having a chance. Black, or yellow, no matter what he is."

"That's what's been puzzling me here," I said. "I never see any blacks." "Well there you are. You're having troubles with the blacks in your country, and you brought it on yourselves. There weren't any there in the first place but you made slaves of them and brought them in." "The English did that," I reminded him. "Yes," he said, "that's what I mean. And here we pushed the Aborigines out."

McKinney the publisher proved less a stuffed shirt than I'd feared. He was quite young for such a responsible job, but had been in publishing a fair time; and in Australia for three years. He was a Quaker, one of only about 30,000 in Britain, and worked and lectured on behalf of the prison visitors' movement, an institution apparently not encountered elsewhere—certainly not in Australia. Its aim was to give lifers a continuing link with the outside world, prone as they are to make a world of their own in prison where they see none but fellow prisoners and officials. He had his feet planted firmly in Australia, was convinced the Suez fiasco had administered the telling final blow to a Britain already fading from the world stage to become "another Portugal, looking back on lost glories and behaving as though they still survived." Harold Wilson held out no hope for him. "We had a Labour Government after 1945 and the Establishment continued to rule." Australia he saw to some degree as "a new America in the making," although he questioned whether it had the economic potential. The vast Australian desert was "the emptiest place on Earth, but if it could ever be irrigated . . ."

"How about those steam bores?" "They can't be used for irrigation." "You mean the water is too hot?" "No. Too salty. The salt crystallizes out into the soil after repeated flooding. But it's not too salty to water stock or even for human consumption."

We talked about the Aborigines. He too had at first been shocked at Australia's indifference to them, but soon adopted a "live and let live" philosophy on the subject. The Aborigines were a dying race and the Government was quietly letting them die. No use getting excited about it. "There is no race prejudice in Australia, or no more than among English-speaking people generally. Australians are merely indifferent, that's all."

"On the contrary I feel there is more race prejudice here than in South Africa."

159

"Not a bit of it," he said firmly. "An abo could come in here and sit down and be served with no more trouble than an occasional surprised comment, much as one of your red Indians would excite if he came in with a feathered headdress. They intermarry freely with whites and nobody thinks anything of it."

I brought up the almost invariable use of the lower case "a," and how even South African papers spell "Native" with a capital "N." "The American Negro forced us to use a capital 'N' as an acknowledgment of our respect for him as a fellow human. And we count our Negroes. South Africa counts its Natives. But the Australian constitution explicitly forbids census takers to count the Aborigines."

"That will be amended as soon as the Government sees fit to put it to a vote. They're really only waiting to couple it with some other amendment they desperately want a yes vote on. Anyhow, you're reading too much into this. The Aborigine is down because, when the English arrived, he was the most primitive man of his day outside the interior of New Guinea. The soldiers and convicts who constituted the first settlers were the least fitted it was possible to send here to establish a bond with him. So they simply set about exterminating him. Unlike your red Indians he had no bow and arrow; so he couldn't even fight back. Unlike the Maori, who had been so advanced he deliberately colonized New Zealand and who actually defeated the invaders and forced them to sign a treaty guaranteeing him certain rights, the Aborigine was not a warrior. Now he is paying the penalty of his backwardness. There are people who maintain he is potentially the equal of the white man; and whenever a young Aborigine does well in school they feel happy and proud."

"But as you say, he's dying. The koala bear is dying too, yet Australia is doing all it can to keep the koala bear alive. Why not have at least this much concern for the Aborigines?"

"No," with a determined shake of the head. "We don't do as you do in America and pen our Aborigines on reservations. The policy of the Australian Government is assimilation. This means bringing the Aborigines into the same schools with white children. Or, if they prefer living their tribal lives in missions or at a bare subsistence, the Government won't stop them. They can come in and be assimilated or stay out in the desert and —" He shrugged.

"You feel this is better than South Africa?"

"Much better. South Africa has apartheid, special Native schools, segregated areas where they must live. We have many South African migrants in Australia, and all have varying degrees

160

of guilt. The guilt is in inverse proportion to the opposition they showed toward apartheid. Here in Australia no one feels guilty. We have no segregation."

"Not physically."

"Not at all. You can talk to them. You can visit the missions. You can visit their neighbourhood in Sydney."

"But as a social worker. No thanks. What I want is to find a— well, some white person who has more or less cast his lot in with the Aborigines, who, if he approves of me, can bring me into their company on a footing of equality. My greatest disappointment in Australia is, where can you find people interested in the Aborigines, not as social worker 'cases' or part of their pastoral 'flock,' but as fellow human beings who have a life and culture that would be fascinating to know and understand?"

I told Jess casually we were looking for a furnished place to rent, preferably before next Tuesday when Candi's classes begin. Just as casually he answered that he thought he knew of such a house in Elizabeth, owned by a lecturer at Adelaide University who is taking his sabbatical leave this year. He will talk to him about it and call Fred at the campground. Only now that I've had a look at the want-ad section of *The Advertiser* do I begin to realize what this means. People advertising for flats and houses— furnished ones especially—speak with a note of desperation bordering on panic.

23

JANUARY 31: We spent last evening with our prospective land-lord and his wife, Mr and Mrs Sprague, and with Jess and Milli-cent Southeby (it rhymes with southerly) who introduced us. It was a lucky strike my speaking to Jess. He and Sprague are fellow bird fanciers and Jess had promised to care for the Sprague birds while they are away, which is how he knew their place would be empty. They hadn't meant to let it, though, but Jess talked to them and they agreed to look us over; and towards the end of the evening Mrs Sprague was showing Peggy how different things operate.

We drank shandies made with Coopers Stout and had a pleasant conversation about Australia's north and its lack of development, for which Sprague blamed the climate and Mrs Sprague the con-centration of land ownership and lease in a very few hands. Sprague is a big fellow, tall and barrel-chested, in his middle 40s; comes from New South Wales; has been at Adelaide five years, and looks more like a truck driver than an academic. His wife is also tall but thin, with a tense, nervous face. She was born and raised on a cattle station in the Northern Territory, off "the bitumen" between Darwin and Tennant Creek.

The land there is treeless and bare of all save scattered short shrubs, with low mountain ranges that look like hills. It is always hot, the two seasons being the "Dry" and the "Wet." A single day during the Wet may have 15 inches of rain; in the worst of the Wet all work stops. A typical day, except during the brief winter, begins with sunrise when, until about seven, the sandflies bite, fol-lowed by flies until around 4.30, followed again by sandflies till seven; and the mozzies all night long. You sleep with a fan; the mozzies can't get set in a breeze.

Sprague, who did most of the talking, seemed to know as much about the north as his wife who came from there. All of his travel has been by plane which he feels is virtually the only way you can travel in the far north. He spoke of Cooktown which once had a population of 80,000 and now less than 3,000, of the billabongs, and the rain forests so heavy they hide the sun, and of Tennant Creek, a town of perhaps 300, mostly unattached gold and copper miners.

They were both visiting Tennant, staying at one of the hotels— a place of narrow fluted iron with steel supporting members that carried the faintest whisper from one bedroom to another, and had, furthermore, a peephole cut in every bedroom wall—when a shop assistant, a miner's wife, won a £30,000 sweep in the Melbourne Cup and announced it would be free drinks for all. Somebody brought the hand-operated mine siren into the pub and every so often one of the miners would wind it up. It made a dreadful din. Then, early the next morning, they were awakened by a terrific explosion. Someone had put three sticks of gelignite inside the washing machine in the publican's wash house. The blast vaporized the washing machine and tore the wash house to bits; it also woke the woman who had won the sweep. She had a sudden dismaying thought: what if the blank, blank, blank telegram wasn't genuine! She knew only too well such a hoax was possible in Tennant Creek, and her bill for drinks was over 600 quid.

Sprague is a polite, non-argumentative talker who sets off to tell something and gets lost (losing most of his audience also) before getting it said. Thus the question of red China came up. "Are you afraid of China?" I asked. "Most Australians appear to be." Both of the Spragues said they weren't and they'd explain why; and Mr Sprague began with a character sketch of Mao Tse-tung, then ended with a rambling dissertation on Australia being the heel of Asia as Italy is the heel of Europe. Asian civilization was older than Western, and better able to exist peaceably; whereas the West during its relatively brief history had repeatedly been "drowned in rivers of blood." Australia must trade more with Asia. "The Common Market. Don't get me started on that or I'll talk for three days." I believed him. "We all have to live on this terra firma. We are all human. The peasant in Peru is as good as I am."

Mrs Sprague's explanation was simply that the Chinese are too preoccupied with their internal problems to invade Australia. Australia needn't fear them because they aren't strong enough without Russia's help and Russia won't be so foolish.

I asked if they'd ever questioned the policy of assisted immigration, but they hadn't. British migrants wouldn't come to Australia

unless they were paid to come. It was as simple as that. I'd like to have argued the point but instead we got switched over to radio, the tawdry fare of American revivalist preachers and teenage pop singers.

"But there are three ABC networks," said Mrs Sprague.

"And the first and third broadcast the same programmes," I said. "I can't recall ever hearing the second but I understand it broadcasts nothing but Brahms and Beethoven." This they agreed was true. The second network was somewhere out there and it did do nothing except play classical and semi-classical records. To tell the truth I'd like to hear Brahms and Beethoven. It would be a change from the Melachrino Strings.

"What about this?" I asked. "You pay $5.50 for an annual radio licence. This brings the Australian Broadcasting Commission 12 to 15 million dollars a year from radio listeners alone. Don't you feel they ought to give you something for that money?" They did in a way, but nobody expected his radio tax to be used for radio, any more than his petrol tax was spent on roads.

The Assistant Programme Director was politely tolerant. He didn't argue when I said the radio programmes were worse than

164

*New Zealand's. He thought this was inevitable with the emphasis
Australia was putting on TV, but there would eventually be a
drift back to radio and then the programmes would get better.
Right now, he said, there wasn't enough listening to warrant
spending money on it, and such money as ABC had was needed to
pay the high costs of establishing an Australian TV production
industry instead of having to rely so heavily on American and
British imports.*

"Then you do have some interesting local TV programmes?"

*That depended on what I meant by interesting. A big audience?
No. Controversial? Well, this was what they tried to avoid on
ABC.*

*"What about the radio licence money?" I asked. "Don't you feel
morally obliged to spend that money on radio?"*

*"Not at all," he said. "We don't even spend it on radio and tele-
vision combined. It goes into the general fund as Government
revenue, to be spent on M.P.s' salaries, trips to Malaysia, Woomera
rockets, and paying the butter subsidy. The Government allots us
money each year quite independently of the licence fees."*

*"And that sum doesn't equal the licence revenue. About what
proportion of the revenue would you say? A half? A quarter?"*

He wouldn't say.

"A tenth? One per cent?"

*Still he wouldn't say. But what was I grousing about? The Govern-
ment also levied an excise tax on valves and none of this money
went into radio or TV. All the same I felt there was a difference if
only a moral one. A licence to operate a receiver, I had supposed,
was levied in order to make some radio and TV possible without
putting it in hock to the commercial sponsor. I waved in the direction of the University.*

"You have lecturers over there. Why don't you use them?"

"We do, on TV."

"Why not on radio?"

"Nobody listens to radio. They're all watching television."

*"I heard a series of lectures on American literature over the
Voice of America short wave radio recently. Couldn't you sponsor
such a series on Australian literature?"*

"We do," triumphantly. "On the University of the Air."

"That's on TV."

"My word."

"It wouldn't be better on radio?"

*"No. On television we can illustrate the lecture with photo-
graphs and drawings. This makes it more interesting."*

165

The conversation drifted back to the subject of Australia having been settled by convicts and what a depressing effect this must have had on the country's development. Australians persist, without saying so openly, in comparing Australia with the United States. Convict settlement seems to help explain why Australia is so far behind. They were surprised to hear that Americans, despite their fabulous wages, are generally in debt on hire-purchase. Sprague knew an American who had come over to work for General Motors, stayed 18 months, and was going back because over there a camera cost only $50 compared to $100 here, and his U.S. salary was twice as high. "I took a step backward when I came here," he told Sprague.

They were secretly pleased over America still being second in the space race. Sprague forecast that when the Americans got to the moon they'd find the Russians there ahead of them, if only by four hours. "It must be terribly frustrating for your scientists," said Mrs Sprague sympathetically. "I don't know about that," I said. "They're doing all right, dragging down something in the neighbourhood of $90,000 a year." "But that's only money," she protested, "when what they want is a feeling of accomplishment. You have to feel you're achieving something if your job is to seem worth while." "How many of us achieve anything in our jobs? Do you?" "Yes; in a good day's work, I do." "So do they. They do the best they can and pick up $90,000 besides." "That," said Sprague, "is what's the matter with America. You think only of the dollar. Australia is fifteen years behind you there, some say twenty-five."

FEBRUARY 2: Candi was happy about her first day of school, despite the heat. We drove her in and saw what appeared to be a great yard full of teachers, all in long pants of the same shade of grey, white shirts, and maroon neckties. To the right was another long yard full of bicycles. These weren't teachers as it happens; they were boys in their school uniforms. None, apparently, drive to school in cars. Candi's summer uniform consists of a Macbeth plaid frock, brown lisle stockings and lace-up shoes, and—should hat-wearing be compulsory—a straw-boater with maroon sash.

We hung around Elizabeth all day to take Candi back to camp, and will have to do this for the rest of the week until the Spragues leave. The more I see of Elizabeth the better I like it. Yet, judging by the people I talked to today, I seem to be in the minority. Actually, though, there weren't so many I talked to. There was the plumber working on a clothes boiler in one of the new houses. He declared he wouldn't live in Elizabeth: "Too many poms." To be

166

sure he came from England himself but this was back in 1939. The appliance store manager from whom we bought a radio tube—Beveridge by name—also comes from England. He's not happy with Australia in general, for the usual reasons: too quiet, no real pub life, can't smoke in theatres. He endures Elizabeth because his house is air-cooled but he still hasn't sold his England home and may go back. The bank teller, Buckminster, who is Australian, dislikes Elizabeth because it doesn't have a river. In Albury, New South Wales, where he comes from, he lived on the Murray River. Here too the desert wind plays hob with his hay fever. "The poms don't bother you?" Beveridge had told me that more than two out of three Elizabethans were English migrants. 'The what?" "Poms." "Oh no. I married one."

Pom or Aussie, everybody in Elizabeth has tiny children. Buckminster said he'd given up trying to shop Friday nights. The kids raced through the stores on their tricycles. Did he, I asked, know of a single family which didn't own a dog? Except for himself he could think of none.

We fixed up our account and Buckminster introduced me to his manager, Mr McPhee, a man only slightly older than he. McPhee has lived in Elizabeth three years, moving out from Adelaide, and likes it a lot. He said the running down I'd encountered could be due to the English who gripe about any place they live in, England most of all. Then, too, he said, some ten years ago English people bought the first Housing Trust homes, sold them at a handsome profit, and went back to spread the word about the gold to be picked off the streets. Later buyers hadn't found their homes to appreciate so rapidly.

On our long drive back I noticed quite a few tracts going up below Elizabeth, another proof to me how Government initiative in business can be an actual stimulus to private enterprise. Without Elizabeth's pioneering I doubt whether private builders would risk putting up speculative homes on the desert. Their designs are more up-to-date, especially in the freer use of glass, but the houses are crowded much closer together.

FEBRUARY 8: Yesterday we completed a week in the new house, counting Sunday night as our arrival. Actually the house is not so very new; the design is certainly not. The windows are too small and too few. There is no permanent clothes storage, just a wooden wardrobe in each bedroom. The Spragues said the separate wardrobe was a normal piece in every Australian bedroom suite.

The bathtub is large and relatively unscratched. It is not one piece either, but is tiled in and takes ages to fill. Perhaps it is tubs like this which make a butler or maid such a necessary character in British fiction. "Your bath is drawn, sir—or madam" seemed the ultimate in unnecessary service when it needed only two minutes to fill one. The tiny trickle from this "instant" electric water heater cries out for the services of a butler.

The toilet, consisting of a porcelain bowl and a separate sheet metal tank fastened to the wall above it, is in a coffin-shaped room of its own; its flush, reverberating off the close bare walls, is deafening. Strategically located right behind and slightly above the neck of a person seated there is a set of unclosable glass louvres. If the wind Buckminster complained of blows cold in winter—as I'm told it does—that little room is going to be no place to sit around in reading comic books.

But the question of heat in the lavatory—as the little room is called—may be academic. The only source of heat anywhere in the house is a fireplace in what is called the lounge (living room), with an opening of a little more than one square foot. Ceilings are even higher than in New Zealand. There Candi used to be able to flick a fly off by leaping in the air with a swatter. Here she leapt and leapt but could not dislodge a crawling insect. The house is built of brick, with a tile roof, and looks strong inside as well as out. Walls are of painted plaster; floors are carpeted all over.

The interior door-latches—and they are latches, not knobs—are about shoulder height to a husky teenage youth. They and the long narrow doors on which they fit seem designed for a race of Gary Coopers—the thin-hipped giants most outsiders imagine Australians to be. The flesh and blood Australian girl and woman may perhaps be taller than average: her consort is apt to be a trifle undersize.

The neighbourhood continues to be almost unnaturally quiet and dark after nightfall. Most of the residents might be away. And yet children and dogs and radios are audible during the day. Perhaps English people, used to living in close quarters, have learned the value of night-time quiet.

24

FEBRUARY 10: Jess Southeby dropped by to see how we are making out. He left school in Yorkshire at fourteen to apprentice himself as a carpenter at five bob a week. Mother was alone, elder sister was working. Had one younger brother. Finished apprenticeship just in time to be drafted; was among those saved at Dunkirk. He owns both the Encyclopaedia Britannica and the set of Great Books and wishes he could find the time to read them. Has paper work to do on his business, with five employees, to all of whom he gives three-week paid vacations. He says $44-$46 a week is the going wage after taxes, and most men keep families on it. A pound a week would be the family man's income tax on this wage. If he also wants to bring his family under the Government-sponsored national health scheme he pays up to another pound a week premium to a private insurance company. This covers most hospital costs up to 26 weeks and half his bills for doctor visits. Prescriptions for drugs on the Government-approved list cost 50 cents whether he is insured or not.

Jess's speech is salted with expressions like "bugger him," "half your luck" (good luck), "all power to you," and "beggars" (beg your pardon). When he eats mutton or lamb he eats "woolie"; sausages are "snags" (a highly important part of the Australian diet); tea or coffee is a "cuppa," his mouth is his "cake hole." One who eats too much is a "garbage guts"; but a "grizzle guts" is a complainer. He has a "shack" (summer cottage) on "two blocks" near some beach and has a caravan parked there also.

Though he hadn't taken much part in our discussion with the Spragues he agreed Australia must quit thinking of herself as an outpost of Europe and strive to be more neighbourly with the countries around her. "Beginning with New Zealand," I suggested. "Yes," he laughed and told me how his next door neighbour moved in six weeks ago and they had exchanged not a single word

169

before last Sunday when she ran over crying, "Your garage is on fire!" The previous tenant, who had occupied the house two years, exchanged greetings soon after moving in. Then they had no more to do with each other until they were both out in front, picking up the lids to their garbage tins. Jess said: "I notice you've been packing. Do you really think you ought to leave us?"

The weather has been lovely in this Southern Hemisphere autumn. Adelaide chose the time well for its Arts Festival. We arrived early enough to grab a meter, and wandered about for two hours waiting to see the opening parade. Except for various marching bands it was a rag-tag affair of commercially sponsored floats, only one of which—John Martin's—showed any real character or craftsmanship. Peggy and Candi went shopping but gave up before the stores closed, and we were early to art class. We still have the same model. I don't mind but others might. Still they don't say so. They don't talk to or about the model, don't fret over the pose, don't do anything except draw, draw, draw. In rest periods two may whisper together; none walk around looking at others' work, to tell and be told how well they're doing. The outgoing Australian just isn't present. Talking to them, about their drawings especially—complimenting, making suggestions—is like dropping a pebble in a pool of mud. There is no sound, no bounce.

FEBRUARY 20: Candi came home in Friday's heat out of sorts as we all were. The heavy load of homework she's been carrying may also have been responsible. She had a certain amount of catching up to do in Math (or Maths as they call it) and Physics particularly; but the demands on children's out-of-school time is in general far greater here than in the United States. Mr Turk of the Housing Trust says that when his son was in secondary school he would get up at six to do his homework. After school he would play outdoors until tea, and, following tea, be at his books till nine or nine-thirty bedtime. "School children work harder and for longer hours than adults."

The prime source of trouble is, of course, the public exam. It was true in New Zealand but, as Candi was only in Fourth Form there, she had no exam to look forward to at the end of the year and she received, on the whole, a good education. Here, though her foreign language instruction is exceptionally good, emphasis everywhere else is on absorption of formulae and examination proficiency. She isn't being educated in those subjects; she is being groomed to pass examinations in them. If she were to move to another State she would be lost. The exams would require a radically different sort of grooming, the syllabuses on which they are based having no uniformity between one State and another.

There are two final examinations in secondary school. One, called the Leaving Certificate Examination is, so to speak, the key that unlocks the gate of the school yard. A child who has not attained the legal school leaving age must pass it to be allowed out. It is supposed also to be highly valued by employers. The second examination, for Matriculation or Leaving Honours, might be compared to the cooling off period in a labour dispute. Its primary purpose is to keep a child out of university for another year or two, on the premise that at the age of 15-16 when he passes the Leaving Exam he may be academically prepared for university but is not otherwise mature enough.

As might be expected under such a system, the examination counts for everything. Apart from attending classes physically, as required by law, and behaving himself, a child has no obligation except to pass the exam. There is very little recitation, almost no teacher-pupil discussion. Answers to Maths and Physics problems are given in the textbook, and I note that Candi has got into the habit of consulting the answers before seriously setting out to solve the problems. The other side of this coin is the student who may be a good scholar but fears and does badly in examinations. Yet he too must stand or fall by them.

FEBRUARY 26: Peggy and I went into Adelaide yesterday to buy birthday gifts for Rick and Will Austin, and a dress Candi saw in John Martin's. She wants to attend a house party next Saturday given by one of her classmates. This I believe is also the night of the annual German Club party to which we've been invited.

We had a hotel lunch. The waitress, a Scot, washed silverware at the cash register between serving meals. Plates were taken from the tables and the cutlery was dropped in an oval dishpan of not very warm water, past which customers filed to enter the dining room. She swished the things around, took them out and dropped them in a bucket of rinse water, also standing on the counter. Then she got a dish towel from the cook and dried them by the handful. What happened to the plates and beer glasses I didn't see.

MARCH 5: It was cold Tuesday, colder than Monday. Wednesday was still cool enough that the Elizabeth postmaster was complaining cheerfully about the summer getting away without there being any. "We usually have a fortnight of temperatures in the high 90s but the last few years the weather has been unusual. It was cool

171

most of last summer too." "You like it hot, then?" "Ah, yeah. You store up heat to carry you through the winter."

I guessed correctly that he came from South Australia. So did one of the girls working for him. The other is from New South Wales. We joked over finding three Aussies together in one place in Elizabeth. "Like hitting the jackpot when you pull the lever. You sometimes feel lonely?"

"We're a dying race."

Yesterday it began to warm up, grew too warm at night, and is uncomfortably hot and humid today. The postmaster is pleased. The new proprietor of the 4-Square Grocery—three months here from the Midlands—was not, as he cheerfully admitted. "I thought that was why you came here, to get some of this heat." "I didn't. A lot of them say they do. I left because I was squeezed out." "Down in the Midlands? I thought conditions were still pretty good there." "It's worse in the north but the little retailer is getting squeezed out in the south too by the giants. You can't make a living." "Still this 4-Square of yours is a chain." "It's not the same thing. I'm a member. I own part of it. They simply do my buying for me. I tried to buy into one in England but they wouldn't let me. There's no longer any room in England for the little man. That's why I'm here." He had meant to get out of the business for good after selling his shop in Worcestershire. He got assisted passage. "Everybody gets that." But no promise of employment. When he couldn't find a job there was nothing to do but reinvest his money in the business.

Working hours are shorter here and the profit margin is longer: 17 per cent compared to ten per cent in U.K., and a 48-hour week compared to 80. They had to stay open evenings and Sundays to compete with the chains. There was no self-service and the shop was about half the size of his present one.

We picked up Harold and Dierdre Austin for a picnic at Victor Harbor, a beachside resort about 60 miles to the southeast. The day was still perfect, just warm enough to make sun and shade equally comfortable. We drove over brown rolling hills with occasional patches of gum scrub and a most refreshing absence of outdoor advertising. Not a sign anywhere big or small. No hand-painted come-ons to see prehistoric monsters, no burma shave jingles, no information about the distance to this or that hotel, not even a service station warning or a Bull Durham paint job on a barn. No barns in fact; and only one paddock of sheep; and two temporary roadside marketing stands offering strawberries at 50 cents a punnet." "What's a punnet?" "Oh, a little box about this

size," gesturing with the hands. We picnicked in a wind shelter on the beach and had the Governor's summer residence pointed out to us deep in a clump of exotic trees.

I was surprised to learn that the Austins, who have lived here so long and who had entered into the spirit of the RAA picnic with what seemed a truly Australian will, don't really think of this country as their home. At the end of the day I asked Harold, "Do you consider yourself an Australian?" "Good Lord, no!" he said feelingly. "You don't find the Aussies much the same as the English?" I pressed him, for to me there's hardly a shade of difference. "Definitely not. They don't like the English. They resent us." "Resentment apart, which anyone might feel toward a newcomer, what sort of people are they?" "They're not friendly, not sociable like the Englishman—outside London, you understand. You go into poob in Manchester, everybody greets you. Here they don't. In England as soon as you move into a new house the neighbours are around wanting to know your business. Here your next door neighbour may not even say good day. After we'd been in our house three years, without exchanging more than a cool nod with the men on either side of us, I saw one of them out in the yard.

" 'What rates do you pay?' was the first thing he said. 'I don't pay any,' I said. 'You mean you haven't paid rates in three years? Haven't they sent you a bill?' A week later I got a bill. For the whole three years. With a notice to come into Council and tell them why I hadn't paid rates before. 'You didn't send me a bill,' I told them. 'It's not my business to ask you to.' 'Well, you have your neighbour to thank for the fact that we have now,' " they said.

"They never ask you to come in their house. In England when you call on anyone they always ask you in for coop of tea. They're supposed to be great betters but they hate to pay up. They're poor losers too. They can't stand having England win at cricket test. We always come out for England, not because it means so much to us, just to even things up. When we barrack for England they say, 'That's the way with you poms. Why can't you be Australians?' "

Young Dr McCulloch was an Ulsterman who migrated in search, apparently, of wider opportunities. His wife, of Dutch parentage but born in Java, was also a physician. They met at Dublin University, had three children, another on the way. They toyed with the idea of going to Rhodesia and were glad they didn't. During his first five years in Australia Dr McCulloch practised in Victor Harbor but was happy now to be out of it: the narrowness

174

and petty feuds of small town life. By contrast Elizabeth, where nobody was part of an old family, was free and comfortable; though he found in its uniform box-like prettiness a lack of character. I thought it would acquire character in time; we had towns like this all over America in different stages of development; Elizabeth made me feel quite at home. He said the migrants often come to him with half-real, half-imaginary ailments. Their bodies are here, their arms and legs, but their minds are only half here; half is still back home. They'd like to go back, realizing they can never be wholly at home in this foreign land, but they are afraid to, fearful they will no longer fit in there either. "Migration is a traumatic experience. One migration in a lifetime is enough."

25

MARCH 7: Candi's party was a great success, Ernestine having thoughtfully and, by dint of enormous effort, assured an actual over-supply of boys. They stomped, they drank lollywater, Candi confining herself to punch in the interest of her teeth, and ate smoked oysters. Candi ate only two. She was "put off" them by one of the boys pretending they were still alive, etc. Two of the couples — Ernestine and Fran and their boy friends — were "mushy" and went off by themselves to neck; but the others mixed freely enough. Apparently the guest list consisted wholly of migrants. At the beginning they grouped Australian style, girls on one side, boys on the other, until someone called attention to there being no Australians present. Then they alternated in seating but still were stiff and untalkative. When the band arrived they adjourned to the tiny garage and the noise of two guitars, a drum, and a vocalist, all hopped up by amplifiers, made conversation impossible. The party really got started only after the band's exodus; then they danced to records and had a lot more fun than at any school social—where the worry of wondering whether she'll be asked to dance outweighs all else in a girl's mind.

Kurt and Ilse Fechner had almost given us up at the German Club. We got lost trying to find the hall in the dark and didn't get there until nearly ten. So we missed the singing, but otherwise the party was just getting started. Sophia and her husband Paul, who is a dead ringer for the late President Kennedy and even speaks like him, ending every sentence on a rising inflection as though asking a question, had also arrived late. We sat with them and the Fechners and drank beer while the dancing went on. Paul had little to say of Sydney except he thought it the most exciting city he'd ever been in—which is perhaps an odd comment for one who was born there. But he evidently lived most of his life in England. His parents were Irish.

Next to the Fechners was a young Belgian couple, Georges and Charmaine, who have been here only six months and speak little English. Like everyone else at our long table Georges is a friend of Kurt's, works with him as a mechanic. I bravely attempted to talk French with them and they, inspired by my example, called on resources of English they had never suspected. They wouldn't dance. Charmaine got dizzy, they said. I asked if they had children. They do, two boys, 1 and 2, of whom Charmaine had pictures, both very charming. (Too late I thought I should have said, "Charmant!")

Meanwhile the dancing progressed from polkas through waltzes to German songs, which the male dancers all knew by heart and sang with feeling as they danced. Then it moved to twist, and Georges and Charmaine were on their feet, spinning, stretching handclasped arms. It wasn't twist actually; it was the dancing young people used to do in the U.S. just after the war. Anyhow this was their music; and Bert too, another German we met at the picnic, was dancing it with Ilse.

We met the president of the club (and learnt it is over 100 years old) and a gentleman whose grandfather settled in the Barossa Valley that long ago. He was Minister of Education in South Australia until the war, when he was ostracized for his German background. We met a Mr Hesse whose family has been here even longer —since 1838—yet he seemed to speak with a trace of a German accent. The trouble is, of course, that precise English often sounds Germanic. On accents—both Kurt and Bert have learnt Australian English. Bert's last name means "paint beer" in German but as he and Kurt pronounced it I thought they were saying "pint beer."

The evening ended, after the four-piece orchestra played a jazzed-up version of *Now is the Hour* which kiwis would deplore, with everyone standing around our table, singing, and drinking the last of the beer. Pitcherful after pitcherful was drunk during the evening. Charmaine drank at least one. Beer, I learnt, is the national drink of Belgium, where the monks brew it so strong two glasses is as much as anyone can take.

We got home to find Candi in bed and Jess outside in his car with a real old Australian, though not so old in years. Early 40s, I'd say, since he served in the war, but younger looking. Unmarried, he lives with his mother in Burnside. Both of Peter's parents descended from settlers who came in the second ship either to Australia or South Australia. The difference would be important in many new and old Aussie eyes as South Australia is the only State without a convict background.

There is a widely held theory that convict settlement had much to do with forming Aussie character. Sophie, who comes from Lithuania, touched on this at the party when she said South Australia was the country's melting pot; and this was because free settlers, including the Germans, hadn't the feeling of inferiority which the convicts bequeathed to the other States. Hence they hadn't the average Australian's fear and dislike of strangers.

I have heard the same convict legacy given credit for the legendary Australian contempt for authority, as is told of the Australian general—Monash probably—who was escorting a British colleague through the diggers' camp. Soldiers lounged around informally and looked up with only casual interest when the two officers went by. "Aren't your men even going to salute us?" asked the horrified Englishman. "Oh," said Monash lightly, "if you wave at them they'll wave back."

"What the Puritans are to America," said Dr Dunhill, "the convicts are to Australia—a hook on which you can hang any theory you please about the country and its customs. One of your thirteen original colonies was founded by a religious sect called Puritans. This name didn't stand so much for purity in themselves as it did for their revolt against the frivolous excesses of the English court. Even so, they founded one only of your colonies. Others were founded by Quakers, Catholics, convicts, and representatives of the decadent English court itself. But whenever a writer or lecturer wants to account for one or another trait in American character, however diverse they may be, he goes back to the Puritans. So it is with us and our convict past, and you can prove as many different things—nine times out of ten the same things!—with convicts as with Puritans."

Besides his colonial ancestry Peter is also descended from Barossa Valley Germans. He says many of these people, though they were among the State's earliest settlers, spoke only German and sent their youngsters to Lutheran schools where all the instruction was in German. Their sympathies were so divided during the war that some would stand for *God Save the King* and remain standing to salute and shout, "Heil Hitler!" There are no exclusively German schools, now, although Lutheran Church services are still given in German; and Peter guessed there might be 200,000 in the valley today who speak English but continue to "think in German." The Barossa Wine Festival in the autumn is a colourful event. Vintners make free wine available to all, so liberally that it really does run in the streets.

178

Peter has a strong attachment for Adelaide and its traditions; deplores the passing of old colonial structures. The residence of Captain Sturt, an early Australian explorer, was bought by a new Australian who removed the old slate roof and replaced it with corrugated iron, grubbed up the trees and vines which had been part of the original garden, and in general desecrated the shrine. Belatedly the Historic Trust reclaimed the dwelling and set to work restoring it. "But you can never restore a thing completely," Peter said. "How can they ever put back the trees?"

He wants to see England because he likes old places. Has no desire to see America unless it might be Kentucky where he imagines colonels live in colonial mansions and darkies in livery bring them mint juleps. It went hard when I told him it wasn't so. Nothing else in the United States interests him. So we sat outdoors with beer and sandwiches until early morning. It was a lovely night and no mosquitoes. The ants, too, which climb over you in the daytime if you stay in one spot outdoors, had gone to bed.

MARCH 14: Friday (day before yesterday) being a pleasant day with sunshine but not extreme heat, I bought some timber to finish Candi's desk. I started to say "lumber" when I was ordering it and corrected myself. "Say lumber," said John Denby. "They have me listed as a lumber merchant in the Lions Club. The American influence." He had trouble recalling my first name again. "One of those Yank names, Mac or something."

"You're not English yourself any more," I kidded him. "You're Australian. You probably hate the poms as much as anyone."

"I do, too. Nobody is more Australian than the converted Englishman, and nobody gets to be more English than the Aussie or Canadian who settles in England." He went on: "And why not? I'm happy here. A better job than I could ever hope for in England; more holiday time, three weeks at Christmas and four days at Easter; a night a week at the pub, a Sunday soccer match, a perfect climate, and the beach close by. That's all I want from life."

I dropped by at the Fechner's yesterday; didn't go in. Ilse had her hands covered with mincemeat; Kurt's were covered with grease from a car he was working on. Both were excited over a Shell petrol station Kurt is to manage, starting three-four weeks after Easter. His meeting the Shell representative resulted somehow from an accident he had on the job and which is keeping him home now. But in his excitement his English got so garbled that I couldn't understand his explanation.

They'll both have to work at the station, and for longer hours than he is working now—including Saturdays from 8.30 to 1.00—

179

but their hopes are high for making plenty of money. Kurt quoted his father as having said: "Even a blind chook finds piece of corn once in awhile."

So this is what Australia can mean. Kurt and Ilse could live their whole lives in Germany, or anywhere in Europe, without such an opportunity. The Shell representative said he preferred new Australians because they understand what service means. To the old Australian, Kurt explained, service is like a piece rubber. And he demonstrated by stretching his hands apart.

I came home by way of Morphett Road past the cricket ground where play was going on—presumably among old Australians. And I bought gas from a young old Australian who was willing enough to check the oil and battery but seemed not to know how to go about it.

This evening they broadcast the last of one of the few listenable radio programmes, called *Any Questions.* It had a panel of four in Sydney (including one American migrant of some years' standing) who answered questions asked from the audience. Tonight a questioner asked: "In light of the rising proportion of pregnancies in the 13-to-15-year-age group, should we return to the custom of chaperones?" The American woman replied, with brittle self-assurance: "What we should give them is, not chaperones, but contraceptives"; and the other panel members allowed they could add nothing to this advice.

This too is Australia's brave new world, where the liveliest intelligences show the utmost courage over—the continued dispossession of the Aborigines from what little land has been left them? Politics, at home and abroad? Public morality? None of these. In New Zealand the most controversial issue of the day was modern art. In Australia it is sex and censorship.

"In the morning I went to a meeting of the Uni literary society. They had a sort of debate about censorship with a lecturer in English, a Scotsman, and a lecturer in Politics. The only thing was, it wasn't really a debate because they were all on the same side— against censorship. And they all liked the sound of their voices so much that there wasn't time at the end for the students, who had arguments in favour of it, to state their views. The English fellow especially seemed to have such a taste for pornographic literature. He read out this crummy poem that had absolutely nothing to recommend it as far as verse goes. The only thing it was slightly sexy. He got this mischievous gleam in his eye as he read it and then he said if anyone wanted to read Lady Chatterley's Lover,

Another Country, The Group, etc., etc., AND etc., he would be glad to lend them, so it looks like he possesses the lot. I would hate them to abolish censorship because it would deprive him of so much pleasure."

Denby told me this: A well-advertised contraceptive in England, Durex, has the same name as a brand of cellotape marketed by Behr-Manning in Australia. Australian office girls and retail clerks in contact with British migrants must be warned about this; and indeed the word "cellotape," which I can't recall seeing in the United States, might have been coined to get them over the difficulty. This still doesn't resolve the confusion for the migrant who has seen Durex featured in chemists' window displays and on large outdoor signs throughout England. A friend of Denby's, a Czech who lived in London before coming on to Australia, wanted to buy the contraceptives and casually asked for Durex as he'd been used to doing in England. The girl behind the chemist's counter inquired, "Will the half-inch size do?"

26

MARCH 20: Sophie and Paul Gallagher have a place much like the Spragues': small, cramped with too much furniture, and soundly built. A fine lawn all around, green and closely mown. A wall-to-wall carpet on the lounge floor of which Sophie said: "It's warm on your feet. It cost £50. Paul had to work two weeks to pay for it."

Paul talked at length about Australia's underdeveloped state and the likelihood of Indonesia or Japan moving in to fill the vacuum. "They could do it too. They'd put millions of men to work—like ants—digging one canal across the country from east to west, and another from north to south; then run branches to irrigate with. Britain and the United States ought to put up the money to develop Australia and keep it out of the hands of the Communists. It would be a good investment."

"Would it yield the return of—say—bubble gum or television?"

"I don't reckon it would, but it has to be done and we Australians will never do it. We prefer easy living, sitting in the sun like we're doing now. Why worry about tomorrow? It's the climate that saps our energy. Look at the difference between the North and South in the United States. The southern States are just like Australia. No ambition, no initiative. Where does all your energy, your drive and ambition come from? From the cold northern States. The trouble with Australia is that the whole country has a warm easy climate."

He recalled a visit some years back of the British novelist J. B. Priestley and how he let his hair down in an off-the-record talk with a reporter in Darwin. When this was headlined in a Sydney paper it caused a sensation. One incident Priestley cited: At a certain hotel in Sydney or Melbourne he didn't like the claret served him and complained to the waiter. The waiter poured some in a glass, tasted it, said, "Nothing wrong with this," and walked away. "That's Australia for you," said Paul.

I mentioned the actual lack of fresh water in the country, without high mountains to catch the rain or big rivers. I'd heard that the total run-off of all the mainland rivers was less than half the Mississippi's alone. Paul waved the lack of rivers away and proposed to fill his canals with de-salted sea water. "It can be done, though it needs much more capital than Australia can provide. It's up to American and British investors to furnish the capital."

"Australia needs us migrants more than we need Australia," said Herter. Australia would still not be anywhere except for them. All of the country's recent progress was due to the migrants.

"Surely not all," I protested. "The natural resources must be partly responsible." "Partly," said Herter grudgingly. "But we had to furnish the brains to utilize the resources. You can't think of a single Australian who is outstanding in any way. He resents newcomers. But where would he be without us?"

APRIL 1: A sergeant in the traffic police stopped to comment on a sketch I was making while parked on Hindley Street. He knew the story of the old building I was sketching, a brown three-storey castle of turrets and deep-set mullioned windows. It was an unlicensed hotel at which country people stayed when they came to town and where they were liable to be fleeced by city slickers. The Sergeant's father used to stop there. "Did he get fleeced?" "No. He was too smart."

The Sergeant was disappointed not to get into the Criminal Investigation Bureau. He had passed all the examinations; yet others went up past him, even some he had broken in. He blamed it on "sectarianism" which he said is very strong in Australia. Having gone to the right college—St Peter's in Adelaide, Scotch in Melbourne—meant everything. "You see them come up, sales managers at twenty-one. It's the old school tie."

I said English migrants often came here just to get away from that sort of thing. He knew that of course; still he wasn't too unhappy. He had intended to be a teacher but was satisfied with his present choice because "I can't think of any other career in which I could be of greater service to more people." I wonder in how many of the world's cities would a policeman engage in a long, casual conversation with a stranger.

APRIL 13: Kurt has been going to school with Shell in preparation for taking over his new station five weeks from now. I asked

him what he'd do when he got rich, go back to Germany? No; firmly. He was through with Europe for good. There was no freedom, no elbow room. (He pushed out his elbows.) You had to carry a passport all the time, and he could never hope to own a business of his own.

"I don't mean to stay," I said; "just go back for a visit. Wouldn't you like to take a trip back to Germany?"

He might go back for a visit, three or four weeks with his family, but no longer.

And see your old friends.

No. He had no friends there any more. If he had a few quid they might be friendly but when it was gone they'd go too.

Do you find Australians better friends than the people back in Germany?

Yes. Australians were more helpful when you got in trouble. Even if they'd never seen you before they'd pitch in to help you out. His house was the first to be built on his street, a dirt track then evidently. Others moved in. His car got bogged once. They went to work to get him out, stepping in the deep mud with their best clothes on. He thanked them. They said it was a pleasure. In Germany not more than one person in a hundred would do as much, even if he knew you.

Kurt's only complaint about Australia is the lack of social life at night. In Frankfurt a man and wife could always find a place to go for a beer and conversation, music and dance, but not here. Even the new Australians seldom get together in social affairs, and when they do the old Australians won't join in. He thought the Aussie women would like to. It was the men who were against it. They never talked soft to their women like Europeans did and they didn't want their wives talked to that way by other men.

APRIL 25: Today is Anzac Day. There were several short sermons devoted to it in church this evening, sketching its history from the call-up of 20,000 volunteers in 1914, through their dispatch to Suez, and then to Gallipoli. During the supper after the service I was introduced to a young American migrant. He has been here a year and came, so he first said, because he could not get employment as a teacher in the U.S. Later he amended this to say that he couldn't get a subsidy to cover his tuition and living expenses while studying to become a teacher. This went against the grain since, once educated, he would be an extremely valuable member of society.

Here in Australia they recognized this. He had corresponded with the Department of Education before leaving Boston, and when he got here they took one look at his credentials and put him on the payroll. He didn't think it an out of the ordinary thing; he wondered more Americans hadn't thought of it.

Friday noon at Candi's school a special service was held in honour of Anzac Day. Said the speaker of the occasion, representing the Returned Servicemen's League: "They sacrificed their lives in war, and when you take a stand against war and say war is wrong you are saying they did wrong. But what they did must have been right because they sacrificed their lives doing it. Let the people who agitate against war sacrifice their lives for what they believe in and we'll listen to what they have to say. These men did. They were right in doing it. And war is right."

I went directly to Cheshire's on Little Collins Street where I had arranged to meet Tony and Lester for our customary morning coffee. Lester brought along an old friend, Bill, who was in Melbourne to be interviewed on his application for an exchange teachership in the U.S. He now teaches in an infants' school in Canberra, a city he professes a great fondness for: wonders why all visitors hate it and all established residents love it. Lester, whose friendship with Bill dates back to the days when he too was a Canberran, said it was because the residents hated the visitors and wanted to keep the place exclusively for themselves.

Bill's expenses were paid for the Melbourne interview. He was given a railway ticket and, travelling on Sunday night, got the train which furnishes foot-warmers for lack of any other heat. These are large crocks or tubs of hot sand, two to a compartment. The passengers rest their feet on them.

Bill's father is a teacher, his two brothers—one deceased, the other a lecturer in philosophy at Monash University—also. This academic environment is probably responsible for his sardonic wit and generally quizzical attitude. He questions many of Australia's sacred cows, including Anzac Day and the pronunciation of Canberra: it was mispronounced "Canbra" by the Governor-General's wife who christened the new city; and, she being a Lady, no mere commoner would presume to correct her. So it's been 'Canbra" ever since.

Lester said that Anzac Day, for the great majority of Australians, really was the One Day of the Year, a day when people who normally were scornful of its supposed ideals were momentarily ready to fight for them. Bill cut Lester's majority down to one-sixth of the population and said most of them would be small boys. I tended to string along with Lester and asked Tony what about England, did they have such a day? November 11th was the closest, he said, and it meant no more to them than to us; but even he would march on Anzac Day in Hobart, in the face of his fellow Britons' jeers.

Yet when I happened to joke about Sir Bob's celebrated apostrophe to the Queen, with its high-flown language and obvious insincerity, Bill's cynicism vanished and he almost took offence. And Lester backed him up. I realized I didn't know Australians as well as I thought I did; for surely a people as unsentimental as they wouldn't be taken in by it? But they were, and in the end succeeded in convincing me that the old hypocrite's affection for that lady was utterly sincere. Tony said, if this were so, how could Australia under his leadership have ditched Britain so heartlessly on the purchase of those swept-wing fighter bombers? Bill's answer was that countries were one thing and people another. Sir Bob's adoration was for the Queen as a person and he didn't feel he was hurting her personally when he let Britain down.

APRIL 27: Candi returned yesterday from her French weekend, vowing she had never in her life had such a good time. She was one of eight in her class who attended, together with representatives from two other State schools—Adelaide Boys and Seacombe —and three public schools. They stayed at a Methodist retreat and hostel in the Adelaide Hills and crammed a great deal of instruction, practice, and testing into what was essentially a gay adventure. There were dictées, oral and written quizzes, vocabulary games, French films, records, songs and poetry, French conversation almost exclusively, hikes, volley ball, tea breaks, and late bedtimes. The teachers, one with each class, presumably contributed their time; and each came prepared to conduct a seminar: on La Fontaine, *Le Petit Prince* of Saint-Exupery, Jacques Prévert, the subjunctive, etc.

Peggy and I viewed the touring exhibition of current Australian art, which I found disappointing. There was a fine picture by a certain Mathews (his only contribution), hung cheek by jowl with a huge collage of toys and pieces of junk which excited more public interest than all the other exhibits put together. There were also two excellent pictures by Margo Lewers and one uncatalogued work by an artist whose name I recognized but can't recall. Gleghorn, from whom I expected much, was represented by a single large picture and it was pointless. Blackman exhibited a collection of faces, Nolan a smeared-over Aboriginal and a man seated in a pool with his head in a box, Drysdale a slick Norman Rockwell portrait of an Aboriginal, Boyd two pictures I'd already seen and not the best. Apart from these and one or two others, all paid their respects to the school of abstract expressionism, using one of the several well-worn pathways to arrive there.

Upstairs, to which a Dutch migrant guard dragged us, the National Gallery's old favourites were on display. Here in Hans Heysen landscapes, highly burnished still lifes, travel records, and illustrational figure groupings the sameness was apparent to anyone. The tricks were different: pink skies instead of scorched and blistered paint; but the mediocre painters had mastered them. The bright spot among the old favourites is a self-portrait by Colonel Light, founder and planner of Adelaide. A superb piece of work and he did, the guard told me, other pictures in the gallery collection. I hope some time to see them.

The guard, who is studying painting with a private tutor, has been here fourteen years and especially likes the climate. Besides, he couldn't afford to go back. He is in his 40s, married to an English girl, and has a family. He was in the Dutch merchant marine in the early days of the war, plying as a neutral to Hamburg, Amsterdam, Rio, and Southampton. His ship was held in Southampton for inspection and then, against the Captain's wishes, sent back to Holland just prior to the Nazi invasion. He was conscripted for labour service and chose to work in Norway rather than Germany. He was there six years and remembers it with particular fondness. He'd like to return to Norway and would if he could get a job there. "The people were so simple," unlike the Swedes who were aloof.

"What about the Australians?" "They're like the Norwegians in a way. When you first arrive they take you in." He'd been told they were more friendly in Western Australia but found this was only surface friendliness, asking "How are you?" and not really caring what you answered. He has a few good friends among Australians. But most of his friends are among Italian and German migrants. He feels more at home with them; they make him one of them. "The Australians are too casual." "What do you mean by casual?" "They couldn't care less whether you're there or not. They're just casual."

MAY 2: Reverend Homer Wagstaff came to Australia from Oregon because the job in his church was offering and a friend was planning to go into business here. After his plans were laid the friend backed out. Now, after two years, Wagstaff has pretty well made up his mind not to stay permanently. Even in university circles he has found no intellectual ferment except, fleetingly, among the students before they get married. "What do the students think about?" I asked. "Oh, the white Australia policy, for one thing," he said. He got himself in hot water with the church with one of his sermons devoted to the Negro revolt in the U.S., in which he touched briefly on the parallel with white Australia.

Apart from their refusal to think, he finds Australians very nice people, easy going, not quarrelsome, and not puritanical in matters of sex as he thinks Americans are. Yet, he has not, he says, made a single friend here; whereas everywhere else—including Argentina where he spent a year—he has made numerous friends. Friendships in Australia he says are lightly acquired and as lightly relinquished. No one ever calls on him: he must do all the calling. Australians just don't make an effort to keep friendships alive.

"He spoke pretty slow at first for my benefit but then I asked if he had read that book Australie *and he really got going. He says it wasn't written by an Australian. It was written by a European because all the European prejudices were so obvious in it. It was*

188

quite surprising how pro-Australian Monsieur is, seeing he can't even speak any English. But apparently they have French grizzlegutses here just like pom ones and he really deplores them. In that book Australie it says that fashions finish in Australia or something, and Monsieur said this was absurd. How could they wear the same fashions at the same time when the seasons are different? And anyway in France if you go a few miles out of Paris they're more backward than in Australia. Also it says in the book that Australia is the only tropical country where white men work, and he thought that was absurd too. He has been in Africa and South America and he worked just the same as here."

27

There are three different track gauges on the Ghan, so called because until quite recently camel caravans with Afghan drivers carried freight from the railhead at Oodnadatta northward. From Adelaide north-west to Port Pirie for 100-odd miles the wide gauge track which South Australia shares with Victoria is used. The route is over flat land between two ranges of low mountains, passing grain silos and stock pens and wheat fields. From Port Pirie for some 300 miles north to Marree, running along beside the Flinders Ranges, the track is the standard gauge adopted by New South Wales. And very much rougher to travel on. And from Marree, past the dry bed of Lake Eyre where Donald Campbell broke the world's land speed record, the roadbed is slightly less rough. The track for the remaining 600 miles north-west to Alice Springs is the $3\frac{1}{2}$-foot narrow gauge adopted for reasons of economy in the Northern Territory and the other three Australian States.

MAY 6: Our compartment companion this afternoon was a retired sheep farmer going to see his son who manages a large cattle property on "the Katherine." He himself had 3,500 breeding ewes on 12,000 acres near Broken Hill—a sufficient number, he reckoned, for a good living, to pay for one's children's education, and have one trip a year. He contracts for the shearing to an individual who hires and supervises the gangs—all men; no women as in New Zealand—many of whom earn $90 a week and work nine months a year. The clip is sent to a broker in one of the capital cities, the choice of broker often depending on how deep in debt the grower may be to him. More important in determining the price is guessing what city auction to send it to. Many growers divide their clip between two cities. Sheep are culled when they have six teeth (three years old) and go to the feed lots near the cities to breed fat lambs.

Coming up through South Australia north of Adelaide I saw many of these feeding paddocks, or stubble paddocks, where ewes and their lambs were cleaning up on the stalks from last season's wheat. Some of the lambs, hardly bigger than a chihuahua and dark in colour, were only a few days old. Still they loped about after their mothers.

The wool grower's son, educated at a private agricultural college in New South Wales, served his apprenticeship in the cattle business as a jackaroo. While learning how to repair pumps and do every handyman job on a station, he looked forward to station management and ownership. The station on the Katherine, a prize bull breeding farm, clears him $6,000 a year which he is salting away to buy his own place.

Though they are so far from other farmers that their nine-year-old daughter has none but black children to play with, they are never lonely. They make, as his father said, their own entertainment, visit one another, and hold competitions among the several stations. They subscribe to the Flying Doctor service, which doesn't come too high yet gives them treatment and hospitalization as well as a radio transceiver system to communicate with one another and receive lessons from the School of the Air. Both the Flying Doctor and School of the Air are headquartered in Alice Springs.

I supposed the wool grower must eat quite a lot of mutton. "Yes," he said, "we do eat a fair bit of meat. I won't knock a steak back, but I prefer meat."

MAY 7: An elderly lady taking the air on the back platform between our car and the crew's quarters said the geologists attribute the gibber plain over which we are travelling to Australia's great age. "They say it's the oldest land in the world, and the gibber has been broken up by centuries of erosion. It stretches over thousands of miles, not only here but throughout all Australia. It was once all porous rock and during thousands of millions of years the water seeped through it, down and up again; it evaporated and formed a new rock layer and that's what the gibber is from. I don't know much about it but that's what they say."

She pointed to an abandoned roofless house we were passing. "When the country was first settled they used to build their houses out of this peasey stone. My mother lived in a peasey stone house with bare dirt for a floor. They used the gibber and mixed it with soil and water to make building blocks. All the buildings you see along the line are of peasey stone."

MAY 8: Finke, on the Ghan where it crosses the world's oldest river, is a long wooden depot beside the track with a fabric water bag and spout hung from a hook in front and a corrugated iron fence along the back. Behind the fence stands a neat row of houses in this near infinity of space, each house completely surrounded by a fence. None of the passengers knew the why of the fence except that it was the Australian way. A young man in bare torso and shorts was doing handyman's work on his house, but everyone else, black and white, was gathered in front and around the depot—including two black trackers wearing broad-brimmed felt hats, one with a large feather stuck in the ribbon. Many of the Aborigines had a grey ashy pallor which I supposed to have been from dust.

The passengers mostly all got off at Finke, it being our first real stop in nearly 20 hours, but broke records getting back on when the train shifted a few feet forward for easier loading. Brian Guest is leading a group of soil scientists from the CSIRO, on their way up to the Katherine. He says that a posting to Finke is a punishment reserved for those public servants for whom the authorities have no pity. Well, Alice Springs on my first impression could be Finke multiplied, say, fifty times.

The Commonwealth Scientific and Industrial Research Organization, better known by its initials than its name, is also better known for two things it didn't do than any of the host of things it did. Contrary to popular belief the CSIRO did not introduce the small bush fly into Canberra to combat the stinging horse fly. Nor did it develop the myxomatosis plague against rabbits.

Its parent organization, the Institute of Science and Industry, was scarcely three years old in 1919 when the Brazilian doctor chiefly responsible for early myxomatosis research suggested its use in Australia. Seventeen years were to pass however before the first Australian trial was made. When this failed owing to drought conditions, another fourteen years elapsed before the second. The success of this second trial, which wiped out three-fourths of the rabbit population in just two years, was so sensational as to overshadow all CSIRO's other achievements. Thenceforth, whenever the letters CSIRO were uttered to an Australian, his immediate response would be "myxomatosis" or, if he couldn't pronounce the whole word, "myxo" or "rabbits."

European rabbits were brought to Australia by the First Fleet in 1788. But the wild rabbit that was to cause all the trouble didn't arrive until 1859, when a small shipment from England was liberated near Geelong, Victoria. It needed just 20 years to populate the whole of Victoria, another six years to reach Queensland, spreading at the incredible rate of 70 miles a year. Eight years later they were in Western Australia, half way across the Nullarbor Plain; and in fifteen more years, in spite of fences and everything else the Western Australian Government could hurl against them, they had crossed the remaining half of the continent and reached the Indian Ocean. At their peak they were nibbling away sustenance sufficient for 70,000,000 sheep, and this from a land whose soils are none too fertile or too well watered.

CSIRO's greatest and largely unsung achievements have to do with improvement of soil fertility and conservation of water resources. Its study of mineral deficiencies multiplied the potential for sown pastures fifteen times, from 20,000,000 to 300,000,000 acres. It has also successfully experimented in cross-breeding cattle for the continent's tropical north, in techniques for drought-feeding sheep and the use of vitamin supplements, in methods of animal disease control, and most particularly in the introduction of parasitic insects to destroy noxious weeds and other insects. It has carried out low-cost methods of impounding water and reducing its evaporation rate as much as 30 per cent. It has found new uses for eucalyptus timber, notably in paper-making, hitherto dependent entirely on soft woods. It has devised ways in which wool—still Australia's major export—could be combined with the new synthetics to produce a better fabric than either wool alone or synthetics alone.

Finke has a hotel, a massive square building with hipped corrugated iron roof peaking to a short ridge. The roof also reaches over the verandah in front and up along half of one side. The hotel sits in a large unfenced plot of sand, rutted with the curving tracks of cars. Behind is a galvanized water tank and a line of fence posts and line poles; and farther back is the nearly smooth ridge of a low range of eroded hills. A mulga shrub grows all alone in the sand and is the only visible vegetation. Far behind the settlement proper is the Aboriginal camp, a hooverville of tiny shacks called humpies, built of sheets of iron, old bedsprings, and oil drums, just large enough for people to crawl into and lie down. As our train pulled away, the Aborigines were trudging to it, carrying souvenirs of our visit: a nearly new billy can for boiling tea and two rolled-up maps of the Commonwealth Railway Lines which passengers had purchased for 30 cents. Some were carrying babies and some waved as we left, but none either there or here in Alice Springs has descended to begging.

They are fond of clothes and can be quite dashing if the right clothes are available. One woman wore an Adelaide Girls Grammar School hat. Two small girls had skirts reaching to their ankles—cast-offs from some long neglected cedar chest. In Alice Springs and on the job they wear more clothes than most *waijelas* in this hot climate. But when one of them leaves town, I'm told, to go on walkabout for up to nine months, he takes off all his clothes and tucks them under a rock for safe keeping. They are there when he returns. No one else would take what belongs to him.

When I asked why the Aboriginal humpies were so far removed from the rest of Finke, Brian Guest replied for all the Australians: "They're the ones who want them there."

We had a long discussion on the train, starting in the morning, continuing after lunch and into the evening, and ranging over many topics: Australia's relations with the mother country; utilization of her vast untapped resources, especially land; Aboriginal rights in the Northern Territory, the only part of Australia where the Commonwealth Government has any say over them; book censorship, by far the liveliest source of interest everywhere in Australia; Australian nationalism, the flag, and the national anthem. Nearly all the participants were Victorians, although Guest, the most vocal of any, hales originally from New South Wales. He has lived in Melbourne for fourteen years and is still not altogether happy there. He says there are two upper classes in Sydney: the first families and then the moneyed; but in Melbourne only one —the moneyed.

One of our train lounge discussions concerned the recently legalized sale of liquor to the Aborigines. One woman thought it a forerunner to a bill of rights for Aborigines including equal pay for equal work. "All this will mean," commented a cattle station owner, "is the Aborigines won't be hired." Guest thought the same and that the liquor rights would only result in Aborigines filling the public bar while the whites took over the lounge.

"What are you going to do?" asked the woman. "If you educate them and send them to technical high school you must give them a chance to use their skills. Suppose you were an Aborigine and had skills you weren't allowed to use, what would you do?"

"The question is purely hypothetical," said Guest. "I'm not an Aborigine."

"But what do you think they are going to do about it? They outnumber the whites in the Territory."

"If you're thinking of anything like an American civil rights movement," said Guest, "give it away. They'll just get drunk."

194

Everyone who spoke voiced a need for more nationalistic fervour in Australia, for a flag and anthem of her own instead of the British Commonwealth flag with the Union Jack in the corner and *God Save the Queen*. But twice when we were on this topic an old gent at the other end of the club car snarled at us. I had said that in Adelaide Britain's Union Jack was flown higher than Australia's colours, although I believed it to be against the law. The old gent shouted out that the Union Jack should always fly the higher. Again in the evening he shouted over to us to stop voicing our political opinions so loudly. This was when I probed how far Australia would go in fighting Britain's battles. Malaysia, certainly. Hong Kong? But of course. Surely not Aden or Israel? Australia could have no conceivable interest in an area as far away as the Middle East? They seemed to think Australia could. Colonel Blimp undoubtedly agreed with them but their lack of enthusiasm must have distressed him. He muttered, thinking of the CSIRO people, "They oughtn't to be allowed to work."

"Over morning tea in the pantry Miss Poynter, who is about thirty-five and from Cambridge, went on and on about how stiff and formal it is here and how she has never been in such a formal place. I said I thought they got all this formality from England and she said oh no, over there it was nothing like here. She said Australia was a terribly formalistic conservative country and it was because it was a colony. All the English people that settled the colonies got homesick and hung on to things like garden tea parties that were long dead in England. She said the formality here was just another such thing. Also she said the people in England can't understand why Australia, New Zealand, et cetera, don't become republics. England is saddled with the monarchy but she can't see why the colonies hang on to it."

We saw more peasey stone buildings, many in decay. We crossed seemingly endless stretches of gibber — a silicate rock — and laterate, an iron-bearing rock. The laterate is red, the gibber white and the pieces larger. We saw coolibah trees which throw so little shade an ironical line in the song *Waltzing Matilda* goes, "Under the shade of a coolibah tree"; ghost gums and river gums, mulga pruned to the height cattle can reach, doughnut-shaped patches of spinifex where the centre of a patch had died for lack of water and the sand had blown into the space.

Later in the journey the soil turned red as the gibber grew sparser and ceased to hide it; and in the setting sun the hills were a vivid orange. None of the hills was very high; the colour of the flat land changed from silver to red in the changing light. At great intervals we passed lonely occupied houses. The inevitable question is, "Can't better use be made of this land? Why not irrigate it with these artesian bores, drawing from the almost limitless subterranean waters said to lie under the continent?" The answer, said Guest, is the waters are not limitless. Even now they are consumed faster than they are being replaced, and the requirements for stock feeding are nothing to compare with irrigation. Guest says the water is sweet enough for crops but would rapidly be used up. To conserve it and prevent wastage, valves have been installed on all the bores.

Unfortunately, we stopped beside one such pipe where the valve had been left open and the water was spraying out to form large pools. Guest thought the aim was to attract the cattle to the water, but if so it wasn't doing the job. The few cattle I saw were fascinated by the sight of a much bigger lake among gently waving trees a scant 200 yards away. The mirages on this desert are impossible to disprove. No wonder if the cattle are fooled by them.

28

Nevil Shute, I suspect, must have written A Town Like Alice *soon after he came to Australia; and Alice Springs in winter must have had the same effect on him as Wickenburg, Arizona, had on J. B. Priestley. Coming from the English gloom both men were entranced by the sun and both tended to endow the country under the sun with the sun's own virtues. It wasn't that they had never seen the desert before; but the deserts a cultured English traveller sees are seldom places where he feels he could live comfortably. Here in Alice, there in Wickenburg, Shute and Priestley each saw in his desert town with its civilized amenities, including books and ice-cream cones, a meeting place of town and country, a place of rural peace with urban sophistication. To Shute in particular Alice Springs, if he closed his eyes to the mountains whose colours changed by degrees from grey-blue to deep red as the day wore on, was like an English country village. All of the residents were young yet many continued to speak of England as "home." And they were especially fond of him because he was English. Undoubtedly much of Australia's foolish adoration of this town, where "they run the sprinklers all night" and which most Australians have never seen nor ever will see, can be traced to* A Town Like Alice.

MAY 9: The legend of Alice Springs seems to be spreading abroad. A South Carolina weekly newspaper publisher has described it as a place where people never lock their doors. The clerk in the Ansett office laughed over this. Mick McGregor at the jail told of his car being wrecked on one of the desert roads and how he sat with it for days waiting the arrival of a repair truck. He didn't dare leave else it would have been stripped. "A bloke is driving along and sees it. Stops. 'Need any help?' No answer. 'Nobody around, eh? There's a beaut mirror, just what I've been looking for. If I don't take it somebody else will.' " Yet when I asked the landlady for a key to our motel unit she said, "You won't need one. Nobody locks their doors here. Nothing is ever stolen." Possibly this is where the South Carolina publisher stayed. For whatever light it may throw on the question a large notice in front of the jail reads:

H.M. Gaol and Labour Prison
Alice Springs
VISITORS INSTRUCTIONS
The gaoler may refuse admission to person who

1. causes disturbance
2. behaves in disorderly manner
3. commits breach of discipline
4. is under influence of intoxicating liquor
5. is insolent to prison officer

Ayers Rock, a two-day-by-plane or three-day-by-bus trip out of Alice (or *the* Alice as many like to call it) is the largest whole piece of stone on Earth's surface, bright red under certain conditions of light and rising 1,100 feet out of the red earth. It is the symbol of Australia's dead or—as the tourist promoters prefer—red heart. Once there, you climb as much of it as you are able, with the aim of writing your name in a book at the top; or potter around the base, examining Aboriginal cave paintings and chipping off pieces of the Rock for souvenirs. Other trips include two to Aboriginal missions, Santa Teresa and Hermannsburg, both somewhat commercialized; to scenic places such as Trephina Gorge, Simpson's Gap, and nearby Pitchi-Ritchi and the Overland Telegraph Station. Like all tourists we arrived with a fistful of bus and plane tickets for several of these tours and will try to fit them in before we leave.

The bus was so old it was having its last long distance run. It would now stay in Alice Springs for the day and half-day tours of the surrounding countryside which play such a major role in the typical Australian holiday. It frequently refused to start after stopping, and the women would walk a mile or more on ahead while the men by putting their shoulders to it pushed the bus fast enough to get it going again. We lodged at converted cattle stations which, during the drought, had become motels. In Coober Pedy we visited the dugouts of the opal miners. After dinner of the second day we called at one in the process of construction,

198

with the marks of the axe showing on its underground stone walls and the benches hewn out of the walls. On these they would spread their sleeping bags. We went on to a finished dwelling occupied by a married couple. It was furnished with a double bed trucked up from Adelaide. All the dugouts had air vents to the surface and ramps to get in by. Not all were occupied solely by miners. Some housed opal cutters and some—the largest and most comfortable—buyers and appraisers, who often traded Australian opal for Hong Kong jade which yielded them a higher profit. Stones, cut and uncut, and opal jewellery were on sale everywhere above and below the surface; and mounds of tailings were free to be sifted through—as the Aborigines were doing—for opal chips.

Yellow opal is the best, also known as semi-black. (Black opal, the very best—and probably best in the world—is found only at Lightning Ridge, N.S.W.) It gets its name from thousands of golden specks which shine like stars in the dark translucent stone. Potch is opal with no colour, all white or grey. Putty is clear transparent opal with no inner fire. It can be made to look like the better opal by fixing a coloured material behind it. Bodgie is a low-grade opal product known as doublets, made by sandwiching a thin sheet of the true iridescent opal over white or black stone.

Matrix is opal with a slightly rough natural surface which shows its colour when wet but becomes colourless when it dries.

A miner's right costs 50 cents, then $10 to register a claim, both fees payable annually. A claim must be registered within thirty days after staking it; stakes are driven at its four corners with trenches from stake to stake. The hole is three feet wide, six feet long, and up to thirty or forty feet deep. The miner descends by means of notches in opposite walls; he uses a winch to haul earth and rock to the surface. Shafts radiate from the hole to the boundaries of the claim. Many miners have one or more diggers working with them on a share basis, one-half or one-third of what the digger finds.

Ern, a retired railwayman, big and hearty, with deep round soulful eyes that looked directly into mine, and a curly grey beard, wore a battered felt hat constantly and stood up while he talked. He started as a digger and, after learning the ropes, filed a claim on a mine which had been claimed and abandoned by twenty others before him. Out of it he said he had taken nearly $20,000, although through careless use of gelignite some $16,000 was blown into dust. From this and two other holes he had—one worked by his wife and the other by a digger—he claimed to have earned as much in two years of opal gouging as in his previous twenty-seven years as a Government employee. The opals, he said, were found in a layer of "pay dirt"—usually gravel or sand—under rock and above clay. In the autumn after his summer lay-off—which he and several hundred others would take to get away from heat and flies—Ern meant to become a buyer, and hire men to do his digging.

I suggested to Ern's offsider, Jack, that miners might skite their takings. He thought not. Rather the other way round. Nobody ever found any opal but they all bought flash cars. And there were dozens of buyers doing well enough for themselves to be able to live in fine houses. Miners shopped around among the buyers, first paying a classer five cents a pound to evaluate their find. Usually a buyer offered less than the classer's appraisal, and the more a miner needed money the lower his offer would be. Jack sold a fine piece for $60 when he was hard up and later wished he hadn't. He still had a smaller fragment which he swore he'd never part with. It looked good to me. Ern said it was broken by seams, and a large stone couldn't be cut out of it.

The greater part of the miners and diggers were new Australians —mainly Hungarians and Czechs—who arrived, Jack said, carrying a single battered suitcase, and left driving a spanking new car.

*I thought it strange there were not more Aussies since Aussies
liked to gamble and this was certainly a gamble. Ern said the work
was too hard for Aussies, digging and hauling rock. He had tun-
nelled seventy feet for a fiver. Jack too, who reckoned he was well
below average in luck, had earnings of only about $30 a month;
but he liked the climate. The dry heat agreed with his arthritis.*

We attended services this morning at the local church built in
honour of "Flynn of the Inland . . . He Spread the Mantle of
Safety Over Inland Australia." The sanctuary is high and spacious
with light wooden pews and glass walls—a most attractive and
inspiring place. I thought of the church in Adelaide, with its solid
windowless walls, so cold you might have taken off your topcoat
outside in the sun, but you quickly put it back on to go in. Here it
was a pleasure just to look up and out at the bright blue sky. The
Reverend Keith Baylor, dressed all in black with a brilliant accent
of white reversed collar and two white ribbons descending in
front, performed the service. While he administered baptism he
waved flies away from his face.

When Mrs Henriette Pearce, author of Two at Daly Waters,
*arrived in Sydney in 1919 she lived for a time next door to Reverend
John Flynn, who even then "talked always of aeroplanes. His
dream was an aerial medical service, and with indomitable will he
worked through the years to make it the blessed reality it is today."
He was then "a wiry-looking, spare-framed Presbyterian minister
whose great life interest was medical service for people of the
inland." The Flying Doctor Service, almost as widely identified
with Australia today as the kangaroo, was Flynn's creation.*
*The flying doctor at Katherine in Mrs Pearce's time was Clive
Fenton, who flew his own plane to an accident, attended the
injury and put the patient aboard, then set to work with native
help "to clear a patch large enough to take off." He once grazed an
anthill on a forced landing in four-foot grass—not an unlikely accident in this country where the anthills rise like reefs to heights
taller than a man. He walked to a homestead some miles away to
borrow tie wire and galvanized iron, patched the plane, and
returned to Katherine. As a recreation when work was slack he
loaded the plane with bags of flour and bombed the township of
Katherine. This always restored him to good humour. Once in the
face of official disapproval, in a small Moth with a home-made
spare petrol tank, he flew from Darwin across the Timor Sea to
China and back, to tend some ill relatives.*

Last evening, with the McGregors and the editor of the local weekly and his family, we went to film night at the Memorial Club. Children everywhere and numerous babies in prams. Beer was drunk and incredible quantitites of cigarettes smoked. The air was acrid and stale and so were the films, including a U.S. Department of Interior short on sulphur mining, a British plea for city decentralization, assorted comedies and Westerns, and the feature after the intermission (when the children came back from the front rows to get money for sweets) : Joseph Cotten in *Walk Softly Stranger* from the mid-30s. It was a heavy dose, running from 7.30 till nearly 11.30, but there is as yet no television in Alice Springs. And for me the absence of advertising slides compensated for the length, the smoke, the great age of the features, and all the other drawbacks.

Everybody sprang to attention at the sight of the red cape and horse, before the opening bars sounded of God Save *etc., and we were subjected to the first showing of crudely executed advertising slides on behalf of chocolates, small goods ("Don't argue—Hutton's is best") beauticians, furriers, pain-killer, whisky, and laxatives. Again the noteworthy thing about the Australian cinema was the sheer volume of dull advertising inflicted on a captive audience which showed no restiveness, merely stared and dedicated itself to eating. Excepting a feature which was designed to make the hunting of America's disappearing cougar (euphemistically called mountain lion) appear as fraught with danger as hunting man-eating tigers in India, all of the shorts were advertisements: a Ford publicity film on the theme of girls smiling, a phony travelogue to Lord Howe Island produced by Ansett, an equally phony but better executed travelogue of Europe produced by BOAC, a film using travelogue technique to promote Peter Stuyvesant cigarettes, with a plug for Pan-American at the start, and the ghastly slides again. The whole melange consumed over one hour. Then the house lights came on and everybody stocked up on food, after which the same dreary succession of slides was shown a third time. Then and only then were we permitted to see the feature, and it just wasn't worth the combination of long wait, advertising annoyance and, for TV owners, deprivation of the film being shown on their home screens at the same time.*

29

MAY 11: On our way with Mick McGregor this morning to see the Overland Telegraph Station, where in 1871 the wires were joined linking Australia's eastern cities by cable to Europe, he showed us a few typical Aboriginal humpies. One was a brush shelter, actually nothing more than a windbreak, a man and woman lounging on the bare and still cold river bed in front of it. A second, set up on a hillside near a "permanent" Aboriginal settlement of tin shanties, was a half of a galvanized rain-water cistern, a miniature quonset or nissen hut open at both ends and not long enough to cover a sleeper's head and feet. Still another was just a double bed turned upside down. There was about 18 inches of space underneath into which the residents could crawl. A correspondent in yesterday's edition of the local paper complained of these humpies and called on the police to clear them out.

Mick's wife Nora, who nurses at the hospital, said clearing out the humpies drives away "wild" Aborigines who have come to Alice Springs for treatment. Most of the hospital patients are Aborigines. They are separated into an overcrowded ward for full bloods and another ward for whites and mixed bloods. This segregation would appear to be in favour of the full bloods whose way of life is so different, even in hospital, that they can't be kept in bed but must get up and go out of doors during the day, visiting the humpies on the river where their families are staying, coming back to the hospital only for meals. At the very least, on autumn and winter mornings like these, they must get out of the cold hospital and gather wood to build small campfires on the hospital grounds. They often go out in their pajamas and sometimes come back without them, having traded them away.

For a few weeks the papers continued to report a mysterious epidemic at Alice Springs Hospital. There was no lack of care and no discoverable ailment, and in time the papers stopped reporting on it. What was there to say? The babies were dying that was all. They were born, sensed instinctively what they were coming into, and—as Xavier Herbert earlier noted about the Aborigines in his novel Capricornia—*"had lain down to die, as it was the custom of their race to do when life seemed not worth living."*

The Overland Telegraph Station National Park, well out of town, has a swimming pool fed by its own spring. Despite its great historical value, the station was abandoned for many years and had fallen into disrepair. The only people interested in it were some myalls, as the "wild" Aborigines are called, who set up camp there. The attraction for them was the spring, a rarity in the desert. In their concern for the Aborigines the people of Alice Springs induced the Commonwealth Government to establish a special camp for them seven miles away, where they could live and be fed in the carefree idleness they are supposed to enjoy. When the myalls turned down the attractions of the Welfare Camp, preferring to stay with their spring and hunt for their own livelihood, the townspeople addressed another petition to their Government. The Telegraph Station was a priceless historical treasure and a potential tourist attraction; and a park and pool would serve the townspeople also for Sunday picnics. "Two birds with one stone," I observed. "Three," said Mick, pointing to the fence around the pool and spring. "They got rid of all the myalls."

Like the larger pool in Alice Springs this one is open to whites and quarter-castes. Only full bloods and half-castes are forbidden to use it.

"I used to hope that one day I might buy a little house at Alice Springs, but it is forbidden for people like me to live there. Rex Battarbee promised to help me to get a special authorization but it would not have been valid for my relatives, so I thanked him and said no. I prefer to live in the desert among people of my race than alone in town."—Albert Namatjira.

In the afternoon Mick drove us out to see Jay Creek Aboriginal Settlement, some thirty miles west of Alice Springs, one of a chain of Commonwealth Welfare Department camps through the Territory. Mick used to work at Papunya, 300 miles farther west along the chain. He telephoned the Jay Creek superintendent who gave us permission to visit although he himself wouldn't be there. We met and passed him along the way, bouncing over a graded dirt road, while the car threatened to break into little pieces and Nora put her thumb on the windscreen. This was to prevent it shattering if a stone hit it. The windscreens here craze over their entire area after such a hit and turn an opaque white; but not, apparently if a thumb is held against them. We followed the line of the MacDonnell Ranges, a low and fairly smooth-topped string of mountains, with an occasional gap in the wall to let a dry river through. The desert has no ground cover but is fairly well spotted with mulga and ironwood trees, some quite large, and ghost gums along the river courses.

The Jay Creek camp is not large. It consists mainly of houses for the white staff, a school, a large kitchen building and the native humpies out of sight over a hill. On the hilltop are a Lutheran Church and some other iron buildings, whose function was not explained. In fact, whether for fear of adverse publicity or to discourage tourists, the whole atmosphere of the place was one of not wanting to explain anything. Joseph, the assistant superintendent, a new man whom Mick didn't know, opened up by demanding to see our permit, then stated flatly, "You can't visit the native quarters." "Why not?" I asked. "You can get the answer to that from such and such a high poobah in the Welfare Department."

"Could you at least tell me whether you know the answer?" "No." "Will you tell me your name?" "No."

Later we got things straightened out somewhat when Ned, the officer in charge of employment for all the settlements, drove in. Ned said the ban was occasioned by a wish to respect the natives' privacy. Then with Ned, and with Joseph joining in, I discussed the settlement and the future of the Aborigines there. They were cagey in everything they said, mostly wouldn't say anything at all without prompting, and then accused me of putting words in their mouths. But the gist of Ned's responses was: the Welfare Department aims to bring the natives into the white community where they'll earn good wages and live in city neighbourhoods. So far it has had little success. Ned could think of only one instance. A young chap who had been a wastrel and drank a lot, now behaves himself, works in town, and lives in one of the Government Housing Scheme cottages at the Gap.

With Joseph's reluctant consent we visited the kitchen, a large roofed structure open on all sides and surrounded by benches from which the people are served as they line up outdoors. A big wood-burning stove in the centre does the cooking. The dish was a meat stew with damper on top; and a girl was cutting this into small portions. There were flies crawling on it. Another girl was operating a bread slicer, and two girls at two sinks were washing plates. Outside, the people in line each received a plate and sat down on the ground to eat.

We didn't visit the school because Mick was fearful of interrupting the class. "They get little enough schooling as it is." Children, however, don't go on walkabout while school is in—only during holidays, if at all. Mostly not at all. Everyone said it's only the old ones who go on walkabout now, and they arrange not to let it interfere with school.

I met and shook hands with a few of the men, but then we stood around looking at each other unable to think of anything to say. "Ask them if they're happy," said Joseph. "Are you happy?" I asked, feeling like a darn fool. "Sure, boss," said one, and the others nodded.

"When one has experienced innumerable times the extreme kindness and friendliness of the Australians toward foreigners," wrote Bengt Danielsson in Bumerang, *a book which has been translated into French from its original Swedish but not into English, "one cannot but feel completely disconcerted and wonder how they can treat the Aborigines with such a lack of heart. If you ask them about their grievances against the blacks their replies give you the impression that the responsibility for these injustices falls on these latter, for they affirm to you with a unanimous and touching accord that all these coloured people are immoral, lazy, of bad faith, and dirty."*

Driving back to Alice Springs—with Nora still putting a thumb on the windscreen whenever another car flew past—Mick said Joseph was not representative of the welfare officers, most of whom are deeply concerned over the inadequacies of the settlements. The biggest problem facing them is the inactivity and purposelessness of settlement existence. The youth especially suffer on this account since the settlement routine offers no substitute for the complicated initiation rituals. In tribal life these cover a span of months or years and serve to bridge the difficult gap between childhood and manhood. In the settlements, even more than on the church missions, the boys and young men lapse early into lifelong habits of laziness and card-playing.

Mick said that at Papunya, the only settlement in the chain with a good water supply, the local staff proposed to plant and cultivate their own fruit orchards. These, besides furnishing employment, would supplement the settlement diet and, by sale of the surplus

fruit, pay the workers' wages. The bureaucrats at Darwin, the Territorial capital, first asked for elaborate plans to prove the project's feasibility; then turned it down, saying flatly, "It wouldn't pay."

"Pay!" I asked. "Must a welfare project show a profit?"

"Ridiculous, isn't it?" agreed Mick; but he'd been thinking it over since. In the back of the bureaucrats' minds, he believed, was the fear of making the Papunya property too desirable for some greedy white farmer to resist. Seeing profitable orchards there he might pull wires in Canberra—as the aluminium combines were able to do in such old established Aboriginal Reserves as Weipa and Arnhem Land—and dispossess the Aborigines.

When a woman is pregnant no word is spoken nor any notice taken of the infant until it is about to be born. Then a big fire is built and allowed to burn to ashes. The ashes are spread out and the mother squats over them, dropping the baby. The cord is separated by pounding between two stones and sterile sand from the fire is poured over the baby's navel to clot the blood. Among myalls it is said still to be customary for a mother to keep only one twin. The other has its mouth filled with sand. There is never enough food for two.

30

Except in its extreme north, Australia is entirely out of the earthquake zone which engulfs its northern and eastern neighbours. Nearly half the total area of the continent is tropical desert comparable to the Sahara, Saudi Arabia, west Pakistan, and Mexican Sonora. Half of the remainder, the entire north above the tropic of Capricorn, is tropical monsoon country comparable to India, east Pakistan, northern Ceylon, Burma, Thailand, Cambodia, South Vietnam, Taiwan and the southern rim of China, north Philippines, east Indonesia, and the extreme south central lobe of New Guinea. The approximately one-quarter of the country left has varied climates, but all resembling one or another part of the world in which Europeans feel at home.

These are the dry-summer subtropics around Perth and Adelaide, similar to the Mediterranean and southern California; the humid subtropics stretching around the south-east coast from Brisbane to the Victoria border, similar to the American southern States; an inland dry continental strip just behind the humid subtropics, similar to the non-mountainous areas of the American Mountain States; and in Tasmania and southern Victoria a climate very like that of Britain, France, the low countries, Denmark, coastal Norway, and the west coast of North America from Alaska to northern California.

Excepting Tasmania, which is mountainous, these European areas are fairly thickly settled, compared to kindred regions elsewhere. So also is the Australian desert, compared to other deserts. But the tropical monsoon region, in size equal to sixteen average United States, is as thinly populated as the desert. Similar regions in India and South-East Asia have enormous populations.

MAY 12: The Ghan, which prides itself on departing on time no matter how late it may have arrived the night before, was a little late this morning. So we made it with minutes to spare, trudging over soft sand footpaths, toting our heavy luggage. Taxis are impossible to get on the mornings the train leaves.

The desert scene was much like we went through going to Jay Creek. Deep Well, which we reached at 10.15, consists mainly of a broken-down peasey stone house amid splendid white-barked gums stencilled against red sand. South of Deep Well the red desert is dotted with tiny clumps of spinifex and mulga trees, spaced with about the same regularity as the cactus trees of Arizona. In the distance they look like an open forest with a grassy floor, pale green as one would imagine the African savannah to be. The mulga at maturity is fairly tall and quite thin. Its branches sprout upward and out like the spray of a fountain. The foliage is tracery-like and pale green. The trees, because of this, are almost transparent and have a flat rather than three-dimensional look.

Moving on down to Finke we left the red soil behind and got into sandy dunes with no vegetation except the mulga, the acacia with weeping foliage called ironwood, and the red and river gums in the wide flood area of the entirely dry Finke River. The sand is the colour of light brown sugar. The red gums have white bark with large dark spots. As they grow older the heart of the tree often gets eaten away by white ants or dry rot, and in a high wind the lower branches are torn off, pruning the tree. The spinifex is suitable for fodder except that it is extremely dry and stock needs lots of water to go with it. This is why you see none of it in areas where there are water holes close by.

We took on a passenger at Finke, Wilf Davey, a lanky man in his forties with a crooked smile, dressed in a grey business suit and toting a tucker bag. Remembering what Brian Guest had said I supposed he must be an exiled public servant. He said yes, he'd been a bad boy. He's an electronics engineer with the Post Office Department. He spent a week in Finke checking on the repeater station, and will spend another week in Oodnadatta.

I was curious about the life in a place like Finke. While we waited at the station he pointed out the houses occupied by the families of railway fettlers, the postmaster, schoolmaster, constable, and storekeeper. The postmaster had a vegetable garden which we couldn't see. Wilf stayed at the hotel and he was lucky. It had just replaced its old wire mesh bedsprings and lumpy cotton mattresses —such as we had to put up with in Alice Springs—with new innerspring mattresses on coil spring bases. So he slept well and dined tolerably well on cornflakes and leftover stew for breakfast, braised beef and potatoes for lunch, and meat, potatoes, and pumpkin for tea. The last night of his stay they barbecued half a steer, having sent one of the black trackers out to gather wood from the numerous dead standing trees on the desert. He says there are about twenty adult Aborigines, their acknowledged leader being the black tracker with the badge on his hat called Brownie. When Wilf arrived he noticed them paying very close attention to the way he walked. This, he said, was each person's mark of identification, his fingerprint. They could afterwards pick out his tracks from a hundred others.

Black trackers have little work to do in the police force today; the office is maintained largely for sentimental reasons. Brownie's last assignment was a month ago when an Italian migrant stabbed another railwayman with a putty knife and fled in a car. It was no trick at all for Brownie to track him after he abandoned the car. He and the other Aboriginal men are mostly kept busy at chores around the township, collecting and cutting firewood, and accompanying the white officials when they travel, to be sent for help if a vehicle breaks down. Even this isn't strictly necessary. One of the cars got bogged while Wilf was there, and the driver sent a couple of "boys" back for help. They walked until they were concealed by a ridge and sat down to wait for the help they knew would arrive when they were found to be overdue.

"*After lunch it was such a beautiful day—around 80 degrees—and it was a holiday so Mary and I decided to borrow a couple of bikes and go for a ride. We rode all the way to Henley, which seemed like about 100 miles, and Mary has an aunt and uncle that live out there so we decided to stop for a drink. The White family were all surprised to see us and especially to hear that we had ridden bikes. They reminded me of the family in that play* One Day of the Year, *they really did, except for the play's idiotic psychological problems. The lady was there in her apron and she apologized for the house because she had been working and hadn't had a chance to clean it up. The house was typical, too, with a big verandah in front and small windows and high ceilings and floral carpets. The kitchen was very small with one door leading to the back porch where there was a cat and a box of kittens, and there was a large table in the middle with stove, fridge, and cupboards spaced around the wall.*

"*When we first got there Auntie Edith made Mary and me a cup of tea and pretty soon Uncle Ben came in all dressed up in his best suit, the coat of which he quickly took off because it was so hot. He had been in this Labour Day parade. We saw it on TV and I think*

211

he was carrying a banner. Anyway Auntie Ede rubbished him about where he had been all afternoon since the parade ended. No, she didn't have to ask, down to the pub of course. He was big and jovial looking with thick iron-grey hair and he said oh, go on, he'd only been there about five minutes.

"All this was like the play except for one great difference. In the play everybody hated everybody else and they just kept trying to hurt each other, but here it was just the opposite. Everybody was happy and friendly and joking.

"Anyhow Uncle Ben went to the fridge and cut up some meat from the eternally present Australian cold joint, and buttered some bread and had it for lunch with tomato sauce—something like ketchup only spicier. He made these rather corny but nice jokes about the cat being a trollop and Mary's swag of boy friends. Then Mary, their twelve-year-old daughter Gillian, and I went for a walk down to the beach. There were all kinds of people there and these funny sort of jellyfish about three inches across and not poisonous or anything, and they were all over. When you stepped on them they went just like jelly in a dish.

"We stayed there for tea which Uncle Ben dished up—and cooked I think. It was two pork chops and cabbage and mashed potatoes, and ice cream for dessert. Then we did the dishes and Mary and Gillian and I had a water pistol fight—not a fight really, but Mary got a water pistol and Gillian filled a plastic salt shaker up with water and it seemed like it was always me that got squirted. Then Uncle Ben took Mary and me back to college. He had this old Holden and he tied the bikes in the boot.

"Anyway, they seemed just such a nice, typical One Day of the Year *sort of Australian family. And when we got back to college Mary told me that the two eldest daughters were staying with Mary's parents because they couldn't stand their family, and one of them, Tania, tried to kill herself just out of spite."*

Wilf is not on the whole too fond of Americans, who are apt, he said, to "blow their bag." Yes, I admitted, this was our own picture of the Yank abroad but had he actually met any? He thought and said, "Yes, one." He was a young railway worker forever skiting about how much better things were in his country; and no matter what a job was, he said it was better done in the States. He soon failed to make friends but this didn't have any effect. He was a Mr Universe in appearance and repeatedly squared up before one of the long wiry Aussies with the invitation, "Hit me. Go ahead and hit me." His stomach muscles were like steel cables.

Finally one of the little fellows shot a lightning fist to the American's jaw and knocked him out.

He could have made some friends then, when he came to, by admitting the better man of the moment had won. Instead he cried foul, and lost still more friends. Seeing the boys at poker he offered to join their game. Could he play? He could play any game. In ten minutes he'd lost $106. Still he wouldn't admit he'd been taught a lesson whereas an Aussie, Wilf said, would win instant sympathy by doing so, saying he was out of his depth playing with such experts. They hadn't cheated, though he appeared to think so. They had merely made their bets and played their hands too rapidly for the American to have a clear idea what was going on.

"The term 'Yank'," said Wilf, "is something like 'bastard.' You can say 'you old bastard' in one tone of voice and have it sound like admiration. Or you can say 'you bastard' and have it convey hate and contempt. We're forever being told by Americans how they won the war for us. That's when the word 'Yank' expresses something not quite the same as bitterness, although there is bitterness in it, but more like what we feel when we call a man a bastard—and mean it."

He asked how true and typical the following anecdote was: A friend of his, Harry Evans, was given a Fulbright scholarship for three months at the University of California, Davis campus. He found when he arrived that the faculty wives had laid out his own wife's social programme for practically every day of her stay. Was this unusual?

No.

Evans had trouble getting a decent cup of tea. He was very particular about his tea. When he had it at home it was always made in a pre-warmed pot set close to the fire so the water was freshly boiling when it was poured on; then steeped just below the stage where the tannin would be extracted. A Doctor Imbert took Evans under his wing and promised to find tea made to suit him. He took him to a flash Hollywood bistro and carefully instructed the *maitre de* that his friend was British and was very particular about his tea. The *maitre de* understood perfectly; he would even make it with his own hands. With a snap of the fingers he had two tea bags brought, broke each one open and poured its contents into the guest's cup, staring straight into his eyes while he did so. Evans stared back. The *maitre de*'s stare was one of inquiry, to satisfy himself everything was being done properly. The Aussie's stare was one of pure horror.

When the bags were empty the *maitre de,* with another snap of the fingers, ordered water to be brought, and it was brought—in a metal pot on a metal tray, all the way from the kitchen where presumably it had stood waiting its call. The *maitre de,* holding the pot high above the cup, poured a long slender stream of the by now tepid water on the tea leaves, stirred them vigorously, and handed the cup with a flourish to his astonished guest. Harry Evans cast one quick glance at the contents of the cup—pale coloured water coated with a thick matting of soggy black vegetation—and as quickly looked away, barely repressing a shudder. Not once again during his stay at the University and his subsequent cross-country tour did he dare to ask for tea.

He travelled with wife and children on a budget of only 25 dollars a day, so they lived mainly on hamburgers, beefburgers, cheeseburgers, steakburgers, burgers of every description. He grew quite fond of burgers.

Our lunch was supposed to be baked fish but tasted more like it had been boiled with the laundry. I realized that ever since we left California I have not had a really first rate light lunch, that in fact people in this part of the world don't really think of lunching out, only dining. I've had some good dinners, making allowances for differences in national tastes, but even the cafeteria lunches don't compare with the Copper Coffee Pot or Loop's or Bob's or Howard Johnson's—not to mention the Wigwam in Royal Oak, the Pontchartrain in Detroit, and Angelo's in Monterey. Or any place on Fisherman's Wharf. What wouldn't I give for a dish of Howard Johnson's fried clams, with crisp french fries—not the soggy, white, flabby things called chips. And red cherry pie—without pits. And thin crisp soda crackers. And a tossed green salad made of bite-size bits of crisp lettuce, romaine, escarole, watercress, parsley, cucumber, radish, shrimp, and slivers of ham and chicken. And a bowl of chili. And a stack of buckwheat cakes with maple syrup. And a glass of ice water.

214

31

JUNE 2: We had our first Australian visit from the elders yesterday, two Salt Lake City lads living in a flat in Elizabeth. The flat, though new, is unheated, lacks a fireplace, and has bare cement block interior walls; so they've been cold. Both are recent high school graduates who are paying their own expenses—as hundreds of their fellows do in other parts of the world—to preach the word of Joseph Smith and Brigham Young. Australia to them is purely a field for missionary work, otherwise noteworthy for its backwardness, slowness, and difference in language. Both wore black suits and rode bicycles; if they need a car they can rent an Anglia from the church for $32 a month of their own money, plus gas, oil, and repairs.

There is no Mormon mission to the Aborigines, to the Bantu in South Africa, or to any African people except some 2,000 in, I believe, Nigeria who addressed a special appeal to Salt Lake City. This is because the blacks, of all the world's races, are not children of Israel. Black Polynesians are, and so are black Indians, but black Africans and Australians are not. "They aren't receptive to our message," one of the elders explained. He'd tried it out on a couple of young mixed-bloods waiting for a bus at Gepps Cross, and confirmed this tenet for himself. They were indifferent.

Hakon Mielche's Eventyrets og Fremtidens Land *(1961)* has *been translated from its original Danish into Finnish, Norwegian, French, German, and English. It must therefore be looked upon by many different people as an accurate picture of Australia. It reveals Cairns as a place where—apart from a single garment—the males wear nothing but shorts; but everyone wears a broad-brimmed hat inscribed with fancy names like "overseer" and "drover." Tourists are "shocked at first at the sight of so many hairy male chests covered with abbreviated singlets." I saw no such*

215

hats in Cairns with or without inscriptions and only one hairy chest and one pair of shorts. The chest and shorts were both on the same fellow passenger and he was remarkably conspicuous. The residents mostly wore coats and sweaters. Mielche writes of "inhospitable aborigines, whose women were very like chimpanzees." These were what the first white settlers found. Have they since improved? On a plane Mielche watched "an old full-blood aborigine" eating sweets: "like a chimpanzee, he took them one by one in bent, wrinkled fingers and peeled off the paper with simian movements." Then when "he looked up and smiled a toothless smile at the stewardess" and she smiled back, our author "loved her for it." Nevertheless he couldn't help recalling an airport in "one of the southern states of America" which refused to serve coffee to "one of the country's foremost young sculptors, because his complexion was chocolate-coloured."

JUNE 10: Yesterday was the coldest day in six years, one of a series of sub-freezing nights and early mornings, with clear skies. We can't hope to keep warm except either in bed or a sheltered sunny corner outdoors. The fireplace isn't big enough to heat even the lounge; the kerosene heater stinks and requires more breathing air than it is prepared to repay in warmth. Most of the warmed air rises to the high ceiling indoors. Outdoors, dressed in heavy long underwear and wearing a wool suit, with a pullover (called a jumper), it is pleasant in the sun.

I now realize how fundamental the open fire is in the difference between British and American living habits. An open fire, even in California or Florida where houses might not be centrally heated, is a purely social event, like a barbecue; as a primary source of warmth a fire is almost wholly literary. People in British books come indoors from a fox-hunt and warm themselves in front of one, but they are literary people. We never think that, in order to get really warm, they must be careful not to shed a single layer of their heavy clothing. The characters in a British detective novel who can always find a convenient fire in which to burn embarrassing documents—are peculiarly British largely because of the fire. We see them smoking a pipe and lounging before a fire, standing before a fire. Even the novelist is probably sitting before a fire as she writes—as I am sitting now—with stiff frigid fingers and wrapped up in rugs.

JULY 23: After a tedious spell of miserable weather—one good day in the past three weeks—spring seems on the way. We've burned bag after bag of coke, mallee roots, and sawdust logs, and

216

Mossgail Street

are now starting on a new 150-lb lot of roots. But the sun is out in a perfectly clear sky and the air is soft and moist.

Candi has finished her mid-year exams and done reasonably well in all save Maths. Her August holidays are next week. We plan to visit Perth and Kalgoorlie, taking the train across the Nullarbor. Meanwhile, when I haven't been busy stoking the fireplace, I've been reading. I re-read *The Fortunes of Richard Mahony* after thirty years, having forgotten everything about it except that it was Australian and its author, Henry Handel Richardson, was a woman. I'm afraid the second reading has made no more impression on me than the first. I can't say the same for Patrick White's *Tree of Man* and *Voss*. Both are simple epics, one the story of a man (whom White studiously refers to as "the man" and "the husband") and a woman ("the woman" and "the wife") and their son and daughter; the other the story of an expedition into the interior in the early days of New South Wales colony. The man and woman are Adam and Eve, one of those timeless stories of simple people recounted with far too many words, and too many of the wrong words, precious words. Nothing happens of course because if it did, or if even the nothing were told in fewer words, it would not have the true epic quality. The exploration epic is also too wordy, and nothing happens in it either. No doubt it is based on an actual expedition whose participants never returned; and no doubt it inspires feelings of patriotism, which help create for the book its status of a classic in the minds if not the hearts of Australians. Perhaps this is the cause of my blind spot toward White: I have no Australian patriotism for him to appeal to. Unlike Tom Collins and Xavier Herbert he doesn't strike me as a genuine Australian.

Herbert's *Seven Emus* (1959) is a short novel, one-third the length of *Voss* and one-fourth *Tree of Man,* made even shorter by having no epic pretensions. It was evidently not a great success; the copy I borrowed from the library was a first printing and still in good condition. This could be due, in the first place, to its having nothing in it to feed the Australian legend, the contrary rather; and in the second place to the twenty-year gap between it and *Capricornia.* 1938 when *Capricornia* appeared was too early for London to be up and about looking for an Australian legend.

Rigby's Romance, one of two parts taken out of the middle of Tom Collins's Such is Life *to bring it down to publishable length, is an essay on socialism in the form of dialogue, as Galileo's* Dialogues on the Two Systems of the World *was such an essay on physics. Galileo provided a little less sugar coating but not very much less; and Collins had Galileo in his thoughts. He begins one of the concluding chapters with his spokesman for socialism, Rigby, saying:*

"It moves, Tom."

"I know it does, Colonel, but we needn't force that fact on an unscientific public. Galileo got into trouble through not being able to keep the same item of information to himself. Let it move."

Xavier Herbert's Capricornia, *written forty years after* Rigby's Romance, *is much stronger meat both in its sermon and its story. The sermon is on Australia's miserable treatment of its Aborigines, not in the dim distant past but at the present time. Australia's literary magazines and critics were affronted by the "excess of tragedy" in the book and the artificiality of the characters' names. The tragedy probably seemed excessive to them because it reflected adversely on Australia. As for the preposterous names, a*

*judge is called Pondrosass, two police officers Settaroge and
Tocatchwon, three police troopers are McCrook, O'Crimnell, and
O'Theef, two lawyers are Nawratt and Niblesome, three clergy-
men are Bleeter, Hollower, and Randter. But these and others
like Dr Boyles, Bortells the pharmacist, and Keyes the jailer are
all minor characters and are so named—I suspect—to point up
the similar naming of Aborigines in real life. The story as a
whole, in its sweep, its currents and cross-currents, its fluid
relationships as characters prove themselves neither wholly good
nor wholly bad, is intensely real; and the fantastic names seem to
make it more so by being, in their deliberate spuriousness, aliases
of real Australians. Since reading this book I have less patience
with those in search of the great Australian novel who continue to
twitter over the bloodless yawns of Patrick White.*

Back again to today's sky. It is as I said perfectly clear—not a
cloud in sight. But it is not really blue—the quarter of it surrounding the low-hanging sun is a smoky white. This may be
caused by the moisture in the air, not sufficiently saturated to con-
dense into cloud. Any minute now, however, as the sun continues
to set, clouds will form.

JULY 31: I asked Maurice Sheppard, whose university research
fellowship is renewable annually for three years, whether he'd ever
thought of applying for a Fulbright to the U.S. A new scholarship
exchange agreement allots several thousand dollars a year, shared
equally between the U.S. and Australia. Maurice wanted no part
of it. The United States with its perennial witch hunts holds no
attraction for him, unless it might be the money he could make
and take home with him. Someone told him of going there with
his wife (no children), living entirely off the wife's earnings, and
returning at the end of a year with $6,000 salted away. Maurice and
Diana have two children and could therefore not hope to save as
much, but he'd give it a go if only it wasn't for a whole year. He
was sure it would be a longer year than any he'd ever endured.

He recalled a questionnaire he'd filled out merely to attend a
U.S. Atomic Energy exhibit in Sydney. Had he or any relative ever
been a member of a Communist organization? Etc. Yet there were
no secrets. I thought there might be a difference. Robert Oppen-
heimer had been kicked off the Atomic Energy Commission and
there were certainly no secrets from him. On the contrary, any
secrets there still might have been, he had. The over-elaborate and
largely futile security measures that Maurice had encountered
were just a by-product of atomic fission, that was all. I thought too

219

that if the Fulbright fellowships indulged in such hanky panky some country would give the show away by refusing to play. Maurice half conceded this point. Perhaps, since Diana would very much like to see America, he'd apply.

"The second bloke on the opposition was a red scarf man. I am still not sure whether this meant a Rhodes scholar or that he was just going to Oxford next year. He was the best debater on that side. He didn't seem really convinced he was arguing on the right side himself and this helped. But then he thought he had to support his side so he would come up with these wild statements. Once he said that we shouldn't disappoint the Americans. He had a friend who was in the U.S. at the time that it was announced that Australia would send troops to Vietnam. He said the headlines were full of it and people went around cheering and weeping with joy because at last America had a friend. One country was supporting them anyhow. They no longer had to stand alone braving world disapproval. I thought it was pretty funny really. I mean if that was supposed to make Australia stay in Vietnam we sure must have some pretty depraved ideas. I should think it would make anybody want to turn tail and run out of there as fast as they could."

"But what value would a year in America have?" he asked. "I'd rather go to Africa or some other underdeveloped part of the world, where I'd be working with students who are anxious to learn."

"Yes, and when you finished filling their heads with useless facts to equip them to take the typical British public examination they'd be more undeveloped than they are now."

I was speaking from Candi's experience. When her Australian classmates qualified for university entrance they would have faced such public examinations three years running—the Intermediate, the Leaving, and the Matriculation—each calculated to test the child's total academic knowledge. Students who ran this gauntlet and still retained a scrap of intellectual initiative or sense of meaningful interrelationships must be rare birds indeed. Over it all spread the pall of Commonwealth Scholarships, $200 plus help on books and fees to the top marks in the Intermediate, still richer rewards to those who responded best to mental regimentation in the Leaving and Matriculation. One girl who should have been in Candi's class, having passed her Leaving Examination well enough to earn a scholarship, was taking the year's work and the Leaving

Exams over again. She hoped next time to score among the handful of big prize winners. Shades of Admiral Rickover!

What was so different, Maurice asked, about the American pedagogical method?

"John Dewey," I said stoutly. "They're getting away from him now, moving farther back into the old methods every year, but there's still a lot of John Dewey left, thank God. I always took him for granted. Now that I see what Candi has to commit to memory, not for education's sake but just to pass your public exams, I begin to realize what a really great man he was."

"Still what difference could a year in America have in my teaching Africans? I should be able to do just as well without it. A year could hardly make me a better teacher."

"True. But if you go to Ghana or some other British Commonwealth country, as you likely will, you'll be surrounded. Your own unsupported ideas won't be sufficient. You'll need backing. With a year at Cal Tech you'll have this backing. 'This was how we did it at Cal Tech where they win all the Nobel Prizes.' "

I tried to explain what a travesty Candi's Physics course was. No attempt was made to teach relationships and the meaning of physical phenomena. Instead the whole emphasis was put on committing to memory a wide and virtually non-interrelated collection of laws, formulae, and experimental procedures. The text itself reflected this approach, looking and reading like a scrapbook in which the contents were not written out but pasted together.

We talked too about the lack of a first-rate work in Australian history. There have been several attempts but they are like Candi's Physics text: pasteups of letters and documents of an era, names, and dates. They have no organic unity.

"What's wrong with that?" Maurice asked. "What else do you want in a history book?"

"I want a whole picture of a country and its character as a country, together with an attempt to explain how this character was created. Just as if someone were to ask me about you. It wouldn't do to describe you detail by detail, starting with the right ear and its convolutions; then the nose and how it's bent, which nostril is larger, and so on."

I said New Zealand was ahead of Australia in this respect, with several good histories and far more good books about New Zealand than I'd found in Australia about Australia. New Zealand was perhaps even a special case, more interested in itself than any other place I knew.

Maurice asked Diana, didn't they have a good history text at

Central? Diana said they had none at all. Some topic of general interest came up in her class and Diana asked whether any of the students knew about it. They were contemptuous. "We don't know *that*. That's history!"

Weedon at lunch contrasted civil rights here and in the U.S., contending a host of liberties like picketing, parading, and outdoor meetings—legal in the U.S. as a result of recent Supreme Court decisions—are illegal in many parts of Australia without specific authorization. Trembath said this was because the Australian Constitution is silent on civil rights. These therefore have their basis entirely in English common law. "How can this be?" I asked, "Your Constitution was fashioned on the American model. Surely by 1900 the importance of the first ten amendments as integral parts of our Constitution was recognized?" Trembath wasn't sure. It was touch and go at the time whether the Australian States would federate. Nor could he recall having studied this question, or anything about the Constitutional discussions prior to federation, while at school or university. "We did have some Australian history, but it was always much duller than the English and European history we studied." "But the history itself is not dull," I argued. "No," he admitted. "Just the presentation of it."

32

AUGUST 14: I am looking out on an absolutely treeless desert, flat and level as the ocean, pale pink with patches of low grey-green vegetation. This is the Nullarbor, short for the Latin *nullus arbor*, a name given it by the explorer Delisser. For 450 miles east and west and up to 250 miles north and south it reaches down to the Great Australian Bight, not to a beach but to high precipitous cliffs. It is morning. The sun is hardly up. A settlement came and went, too fast to read its name. Could it have been Daisy Bates's Ooldea? It consisted of a white painted shed by the tracks, one or two other white painted buildings that I couldn't identify, and behind these buildings, neatly spaced in a square, were four trim, white painted backhouses.

The sky is cloudy. But beyond the clouds, which are small and puffy and clustered in thin clumps, the sky is a milk blue descending to green-white. It is pink near the sun and gun-metal blue where the clouds touch the horizon. Off in the distance a small round shape looks to be racing over the ground trying to keep pace with the train. A rabbit perhaps? An emu? A dingo? Surely not a kangaroo? if so it will be the first natural one I've seen. No; just a bush, with grey-blue foliage, one of thousands which my eye singled out to fly along with the train. There are stones scattered loosely over the whole ground, and now and then they seem to have been heaped together in cairns.

We have just passed Fisher, a railway workers' outpost, consisting of some small wooden houses around a large pile of white stones carefully shaped in the form of a cube. Men were standing in their doorways in shirtsleeves to watch the East-West go by. On such a flat plain the railroad bed should be smooth but it is the roughest and most jolting I have yet been on. Often during the night I was awakened by a violent twisting as though my shoulder were being shaken to waken me from a stubborn sleep. It was a long night. The time went back an hour and a half during our westward movement.

The start of our trip yesterday afternoon was like the one to Alice. After changing trains at Port Pirie we continued along Spencer Gulf with its promise of beaches and camping. At dinner we had a glimpse of Flinders Ranges, very blue and very pretty, and with scattered gum trees dotting the flat land in front of them. We are now stopped at a place called Cook, somewhat larger and older than Finke, with a windmill and even a few trees. As in Finke each house, here in the middle of nowhere, has its wire front fence and side fences of corrugated iron; and one of the backyards appears to have a patch of grass. Elsewhere the land is bare of everything save stones: beyond Cook and its fence of electric poles the flat treeless land reaches to the horizon. There are no Aborigines. A sign reads: "Our hospital needs your help. Get sick. If you're crook come to Cook."

When Edward Prince of Wales (later Duke of Windsor) stopped at Cook on the morning of July 10, 1920, his eyes must have lighted up at what they saw. There was the same "long string of two-roomed houses . . . with the two steel lines of the railway running east and west to infinity" which constituted Cook Siding then as now. But there were in addition, spread out across the bleak and cold treeless plain, scores of campfires and native bough shelters called mia-mias. Here he must have thought was a typical settlement of the Australian desert outback. The blacks in particular must have seemed a virile and prosperous race. See how many there were—150 at least, "stripped to the waist, decked in corroboree paint and feathers"—at just this one tiny speck on Australia's vast inland map. And see also how happy they all appeared to be as they greeted him "with a native shout of welcome and the singing of the women; and in a few minutes the Yuala"—the "dance of magic," most spectacular of Aboriginal corroborees—"was in full swing. . . ." They put on "a demonstration of native arts—spear-making and spear-throwing, the manufacture of boomerangs, hair-spinning, flint-cutting, seed-sifting and other primitive Aboriginal handicrafts. A bag painted with the crude effigy of a human body was the target for the spears . . . Two young initiates were brought forward, with their elaborate decorations and head-dresses of string, emu chignons, cockatoo feathers, and paint. And the greetings ended with the booming of the big bull-roarer, the welcoming voice of the wilderness and its savage people."

If there was anything peculiar to catch the eye of the Prince in this picture-idyll of his two subject peoples black and white living amicably together, working and prospering together to build their new country, it must have been the almost complete lack of communication between them. None of the Government big-wigs, railway officials, or residents of Cook appeared to recognize the Aborigines. The only white person who did, evidently, was a frail middle-aged widow camped in a railway van. She circulated freely among them, could talk to them in any one of 188 dialects; her "presence was necessary throughout, there were so many mixtures, uncivilized, semi-civilized, and fully civilized, the last named by far the worst to deal with." In February, when she "was asked by the authorities to arrange a display of Aborigines," she began collecting them, bringing them in from the outer desert with the promise that "my king will give you plenty flour, sugar, blankets, tobacco."

"It had been a trying summer," she writes in The Passing of the Aborigines, "with temperatures for days at a time touching 120 degrees, and unending dust-storms and disappointments. The meat-supply of dingo and rabbit had failed. . . . A new mob was expected for an initiation ceremony, and the camps were hungry and disgruntled . . . I could hear the banging of boomerangs and clubs, and the loud chatter of voices in the men's camps." The authorities hadn't given her an easy job. The sudden reminder to the Aborigines that there was a government theoretically responsible to them as well as the whites opened old wounds. "White-fellows have frightened all our game away and taken our waters," they said. "The kooga will come back when the white man goes. This is our country. White-fellows took it away, and brought their sheep, bullocky, and pony to hunt our totem meat away. You send paper to Gubmint and tell them we don't want white-fellow king. We want our own king and our own country!"

In her years of service to the Aborigines Daisy Bates (this was the widow's name) had inspired such trust and affection that she was able to win them over. She had chosen, in the words of Arthur Mee who wrote the introduction to her book, "to be the last friend of the last remnant of this dying race, the last friendly hand. . . ." Her idea was that "they should be left as free as possible to pass from existence as happily as may be . . ." and she hoped that the right man, a King's Man, would "someday be appointed by Australia to take charge of these people who are dying out not knowing how wonderful life is."

Early in July she "started out to collect the natives at the various sidings within a radius of two or three hundred miles . . ."

travelling *"the line with them in the goat-van of a goods train . . ."* They *"now understood that the coming of the King-King-Kadha (the King's son) meant new blankets and pipes and unlimited food and tobacco, and they were all excited and eager to do their best."*

Daisy Bates, unknown to most Australians and virtually unreported in their history books, is one of the country's truly great historical personages. Born in England amid *"primroses and church bells, green fields and the song of birds, the wild rose in the hedgerows, the little church at the end of the country lane, and a harvest field,"* she lived most of her life far away from the sight and sound of these things in primitive Australia. She arrived in Broome, on the distant north-west coast, when it *"was a quaint and prosperous pearling post in the 1900s with a polyglot population living out on the ships and along the foreshore—Chinese, Japanese, Malays, Manilamen, and a score of European races. I believe there was actually an Eskimo among them. The hotels were full of pearl dealers from overseas, divers, shell-openers, and traders, white and coloured, and night-time was a continuous revelry. At one period, so fast and furious was the racket that I was locked in my room from danger of unpleasantness . . . Even in those days the tribes of the place were but a remnant. My interest in the town natives was confined to those in gaol. They were chained to each other by the neck, and there was discussion as to the humanity of this procedure. The natives themselves told me that it gave them more freedom than handcuffs, and that a piece of cloth wrapped round the collar relieved the weight and the heat of the iron, and left their hands free to play cards and deal with the flies and mosquitoes."* In 1907, in Perth, she assisted at the burial of Joobaitch, last survivor of the Perth tribe which had been reduced in a single life span from 1500 souls.

"When her husband died, she disposed of her cattle station and thousands of cattle and travelled wherever she heard of natives gathering. She pitched her camp along the edge of the Plain, living a mile from the trans-continental railway in a tent and a shed made of boughs ringed by a high breakwind. Here she passed from her prime to old age, walking a mile every day when she was over 70 years old to get water. Sitting at her tent she would receive wandering tribes, coming one day from nowhere to nowhere." This was at Ooldea Siding, 86 miles east of Cook. Although *"nothing more than one of the many depressions in the never-ending sandhills that run waveringly from the Bight for nearly a thousand miles, Ooldea water had been one of Nature's miracles in barren Central Australia. No white man coming to this place would ever*

*guess that dreary hollow with the sand blowing across it was an
unfailing fountain, yet a mere scratch and the magic waters welled
in sight. Even in the cruellest droughts it had never failed. Here
the tribes gathered in their hundreds for initiation and other
ceremonies. When all the waters had dried for countless miles,
strangers came from afar, offering their flints and their food and
their women for the right to share it and live.*

*"In the building of the trans-continental line, the water of
Ooldea passed out of its own people's hand forever. Pipe lines and
pumping plants reduced it at the rate of 10,000 gallons a day for
locomotives. The natives were forbidden the soak, and permitted
to obtain their water only from taps at the siding. In a few years
the engineering plant apparently perforated the blue clay bed. . . .
The waters became brackish, injurious to the engines, unpleasant
to the taste, and gradually seeped away . . ."* and the *"magical Yul-
di-gabbi that had not failed its people in hundreds, perhaps thousands, of generations . . . was a thing of the past."*

*If Prince Edward did happen to see Daisy Bates on that July
morning in 1920 before the royal train pulled away, with himself
at the controls, he must have found her a sight no less bizarre than
that of the Aborigines. Throughout the whole of her life with
them, during which "I lived their lives, not mine," she writes, "I
have adhered to the simple but exact dictates of fashion as I left it,
when Victoria was queen—a neat white blouse, stiff collar and
ribbon tie, a dark skirt and coat, stout and serviceable, trim shoes
and neat black stockings, a sailor hat and fly-veil, and, for my
excursions to the camps, always a dust-coat and a sunshade. Not
until I was in meticulous order would I emerge from my tent,
dressed for the day."*

Cook was still in South Australia. An hour or more and a breakfast later we entered Western Australia. There was no noticeable
difference; the treelessness and flatness still reached out to the horizon; some spinifex mixed with the saltbush and bluebush. Mirages
were numerous and strikingly real—of trees naturally.

AUGUST 15: The land in Western Australia just east of Cunderdin is almost as flat as the Nullarbor but green and wet. We are on
a different train now, having changed last evening from the Commonwealth-operated East-West to Western Australia's Westland.
This train has no heat, having been designed with the aim of keeping the heat out. My compartment has an electric fan and louvred
door and transom to the corridor, and the door faces the head of
the train to receive the full impact of the icy wind whistling

through the open door to the platform. After dinner I tried closing this door at the end of the car, but conductors made a steady run through it all night, each leaving it open behind him.

The dining car was temporarily hitched on at this same end and the connectors made a succession of whistles, screams, and screeches whenever the train slowed down, speeded up, or rounded a curve. Then there was the bounce or jig and rattle of the train. I thought the East-West jolted unnecessarily. This train leapt into the air and twisted. Though I was oppressed with the weight of blankets I couldn't keep warm, for each shake let a new whiff of icy air under them. I slid down and curled up but I couldn't slide very far on account of the pillow. Unless it rested against the wall the jolting would knock it loose from under my head and I had to clutch the case to try to hold it down. The pillow was jumbo size, filled with kapok, and hard. When I covered my head to keep warm it would slip away. The coupling shrieked, the wind cut like a knife, the train stopped with a shudder, started with a series of slips and slams. Despite all this I would drop off in catnaps, wake, and drop off all night long—each time looking hopefully to the window for signs of daylight. After two nights on the East-West in a heated bedroom I was back in Australia.

And sure enough, at breakfast this morning—all the Australians I spoke to, except one lady from Queensland, said they slept more comfortably on the Westland than "that stuffy East-West."

It was mildly sociable in the lounge car yesterday morning, nothing to compare with our marathon discussion on the Ghan. We missed the Victorians, best of all Australian travelling companions. Instead there was a young man from Adelaide, a girl from Perth who has been working in South Australia, three older ladies from South Australia, and ultimately an assortment of people including an old boy born in France who fought for Aussie in the 1914 war. Then in the afternoon we sang around the lounge piano, but the Aussies knew American songs better than their own. As the afternoon wore on the trees began to reappear until by late afternoon the land—still flat—was fairly well covered with them. In the evening after dinner we watched the sky from our darkened room until we got to Kal.

We changed trains at Kalgoorlie, the last survivor of Australia's gold-mining towns, and a far quieter place than I anticipated. I expected to find a rowdy, noisy, gambling, drinking frontier, a western Broken Hill, with two-up schools and S.P. bookies and Kalgoorlie's own famous "dirty half acre" of pubs resounding to the songs and shouts of thirsty miners. I found instead a tall war memorial, an extraordinarily wide Hannan Street bordered with flame trees and parked cars, and—for all it was Saturday night— the hotels more than half empty. A listless few were dancing to an accordion and saxophone, even fewer stood at the bars. The lights playing on the mine shafts and smelter smoke at the other end of the "golden mile" were by far the brightest lights in town!

33

You see poker or slot machines everywhere in Broken Hill, as throughout New South Wales. People sit with a tray of shilling or 20-cent pieces in their laps, playing three machines at a time. Poker machines are legal. Two-up, Australia's own version of heads or tails, is not. It is played in a "school." You know whether the school is open by the street light on the corner. If the light is on so is the game. If a police inspector is due in from Sydney on a weekend (they play weekends only—after 9.00 on Friday, Saturday, and Sunday) the light stays out and the inspector finds everything to his liking. No two-up, no 21, no S.P. betting in the hotels—which stops at noon anyhow—and the hotels themselves in a rare spate of virtue observe the legal 10 p.m. closing hour. The housie is on as usual of course. There is housie every night, paying $200, $80, and $20 on a 40-cent card. Three of the games are run by churches. The 21 game isn't big, mostly for silver, $2 at the most.

At the two-up school as many as 300 on a Friday night will watch the fall of two pennies. A man in the centre "spins" the pennies by tossing them in the air and calling heads or tails. The pennies are blackened on the tails for easy identification. If his call comes up on both coins he wins; the opposite on both, he loses; while two odd coins makes no bet. The school gives him one free play, after which the house takes its cut—a dollar on a four-dollar win. The balance of $7 plays. From time to time a successful better will take a dollar out of the pot, else he'd be sure to lose everything; then the house also takes a dollar. Besides the bet in the centre, which may be covered by several different betters, individuals lay bets around the ring, putting their money on the floor in front of them to be covered. Here is where "you have to watch out for yourself" that nobody grabs this money, claiming a win which isn't his.

Though such schools operate in every Australian city, even Adelaide, the two-up school is Broken Hill's big tourist attraction. It is easy to find, almost next door to the police station, and it serves the best meal "on the hill." But only men, and among men only those outside the newspaper profession, are allowed to play or eat there. The unions believe that publicity given the two-up school doesn't do Broken Hill any good.

And in truth when Chris Priest and his wife Haze took their holidays in Broken Hill they found the miners' interest in two-up waning. These, Chris said, were the wealthiest workingmen in Australia owing to their exclusive reliance on collective bargaining. In Broken Hill, he said, arbitration—Australia's favourite prescription for industrial ailments—was a dirty word; and as a result there was less industrial unrest and fewer proportionate man-hours lost because of disputes than in all the rest of Australia. From Trades Hall, familiarly known as the Kremlin, the unions worked in harmony with the employers to make Broken Hill a showplace among the world's mining towns—isolated by hundreds of miles of desert but sheltered by planted windbreaks from the desert's dust; with parks, an artificial lake, a kindergarten, an Aussie Rules league oval, and their own summer resort on the beach near Adelaide. The last big strike ended with a victory for the unions and collective bargaining, after an 18-months' struggle in 1920; but so fresh was its memory still in the minds of the unionists that appeals for help from strikers anywhere in the world continued to touch their hearts—and their purse-strings too, Chris said, to a total over the years of something like two million dollars.

While paying the highest wages in Australia the four major companies operating in Broken Hill had also done well, according to Chris. Their profits had doubled in ten years; their shares now appeared to the miners a more attractive investment than two-up, where a man used often to "do" a week's wages in an hour. Hence, while pub arguments in other towns were concerned mostly with sport, in Broken Hill they dealt in shares and margins, debentures and dividends, what this or that stock did yesterday, and how much profit they made on another. But affluence had brought troubles in its wake, Chris said; Broken Hill was a town of suicides.

AUGUST 16: Now it's not the worst hotel in town. On the contrary, when we showed our bookings to Andy, next door in Elizabeth, who comes from Perth, she said it was one of the best. Bath and

toilet are down the hall of course, and the plumbing is primitive in them as the furniture and fixtures are in our bedrooms. There is a lift, an open cage operated, I believe, by water power. There is no heat and it is cold in Perth at this time of year. Every so often something bangs just outside our room, a sure discouragement to sleep. The beds sag and have lumpy mattresses. There aren't enough blankets and there are no hot water bottles to be had. The light is a bare bulb hanging from the ceiling. The mirror on the chest of drawers covers part of one window. There is no regular closet, only a wooden wardrobe and it extends over part of the other window. The one good thing is that the water in the wash basin is hot: it was cold and lukewarm on the train. All this is the consequence of restricting the sale of liquor to hotels. Like the railroads in the U.S., which derive their profit from freight, most Australian hotels find caring for people an unprofitable nuisance.

He looked every inch a gentleman and there were a lot of inches. His head almost brushed the ornate chandelier hanging from the 11-foot ceiling of the public lounge. His big frame and long narrow head were spare and bony; his hair, all still there, was untouched by grey. A very rugged face, brown eyes, and a wide mouth with thin lips, and the slightest trace of a foreign accent, picked up no doubt from his parents and elder brothers.

Jan was five when they left Holland. His father was a charming ne'er-do-well, the darling of all the women in their town but the despair of his relatives who, to get him off their necks, took up a collection to send him, his wife, and nine children to Australia. This was in 1913 when Australia as yet had no European migration programme. Whereas in Holland the father had lived like a gentleman and supported his family on his borrowings, they were desperately poor in Australia and the father had to work as a wharfie. Somehow they managed to acquire a block of land in the Sydney suburb of Punchbowl and on it they built a three-room shack of corrugated iron with two bedrooms—one for the parents and the other fitted with three double beds in which the nine boys slept, three to a bed. The bare earth was their floor. For the father this amounted to virtual transportation, as for the convicts of old, but it turned out to be an excellent investment for the relatives back in Holland. He was never able to earn enough money to return.

He still retained his dandy-ish ways. He had his special chair, his newspaper always untouched before he picked it up, and—though he had been forced to work with his hands—at home he demanded to be waited on. If he were thirsty, instead of running himself a drink he would call to his wife, "Wilhelmina! Hass Wasser!" He was so averse to doing anything for himself personally that, poor as they were, he always went to a barber for a shave.

With Jan and the elder brothers working the family had scarcely managed to lift itself out of the mire when the 1929 Depression hit Australia. Banks closed immediately after the Wall Street crash. There was no dole or any form of unemployment or welfare assistance except a meagre work relief called "susso," and this only to family heads, rationed according to the number of small children they had. For Jan and his brothers there was nothing but the soup and bread line. The experience gave them all a leftward bent in their political thinking, and they joined in demonstrations at "the Dom" or Domain, in Railway Square, and on 24-hour vigils to prevent the eviction of tenants for unpaid rent. The thing that angered them most about the Depression was the wastage of human resources. Here were workingmen, tradesmen, and former businessmen like Jan's eldest brother able and willing to work, and here on the other hand were jobs needing to be done, schools to be built and renovated, hospitals, roads, houses —needs which still have not been filled in all the years since the Great Depression.

Seeing no end to the Depression except war, Jan proposed to

enlist in the International Brigade and fight in Spain. His mother was sympathetic but his father was not and, though Jan was his own boss, he gave in to his father and didn't join up. But he still took part in the meetings and demonstrations for the Spanish Loyalists that were held in Sydney, mainly at "the Dom." Some of these demonstrations were so huge and the men stood so close together that a speaker would stand on one man's shoulders, speak awhile, step forward to another pair of shoulders, and so on. Thus no one's shoulders bore too heavy a burden.

At last Jan's eldest brother Heinz, having scorned bankruptcy and paid off his creditors at the unheard of rate of 19 shillings and seven pence in the pound, or 98 cents in the dollar, was able to get a loan and go back into furniture. Jan joined him and stayed until he had enough money to buy an interest in a hotel, first in Punch-bowl and later in St Peters. Then, after a long hiatus, he had finally got back into the business again, managing a brewer's hotel in far-off Fremantle. It was the thing he knew best how to do.

A hotel, I said, to most people outside Australasia, was a place where one spent the night when away from home. Did Jan as a hotel-keeper hold this view? No. He never had. He never thought of a hotel in that light at all. From the time he first got into the business, before the war, a hotel to him was purely and simply a saloon. He sold drinks. The bedrooms overhead might as well have been insulation in the ceilings, just something to fill the upstairs with. The law required a publican to have a bed available to lodgers for each given number of feet in the bar's over-all length. The idea that the beds would be used never crossed his mind. A police inspector called around four times a year to make sure the beds were still there. He would look at the beds, lift up the mattress on one, and perhaps say it needed a new spring. It was pure formality of course, for the spring had never been slept on; but Jan would buy a new spring all the same. Then the inspector would look around the bedroom, notice a flyspeck on the ceiling, and order the ceiling to be repainted. There was in fact no limit to the amount of repair and upkeep he could compel a publican to do.

On the other hand if he went easy, as he generally did, he would tell Jan some story such as that he had to supply the drinks for a wedding, and would Jan put a dozen Haig, a half dozen Gilbey's, and three bottles of Cherry Heering in the boot of his car? When he offered to pay, and made a half-hearted motion toward his hip pocket, Jan would naturally say "forget it." Still Jan was better off than the publican who served drinks after the hour when hotel

234

bars by law were required to be closed. His brother Max used to own such a hotel and he had, in addition to the six regular policemen of his district, other police from neighbouring suburbs dropping in to cadge free drinks. This rather annoyed the six regulars; Max was their pigeon and they didn't fancy sharing him. "Why do you put up with it?" one asked; and Max, who was new to the game, replied helplessly, "What can I do?" He was told. The next time one of the outsiders entered the pub Max pulled him a beer and said, "Redfern's been calling. They want you to report." The fellow choked. "How in blazes did they know I was here?" Soon word got around to the other outsiders that their own stations had them tabbed as off limits and they didn't trouble Max any more.

Max was pretty innocent. He imagined free drinks discharged his debt to the men who turned a blind eye to his sly grog activities, and he made no move to reward them any more tangibly. It wasn't long however before one of the six, the same one who had helped him get rid of the outsiders, took him aside and said, "Look, old man, I'm a bit short this week. What do you say to lending me five quid?" Five quid is ten dollars—in those days one-third of a policeman's weekly pay. Why sure," said Max, and he had the good sense never to ask that the loan be repaid. From time to time thereafter he was approached for such loans.

An after-hours hotel is a less valuable property than one that observes the closing law; and the owner of a hotel that's for sale will invariably affirm it closes strictly on time. There is a way, Jan said, to test the truth of this claim. When he sold his hotel in Punchbowl and was shopping for another he would carry the deal almost to the point of signing, whereupon he and his wife would call around unexpectedly, late in the evening, with "only a few more questions to ask." Invited in, as they just about had to be, they would listen for the doorbell. It made no difference that the owner didn't answer it; if the bell rang frequently the hotel carried on after-hours trade.

During the war beer and liquor were rationed, so what the hotels used to sell in bottles they now sold in single drinks. It was more profitable and it theoretically made the stock go farther; even so, they would sell out an entire day's stock in an hour or two. This was especially true just before six o'clock, the then legal closing hour, when customers would drink whole pints at a time as fast as they could down them, one after the other. They used to make a lot of bricks in St Peters, and the brick dust parched their throats. They'd come in, take a look at the clock, make a quick calculation, and groan, "Only time for five pints!"

Nevertheless there were customers who had formerly bought bottles and whom Jan still felt obliged to sell bottles to. He couldn't do this publicly, so he would tell a privileged customer to go out and around to the side, and Jan would hand him the bottle through the cellar window. Once he was caught doing this by a passer-by who called out, "While you're down there, Jan, hand me up a bottle." He thrust a folded handkerchief in Jan's hand and walked away. Jan unwrapped the handkerchief and found, as surety for payment, the man's upper plate.

One of the problems of the business was, and still is, the wastage of spilled beer when the barmaids filled the mugs. It might amount to three or four gallons a day. Some hotel keepers had very elaborate means of recovering it to serve the next day. It was flat but palatable. Some went so far as to save the spillage on trays and the dregs in glasses, putting it through cloth to strain out the cigarette butts. But State licensing commissions now required a dye to be put in the trays which coloured the spillage purple. Can it have been unconscious republicanism that has made purple Australia's least loved colour? Meat sold in butcher shops but designated only for pets must also be dyed purple.

When the war was over Jan sold his St Peter's hotel, not dreaming that when he went back in the business the price would be far higher than he had received. With his wife and two children he set off on a tour of Australia and, like many another city-bred Australian, saw his first Aborigines. Having also sold their car for nearly twice what it cost in 1940, they went by train to Adelaide and then by plane, hopping to Port Augusta and Oodnadatta on the way to Alice Springs. It was summer and the tourist buses weren't running so they took a taxi. They saw a group of Aborigines and stopped to talk to them. He noticed they all wore a bandage over one eye and learnt this was because of the flies, which clustered so thickly around the eyes that they had to cover each eye in turn to rest it. They stood in dust nearly two feet deep. Back in Alice Springs he asked if something couldn't be done to give employment, at least to the young people. The reply was, "You city slickers come out here and think you know all the answers. They live that way because they want to. Nobody could treat them any better than we do." He thought then of the St Peter's brick makers and how they couldn't get enough beer to wash the dust out of their throats, and wondered why no dinkum Aussie would let his heart go out to the Aborigines at Alice Springs whose throats must have been a whole lot dustier.

They soon got tired of just touring and, seeing an advert offering a three-year lease on the kiosk at the municipal campground in Evans Head, a coastal resort up near the New South Wales-Queensland line, they took the lease. The municipal authorities went to work to fix up the campground in preparation for holiday season. While Jan watched them repair and clean the toilets and baths, the official in charge pointed out to him a patch of wild undergrowth where, he said, "the abos could go."

He had previously seen how Aborigines were restricted to the less desirable seats at the very front in a movie theatre, and how when an Aboriginal child was sent to shop he was made to wait until every white person was served, no matter how late he came in. He couldn't help but feel how exasperating this would be for anyone regardless of his colour. He therefore instructed the girls in the kiosk to serve people in the order of their arrival; and this little gesture was such an unheard-of thing that at the end of the season he was presented with a leather notecase, or billfold, by the Aboriginal leaders.

There were two hospitals in nearby Lismore, one called the Public, and the other the Maternity. The Maternity was a general hospital, and public as well, but it only admitted whites. Jan, when he fell ill, was adjudged a difficult case and taken to the Public Hospital. While he was convalescing he visited the maternity ward just after two babies were born, one white, the other black. The matron said, "These will be their only ten days of equality. We probably shan't see the white baby again but the black one will be back in three months, afflicted with worms."

34

"I can never look down on the panorama of that young and lovely city from the natural parkland on the crest of Mount Eliza that is its crowning glory without a vision of the past, the dim and timeless past when a sylvan people wandered its woods untrammelled with no care or thought for yesterday or tomorrow, or of a world other than their own . . .

"Through it all, a kangaroo skin slung carelessly over his shoulders, a few spears in his hand, strode the forest landlord, catching fish in the river-shallows, spearing the emu and the kangaroo, and finding the roots and fruits that were his daily bread. His women and children meekly followed, carrying his spare weapons, their own household goods, and perhaps a baby swung in the kangaroo-skin bag."—Daisy Bates.

Andy's brother-in-law David sounded cheerful on the phone and has offered to pick us up this evening for a drive. Our foot tour yesterday of the city and riverfront had no surprises—or wouldn't have had before people on the train began telling me what a beautiful city Perth was. It was what I'd previously envisioned Perth to be: a few streets of shops and department stores, a quaint arcade done in the manner of a London residential courtyard, an art gallery in an old brick building to which additions have been made. My strongest impression is of the courtesy of Perth's motorists, in contrast to Adelaide's who have a bad reputation all over Australia. In Perth indeed it is the pedestrians who are most apt to run you down. Flocking out of church and filling the footpath they nearly bowled us over, pushing blindly ahead, bumping and jostling others out of their way. Last night, too, the street below our window was noisier than Sydney's Pitt Street from shouting and whistling youths; and today the footpaths were jam-packed with shoppers, more than Melbourne, Sydney, and Brisbane, more even than on Rundle Street in Adelaide. But school is out, which makes a difference.

AUGUST 17: David and Helen Pell, on no other incentive than Helen being our neighbour Andy's sister, picked us up last evening and drove to Fremantle along the Swan River, up the hill to the Fremantle War Memorial with its view of the harbour, where we saw the British destroyer *Victorious* and the *Centaur* tied to the wharf. We also saw the new Port Authority Building with a ship's mast on top and lots of glass and concrete descending therefrom in vertical stripes. Close at hand is the passenger terminal, far handsomer than anything in Melbourne, Brisbane, or Adelaide; its only rival is the Circular Quay terminal in Sydney, and Perth's terminal shades Sydney's. We went on to the University and drove around the beautiful campus spread along the river; we saw the fine new library, also of glass and masonry, and several storeys high. We saw the Empire Games Village, so much like a California suburb except the construction is of solid masonry rather than California's chicken wire and stucco. But the walls and carports tying the houses together reminded me vividly of Supertino just outside San Jose. Only the shrubs and trees were lacking. We drove on the freeway that connects Perth with its heavy industrial suburb of oil and steel in Kwinana. We crossed and recrossed the river, a real river, rare in continental Australia, whose width in places is up to seven miles. We drove through King's Park, 1,000 acres of mostly native bush right inside the city, and saw the city lights from the Perth War Memorial on its mountain top. All in all it was a lovely and exciting night-time tour of Perth and its surroundings, including the beaches and the oceanside suburbs. Perth is pre-eminently a city that must be seen on wheels. Even downtown looks better from a car than on foot.

This morning we walked down to the river and along as much of the river as there was footpath or roadway, enjoying the sun, for it was chilly in the shade. At noon as we were spying out a tea shop to lunch in we ran into Susan, one of Candi's friends on the ship; and she was as delighted and of course more surprised than we. Just before dinner—this time by appointment—we met and had drinks with another couple from the ship, Sime and Di Carpenter, boilermaker and wife. So it was very much a day of social contacts and the better day for it. Sime says they have a saying in Western Australia: "If you see a good pawm, shoot him before he goes bad."

AUGUST 20: On the boat from Rottnest Island we got into conversation with a forty-year-old bachelor—the type you see so often

in Australia. He was up for his first visit to Perth in five years. He described himself as a drink steward at one of the hotels in Albany, and said the people down there still dress conservatively. It was hardly necessary for him to say so. I could imagine how his eyes bugged out when he got to Perth and saw the super mini skirts, troglodyte bangs, and tan death-mask make-ups. I can't think of very much he had to say. He was just a very friendly fellow, that was all. Liked Americans and Scandinavians and Greeks, didn't like poms, said the Dutch were more arrogant than the Germans. He was typical of the Australian bachelors I've met even to having had a mum until recently, when she died at the age of 84. Has no special objection to getting married but is afraid he'd be unlucky enough to get the wrong woman. The present day equivalent of the 1920s flapper frightens him. He gestured to a girl on the boat, dressed modestly with nothing freakish about her make-up and hair-do, and said she was the kind he'd like to marry.

He thought he'd be taking a trip to Japan the next year, but the thing he particularly wanted to see was a new bridge in New York which he'd read about in the *Reader's Digest*. That and the Statue of Liberty.

Rottnest Island, ten miles out from Fremantle harbour, is such a popular summer resort that holiday bookings are available only on a first-come basis just before the season opens. Otherwise accommodations would always go to the same people every year. The first settlers considered it unfit for human habitation; hence, when a site had to be found for an Aboriginal prison, Rottnest was the obvious choice. Aborigines from all over Western Australia were brought to Perth for trial and sentence, to work by day in chain gangs in the salt lakes of the island or building roads, and to be locked away by night in low, dismal stone cells where they died like flies, at the rate of one death every hour of the twenty-four.

AUGUST 23: Yesterday we joined the Saturday shoppers, covering much the same ground as we have on previous walks, but farther along on Hay Street—the main shopping street—and back on St George's Terrace, the leading avenue of large buildings. Perth already has more such buildings than Auckland, a more populous city, and is building others, including a twenty-story Government Offices Building, one of the tallest in Australia. It is also putting up a new town hall, and besides the country's finest Port Authority Building and ship passenger terminal, it has Australia's most modern airport and terminal as well; not to mention a magnificent House of Parliament on a hill overlooking the city.

I asked the Pells where Perth got the money for all this. They thought some of it came from the sale of land which the city owns along the river. As the suburbs expand, this land is subdivided and usually commands high prices. But obviously much more money was needed, and could only come, they surmised, from Commonwealth tax disbursements. David added that Victorians complain of having to pay for Western Australia's roads. Seeing the splendid roads out of Perth on the way to Kalgoorlie with scarcely a vehicle on them, and comparing them with Victoria's patched-up thoroughfares, clogged with traffic, I'd be prepared to say the Victorians have something to grouse about.

Our hotel continues to live up to form. While Candi was out with Susan this evening, Peggy and I, having neither radio nor television to keep us in our room, went down to view the TV in the hotel lounge. We being virtually the only resident guests the lounge was empty except for some hotel employees, who were talking and drinking at the other end of the room. The TV picture was on but we couldn't hear the sound, even from close at hand, over the conversation. I turned the volume up a bit. Very soon one of the barmaids came over and, without a word, turned it down again.

AUGUST 23: It rained most of this morning but by afternoon when the Pells called for us the sun was making temporary appearances. We drove to King's Park Restaurant where Helen had reserved a table on the outdoor terrace. It was crowded even out there, and inside the large and handsome building there was hardly a vacant chair, let alone a table. The restaurant is a favourite rendezvous for visitors who enjoy the splendid view of the city, and for Perth people themselves who must travel 200 miles or more for most of their other distractions. Perth is a city with all the virtues—clean air, handsome buildings, sensible drinking hours, splendid views, good beaches. It has only one drawback: isolation. It is perhaps more isolated from its own kind than any other city of its size on Earth. Both Sydney and Melbourne are closer to Auckland than to Perth, and Perth is closer to Djarkarta than to Sydney.

It was a mite chilly on the terrace and I kept my topcoat on. The others didn't seem to suffer. We had an excellent local fish, dhufish, grilled without batter, together with a mediocre salad, a pie—called apple but actually applesauce—and strong tea. There were no flies at this time of year, although David and Helen said they are unmanageable in summer. You just don't eat outdoors in the summer, and you don't eat in either unless you have a reservation; the choicest tables, overlooking the city and river, are more or less permanently booked.

I asked David about Perth looking west to Britain, as I'd heard tell, rather than east to the rest of Australia. Except in business he thought this might be true. No more patriotic people were to be found anywhere, he said. When the Queen came out . . . So there it was, as he himself realized. Patriotism was not love of Australia but love of Britain. And Perthites do travel more to Britain than to the eastern States, David says. Many who have never been east have been to Britain. Many others go once to Sydney and Melbourne, feel they've done their duty, and never go again.

When, earlier in the afternoon, we came from the airport north of town and crossed Double View Ridge, one of several dunes reaching back from the ocean, we turned along the waterfront at, I believe, City Beach and it looked just like the beaches north and west along the Pacific from L.A. This was my first view of the Indian Ocean except as it formed a pool of dark among the harbour lights as we viewed them from the Fremantle War Memorial

at night. The water was a beautiful green, greener than I have yet
seen in waves rolling into shore. Every mile or so along these
beaches is a handsome clubhouse for the lifesavers. Much of the
shore is still resigned to dunes but tracts are going up as the well-
to-do abandon the older residential suburbs to Italians and
Greeks.

AUGUST 25: Still shaking from my second overnight trip on the
Westland I have suddenly become aware of the fact that, although
Western Australia contains more Aborigines than any other State,
we have not see one on this trip. None in Perth; none from the
train travelling west; none so far travelling east. West of Kalgoorlie an area of mulga scrub is posted as a native reserve, but the
posters are old and tattered and there are no evidences of habitation anywhere near the railway. The feeling that the Aborigines
are people in a dream and not real people at all is stronger here
than anywhere else. So far as Perth is concerned the Aborigines are
no dying race. They are already part of history with the Picts and
Hittites. There were Aboriginal souvenirs on display in the shops—
and souvenirs would be a big thing in Perth, the first port of call
for migrants and European visitors—but they looked to have been
made in Hong Kong. The people who used to make them are
merely part of a dream.

Adam and Atoms was written and published by William Graydon, a member of the Western Australian Legislature, in order to
publicize the findings of a Select Committee he headed in 1957.
The Perth newspapers would not report the Committee's findings.
The Committee's purpose was to inquire into the welfare of the
nomadic Aborigines of the Western Australia desert. On this
inhospitable land, left to them because at the time no other use
could be found for it, the Aborigines were still contriving to exist.
With only spears for weapons they hunted the scarce emu and
scarcer kangaroo, and the dingoes and rabbits that the Government
pest exterminators overlooked. They did what they could to discourage their own hungry children from eating the poison baits
scattered indiscriminately over their hunting grounds.
   The bulk of the protein in their meagre diet had to come from
goannas—also subject to bait-poisoning—and from wood grubs.
For the most part they subsisted on seeds and roots, and even these
were so scarce that the women and children had to labour from
dawn to dusk at gathering them. They wandered from water hole
to water hole as each dried up. "There is no permanent surface
water in the area," writes Graydon. "The annual average rainfall

is between five and eight inches and the evaporation rate approximately 96 inches. The country may be regarded as some of the most arid and inhospitable in the world. It would be reasonable to assume that no people in the world are less favoured in their choice of habitat." Add to this the blazing heat of the sun by day and the bitter cold of the desert at night, and the environment looked then very grim indeed.

In quick succession the State and Commonwealth Governments took steps to make it grimmer. Britain wanted a rocket-testing range. Australia generously offered this desert and mapped a route over which the rockets could travel without menace to a single sheep or cow. Instead they flew directly over the Aboriginal reserve. A meteorological station was set up in the heart of the reserve, cheek by jowl to the only dependable water supply. It became also a tracking station for the rockets, and 150 miles of roads were cut through the reserve for supply trucks. Four million acres of the reserve were given away in rights for mineral prospecting, these rights being subsequently traded to an overseas nickel concern for shares valued at $600,000. In 1956 Britain tested an atom bomb in the desert just east of the reserve. Efforts were made to warn the Aborigines but, such was their shyness at the approach of white men, no one knows to this day whether all escaped blast and radiation. Those who did hear of the projected bombing thought an enemy was about to attack Australia. The primitive mind could not conceive of a Government bombing its own country.

As a telling final blow to a people who had already suffered so much, the Western Australian Government was preparing to take their children from them. When the toddlers reached school age they were, by force if necessary, to be separated from their parents and sent to a boarding school 360 miles away.

The Committee, noting Australia's relatively generous assistance to other poorer nations, found it "hard to visualize that any people, anywhere in the world, could be more in need of such assistance than the natives of the inland area of Western Australia who were investigated. Their immediate requirements are adequate water, food and medical attention." As a first step the Committee recommended the establishment of a pastoral industry to provide food and employment to the reserve's Aborigines. The Committee estimated the capital cost of such a venture at $200,000 —one-third the value of the mineral rights alone that had been taken from them. The Federal Government turned the proposal down.

35

AUGUST 26: Our table companion at meals is the taciturn Australian one hears a lot about but seldom meets. I tried to start him talking—without asking questions, for he looked as if he might resent questions—but it was pretty hopeless. He liked Perth. It was a clean city and the people were friendly. He wouldn't like to live there, but mainly because it gets too hot in summer. He prefers to live in Melbourne, partly because he was born there and partly because it doesn't get too hot. He thinks Sydney is horrible, and says this after having spent half his life in Sydney. But, except that the people are cold and indifferent, he wouldn't say what was horrible about it. "Melbourne," he said, "is the most civilized city in Australia."

More people have said "God bless you" and especially "God bless" to me in Sydney than any other Australian city—or any city in the world for that matter. Friday on Martin Place I passed a couple of men arguing over something in the Bible—a friendly argument. One had an open Bible in his hands to prove his point.

Although he seldom smiles he is not unfriendly; nevertheless this was the sum of our luncheon conversation, while the two couples across the aisle—also erstwhile strangers—were laughing and shouting away in great fashion. At dinner we were left with nothing to say. We'd met in the lounge before dinner and I'd told him what Malcolm our steward had told me, that our third sitting tomorrow would almost exactly coincide with our arrival to change trains in Port Pirie, and we'd have only about enough time to glance at the menu. This pleasantry evoked no response.

When at the close of a silent meal the time came for tea he complained to the waiter about it having previously been too cool and he liked it hot. I told him then about the tea bags in the pewter pitcher on our Italian ship. He said he'd never travel on an Italian ship anyhow, and he said this flatly as one would who had made his mind up on this very subject a long time ago. I said I missed getting tea in a pot and was disappointed to find tea served everywhere in a cup in Australia. He said the better places served tea in a pot. "Still," I said, "this train . . ." But the train he'd already written off. I said we even got tea served in a pot in the U.S. "With a tea bag?" he asked, with the faintest suggestion of a smile. "With a tea bag," I admitted, "but still in a pot."

Somehow it got close to what he might do for a living. I hadn't broached it; the topic was just there. He said he wasn't being secretive but it always took such a while to explain he'd rather not go into it. I said I wouldn't ask; I'd just imagine he was in some highly romantic field like MI5, and I was prepared to enlarge on this at length; but he showed no interest. So we let it lay and at last he said he'd tell what he did if I didn't ask any more. I implied that I'd cross my heart if he liked and he spilled the beans. He was in med'sin in connection with insurance but it was all pretty complicated . . . "Then you're a doctor?" "Yes."

We kicked the medical profession around then, comparing the degrees here and in the United States, and how a doctor reached the stage where he was entitled to be called mister. This, the Doctor said, only applied to surgeons; but then it turned out that all doctors were surgeons and—I may be wrong on this—the surgeon-mister was a specialist who mightn't do any cutting up at all.

AUGUST 27: Our last day of the trip dawned bright, with us still on the Nullarbor. I forgot to note that yesterday while we were in the lounge Candi spotted a flock (?) of emus and called out in time for me to see them in the distance. But we still maintained our record of having travelled the length and breadth of Australia without seeing an uncaged kangaroo. By the time we had breakfasted, dressed, and adjourned to the observation car the land was no longer flat and trees were rather plentiful. By noon—back on early time now—we had reached the Flinders Ranges, and the rail spur leading off to Woomera. We were still at lunch when we sighted Spencer Gulf.

None of our travelling companions seemed to have noted the absence of Aborigines along the way, in contrast to the Ghan. To my questions they could offer only the vaguest explanations. The Aborigines had been gathered up on reserves and missions. They used to be a dreadful nuisance flocking around the train whenever it stopped, demanding "two bob" (20 cents) before they'd let you

246

take their pictures. A lady from Perth said they definitely had been removed; and after they were gone the goats used to still meet the train to beg for lollies. "Were they their goats?" I asked. She didn't think they could be. They were just goats. But there were no goats anywhere along the line on this trip. The fact is that nobody displayed even a mild curiosity over what really might have happened to the Aborigines.

OCTOBER 23: We had our first taste of kangaroo for dinner last evening. Several months ago I began inquiring about it here, in Alice Springs, in Perth. Barry offered to shoot one for me the next time he went up bush. A local butcher said he'd see what he could do. I hated to leave the country without so much as a taste; and after all, if they're so plentiful they can be slaughtered for dog food . . .

I was told that the best of the kangaroo for meat is the hind quarters, but hardly anybody eats it nowadays. I've seen kangaroo tail soup, processed and tinned in Sydney, on display in a few food stores. It's one of the few Australian foods that gives a list of its ingredients on the label; and one of the ingredients is beef. But I didn't want soup, least of all canned soup, least of all soup containing beef. An elderly lady in Perth told me she often used to eat kangaroo when she was little, and that only certain small species —two to three feet high—are really palatable. She said the meat was quite dry and of a fine texture, dark, and that it made good rissoles. "You call them meatballs." These are fried in shortening and "are nice and moist." The manager of the shop in Alice Springs where Candi bought her koala bear made from kangaroo skin said the meat is very strong in flavour. "Australians don't seem to like it much, but I understand they eat a lot of it in America."

Brian Guest of the CSIRO said butchers in every State except Tasmania were forbidden by law to sell kangaroo unless it was dyed purple. This was because only Tasmania had inspectors to supervise the slaughtering and cutting. Yesterday Reg Thistledown and Dan Starr obtained three thick steaks for us quite matter-of-factly. They had simply inquired and learnt of an outfit which kills and cuts the meat and packs it in ice in a truck for shipment. I forbore to ask details, fearful of hearing something which would put me off it. As it was we ate with trepidation. (How does one get ptomaine poison?)

Candi insisted the meat had a taste, although the only taste it could have had was the vinegar, Worcestershire, mustard, and celery salt in which we had marinated it—or from some mutton broiled with the kangaroo for purposes of comparison. Actually the meat, apart from the marinade and flavour of broiling, had almost no taste—probably for want of hanging. It was exceptionally tender and without fat. Thus it is dry rather than juicy meat, quite edible and satisfying. We cooked only one of the three steaks just in case. We'll have the other two tonight and I hope we can soak some of the marinade out of them.

OCTOBER 25: After two or three cold and slightly wet days the sun is bright again this morning. Candi took a drive to Outer Harbour yesterday with Reg and Bubby and a load of kids in Reg's jeep, and had an amusing time with the steering wheel acting up. The Thistledowns and the Starr family, consisting of Dan and Petra, fourteen-year-old Preston, and eleven-year-old Heather, are getting ready to make a circuit of Australia which will take about five months. During this time the Starr children will study by correspondence. They will take two caravans, pulling one with the jeep; and Reg would like to have our car to pull the other. I told him we planned to sell it before leaving the country, but we're taking a trip to Canberra and the Snowy River Project ourselves as soon as school is out. However we might be able to part with it after that as we won't be using a car in Tasmania.

Reg's father ran a hotel in N.S.W. in his early days, some seventy years ago. Walking back and forth to his house he often tripped over a boulder in the road. So did everyone else. Once somebody had the energy to dig it up, and underneath was a huge gold nugget. He brought it to Thistledown and ordered drinks to be dispensed until the nugget's value was used up. Drinks were free to everybody in town. Strangers were given a free drink and sent on their way. For three years nobody in town did any work— no men at any rate—as they laboured to drink up the nugget. This nugget bought the Thistledown farm which carries, Reg says, 35,000 sheep, plus cattle whose numbers they don't trouble to count.

Our second taste of kangaroo, Saturday, was better than the first, although Candi wouldn't share it this time. Most of the marinade was drained and blotted off the meat and it was wrapped around bread stuffing and roasted. Peggy and I found it delicious, and told our donors so. They seemed pleased, even, I thought, relieved; they didn't act as though they meant to try any themselves.

OCTOBER 30: In Adelaide yesterday noon there were people lying and sitting, eating lunch on the North Terrace lawns. Nice days at this time of year are the best in Australia because the flies haven't reached the stage where you must keep a hand waving before your face.

For the past month a weed with a dozen or more bluish-purple flower heads on every stem has been growing wherever the grass is not mowed or cropped. It covers our back yard and on distant fields and hillsides spreads a violet hue over the ground, like the colour the French Impressionists used to represent shadows. Here in South Australia it is called Salvation Jane because the early herdsmen welcomed it as the first green feed after a summer drought. In Victoria, where the weed was less useful to livestock because rain is more certain and plentiful in that State, it was given a less flattering name.

Candi is into the final stretch of her exams preparation. She has made excellent progress in Maths the last few weeks and should pass unless she is seized by panic on examination day. I still have doubts about her comprehension of Physics; I'm hoping her memory of formulas and laws and definitions will see her through. She has been taking the dry run exams in these subjects, using the bound collections of those given in previous years. For the past few weeks in class she has done nothing else.

249

NOVEMBER 1: Dan Starr and his young German wife Petra called yesterday afternoon. Dan's first wife and the mother of his children died with their third child eight years ago. Petra has been in Australia four years. She came with her mother and brother and still has not accustomed herself to the climate. The hot summers bother her and so do the cold winters. She said she had never been so cold in northern Germany as in Adelaide—indoors. When she went out in the sun she felt warm enough. In fact she surprised her neighbours by the lightness of her outdoor clothing: a single cardigan when they might be wearing heavy coats. But she dreaded going back in and only felt warm when she was in bed. This is still so after four years. She misses the holiday that Easter was in Germany, a season of springtime, whereas here Easter comes in autumn. Dan said spring never means much to Australians. Summer, he said, is not a season to look forward to but to be endured. It is hot and dry; and from earliest days Aussies have hated summer. Autumn with its first rains is the season they prefer.

Dan said he couldn't understand why Americans, who are such nice people in all other respects, have so much racial trouble. He had never been able to make head or tail out of the Civil War. I said our South was like Western Australia. You couldn't find nicer people than the residents of either place, but their treatment of the Negroes on the one hand and the Aborigines on the other was shocking. Starr could see no connection between our Negroes and his Aborigines. Aborigines were clearly a lower order of man whereas Negroes were in every way the equal of whites. He felt Australians were doing everything possible for the Aborigines but the Aborigines were incapable of benefiting from it.

"Maxine Calder is a very pretty blonde student who is quiet. She introduced me to her mother. She is also a blonde, thin and very talkative. When she heard I was American she told me about her visit to America three years ago, and especially about Cincinnati. They took the Greyhound bus everywhere they went, and in this station in Cincinnati where they were waiting for the bus there was a Texan in his broad-brimmed hat; and a young Negro fellow came up and asked him where he was from, and he began to abuse him for the way they treated the Negro people in Texas. Then when he found out that the Calders came from Australia he said, 'Now you wouldn't treat Negro people like that in your country, would you?' She was quite embarrassed because she was thinking of the policy of not even allowing coloured people into their

country. So she didn't know what to say, but it didn't matter
because this young Negro fellow was able to carry the conversation
for everybody. He didn't stop talking and he wanted their address
and said he'd write to them. She didn't especially want to give him
their address. She was afraid he was not a very good type. She said
she didn't have a pen and he said, 'Oh, I've got a pen': but he
never did write.

"She said there was another native girl there with her little
child and she seemed quite embarrassed about this Negro lad who
was doing all the talking. (Mrs Calder called this Negro girl a
'native.') She said they saw this native girl getting a taxi. The taxi
driver first put her bags in the cab, and then a white couple came
along so he threw her bags out and said, 'You get another cab. I've
got a fare.' "

I told Dan my outstanding impression of Australians was their
amiability, and next to this their indifference. I can't say he acted
as though I'd really put my finger on something. He admired
rather the American character which he feels is the best in the
world because it's an alloy of various strains; and he hoped European immigration would do the same for Australia. He said before
the war you would hardly meet two non-Australians in a hundred
on the street. Now it was sometimes hard to find the Australians
among the migrants.

However, in support of my argument Mrs Starr mentioned a
meeting she'd had with an Englishman she hadn't seen for two
years—one of the rocket experts for the recent maximum security
Woomera experiments—and how she mentioned driving up to
Andamooka, getting lost, and blundering into Woomera. She
wasn't challenged, and drove all around the rocket pad. She told
this to the Englishman. "When were you there?" he asked sharply.
"A few weeks ago," she said, adding that it was about 1.30 in the
morning. "Ah well," he said, "there'd be no one on guard at that
hour."

36

"*Betty comes from Hartford, Connecticut. She has only been here three weeks and her impressions are still a bit muddled, but mostly she finds it hard to understand what people are saying. Going through Customs they had to ask her if she spoke English.*

"*After registering at the American Consulate we went to a place called the Manhattan Coffee Lounge because it sounded appropriate. It was a little hole in the wall at the top of a shop and we were the only ones there. I asked Betty about American universities and in particular whether American students think about things. This is what is concerning me more and more about Australia, that people don't discuss things much, or only a few do.*

"*Then she gave me an outline of the structure of a typical student body. You have the beatniks and 'arty types' that wear sloppy clothes and think they are intellectuals, but they just make her sick because they conform more than anyone else and don't have the strength of character to be individuals. Then you have the 'preppy types' that just think about boys the whole time and wear John Crundall of Norwich clothes. And then you get the types like Betty feels she is, that are true individuals, that do and think just what they believe in and don't conform to any sort of herd instinct. You can get in-betweens, too, like a friend of Betty's who liked to hang around with the 'arty types' but was pretty rich and had one John Crundall of Norwich outfit. But Betty thought that all the students did more talking about things and she thought that was because everyone lives on the campus so you can get to know each other a lot better.*

"*She is looking forward to going home, a bit. She couldn't stand to live in Australia. She thinks it is too apathetic. (I don't know where she picked that up from.) They don't get excited about anything here, not even elections. She told her father it was going to become the 51st State and he said Wall Street said so too. That is another thing that makes her mad, that they let Americans control all their big monopolies. And they don't teach Australian history in the schools. We picked up these booklets called an outline of American history at the Consulate and were both getting quite nostalgic about all those battles and things we had studied."*

The Starrs had hardly gone when we had a visit from a James Jeffries: an Australian by birth who migrated to America several years ago and returned last March with his wife and five or six kids to see his ailing father. He apparently meant to settle here again, worked as a fitter for Broken Hill Proprietary in Whyalla up to a month ago, and left because of the wind and dust. He has been away long enough to lose his taste for Australian food. He grouses about it now, feels he's undernourished. "You just have to learn to eat mutton," I told him. "This is a big problem Americans have, overcoming their distaste for mutton. You can't afford to eat beef. It costs as much here as in the U.S."

"Three times as much," said Jeffries, "when you consider relative wages."

He also complains of Australia's lack of political savvy, the arbitration system which he contends Andrew Carnegie tried to foist on the American workers, who would have none of it. Neither would they in Britain or Canada. "But here," Jeffries told his fellow unionists, "you are a defendant on trial in the Arbitration Court and have to prove your right to a decent wage."

He asked what I thought of the educational system. I said on the whole I thought it compared favourably with California. The American ideal was better, but in practice under local school board control the scholars were forced to shorten their steps to fit the dullards. Every pupil was automatically promoted each year; his parents would squawk to the school board if he weren't. They would also squawk if he were separated in any way from all the others in his class, so the pace of the whole class had to be geared down to let the ones who were behind catch up. Here there were as many as twelve so-called streams in every grade, a stream to suit every child's learning pace. This I liked.

Jeffries shook his head stubbornly. This "ramming and cramming" was no good. His kids were at the top in their classes so they must have been better educated before coming here. It turned out they'd been at the top in California too. They are especially good in English, and I conceded this was one subject invariably better taught in the United States than here; the reason being that there the emphasis is on English usage including speech. Here it is on literature and literary criticism—less useful in practical life but easier to tie up in little packets of knowledge that can be tested in a public examination.

Jeffries very much wants to go back to the United States, convinced now it's far and away the best country in the world. He had to leave it to fully appreciate it but, although he recognizes its failings, he gets positively starry-eyed now when he talks about it. Kennedy—the example of an Irish mick reaching the highest office in the world—symbolizes for him all that is best in the U.S. and the world as a whole. His blackest day was the day of "Jack's" murder; and he doesn't for one moment believe the Warren Commission uncovered the truth about it.

His chief regret is that he didn't become an American citizen. He'd led a couple of strikes and the Immigration Department had had him in for questioning. He'd taken the fifth amendment (refused to answer on the grounds that it might incriminate him) on a couple of them. But, I said, you'll have to answer the same questions if you try to get back in. He supposed so; money was the big problem though. "What about your family?" He could bring them back three times as fast working in the States: get a light housekeeping room for $8 a week and eat very well for $12— "pickles, beans Spanish style, chicken Spanish style." His eyes sparkled at the thought of the wonderful food he could eat.

Later on Candi was worried about Jeffries, asked if I'd pay his fare. I said that wasn't going to be his problem so much as getting back in. Would he get back in? "He seems to think he will," I said. "His five kids are all American. But if he doesn't he'll survive. Australia isn't that terrible, is it?"

NOVEMBER 8: Continuing with our rounds of farewells today we called on the Gallaghers, and later on the Sheppards whom we found about to go out and vote. Sophie Gallagher had already voted and deplored the preferential ballot which requires a voter to list his choices in numerical order for every candidate.

On the average at any given election one ballot out of every sixteen is spoilt or, to employ the euphemism favoured by election officials, is "informal." But this is perhaps the smallest part of the price Australians pay for one of the weirdest voting systems ever devised, a system which Sir Winston Churchill called "the worst of all possible plans . . . the stupidest, the least scientific and the most unreal." Under its terms an elector is forbidden to select a single candidate; he is required to vote for his worst enemy if he be a candidate, or lose his vote altogether. They tell the story of the blind voter in this predicament. "Is so-and-so running?" he asked the person assisting him. On hearing he was: "Put the bugger last."

If there are twenty candidates and a voter carefully lists his first nineteen preferences but forgets the twentieth his whole ballot is spoilt and the candidate at the top of the list, whom the voter really wanted, is deprived of his support. If, working his way through the maze of numbers and names, the voter gets all the numbers down but skips a number in the process, so that candidate number twenty becomes number twenty-one, the ballot is spoilt and his vote is lost. If he allots two candidates the same number, nineteen say, the ballot is spoilt; all his patient care with the first eighteen has been wasted.

This naturally leads to the practice of what is called donkey voting (numbering each name in the order it appears on the ballot): and it speaks volumes for Australian patience that only about one vote in fifty is such a donkey vote. Still it helps to give added value to the first places in the ballot. Places are decided by lot, making the choice of Prime Minister in some degree a gamble. To further confuse the voter, party designations are scrupulously left off the ballot. If James Johnson and John Johnson are candidates of two different parties it's up to him to remember whether his man's first name is James or John.

Political parties take advantage of the inevitable voter confusion by making deals with one another for second and lower preferences. The splinter parties in particular make their influence felt in this way, since only those ballots whose first preferences haven't gone to a winning candidate are counted again for second or lower preferences. Thus it often happens that a candidate who enjoys a clear lead on the first counting may fail to be elected when the votes for other candidates have been counted a second or a third time. As Sir Winston said, "The decision is to be determined by the most worthless votes given for the most worthless candidates."

When a voter goes to the polls (and he must go or risk a four-dollar fine) he encounters just outside the fence surrounding the polling place a small horde of party workers, each thrusting upon him a card detailing in carefully drawn pictures exactly what number to put where. He selects the card which puts the candidate he favours in first place and takes it into the booth with him. Only an over-nice concern for appearances forbids him to drop the card in the ballot box and return his unmarked ballot to the elections officer.

But the cards do have the saving virtue of keeping informal votes down around the level of one in sixteen. Without them it would be more like fifteen in sixteen.

Both Sophie and Diana said they took little interest in politics, left it to the men. They voted because they had to, and followed the card handed them by their party worker. Diana accepted all cards (except the Communist) so as not to give her hand away. Maurice also believed most voters went by the card. "How do you reconcile this slavish behaviour with the Aussie who's so famous for defying authority?" He shrugged.

NOVEMBER 12: Candi seems to have got through her Physics and two Maths exams relatively unscathed. At least she felt fairly comfortable doing them—though the Maths left her insufficient time to check the accuracy of her computations. Fortunately she has no exams scheduled for next week. The following Monday she is expected to be back in classes. Not for any good reason, just that there are a few more weeks for the term to run. However, we'll be in Canberra, having rented a furnished house for a week; then to Melbourne by way of the Snowy River Project, and by ferry to Tasmania.

Reg showed up yesterday to ask again about the car. It seems he wants to make a gift of it to the Starrs; their old Austin is about ready to conk out. I told him we were undecided about leaving Australia right away. If Candi passes all her exams she'll matriculate to University; whereas she'd likely be required to do at least another year in high school before an American university would admit her. However I realized I'd half promised him, and if he hasn't found anything else when we finish the Snowy River trip he can buy it.

NOVEMBER 13: Yesterday we made our first real trip over Australian highways, from Elizabeth through Adelaide, the Lofty Ranges and Murray Bridge to Bordertown, where we stayed the night. Our motel room was damp-smelling with an unscreened bathroom window and lumpy beds, and charged an exorbitant rent; but it could get it because its only real competition is the Australian licensed hotel. We arranged to have dinner rather than go on to a café in town where the choice was wider than steak. Our steak was described by the manager: "She fries it in butter. It's tender." So this was how it was done! Australian steak is more like thick sliced ham than sizzling beefsteak. It goes well with eggs as ham does, and may account for steak and eggs being the Australian national dish. The manager was a Dutchman, here twenty years,

who left Holland because of the insecurity. The country had been occupied by the Germans, and the Russians were only a few hundred miles away, and Australia seemed an extraordinarily safe part of the world. Chiang Kai-shek ruled China, the Dutch were firmly in control of Indonesia, and the French and British far eastern empires looked as strong as they had ever been. "Now see how things have changed!"

Nevertheless he thought Holland too crowded and the people too narrow-minded, whereas Australians were free and casual. "A good country to be in," echoed the lady at the next table, and she'd come out from England forty years ago. On balance yes, said the Dutch manager, though he missed the wild animals which were so numerous even on the outskirts of Utrecht. "When I first came here I expected to see all sorts of strange animals—kangaroos, wallabies, koala bears, emus . . . I did at least see rabbits. Now you don't see rabbits any more." But the English lady was sure there were still plenty of kangaroos in the outback. "They'll never destroy all the kangaroo," she said.

37

There were few billboards along the way, none whatever of the big 24-sheeters we used to see standing edge to edge along a busy American highway. Yet the road is busy enough. It is four lanes wide to the top of the Lofty Ranges and is the main route from Adelaide to Melbourne. The few notices I saw were directions to motels, petrol, and roadhouse vendors as we approached the larger towns. Elsewhere we passed through former desert made into grassland by the restoration of trace elements to the soil, and elevated now to dairy production. It is still not prosperous to look at but doubtless returns a good living to the men who acquired the land cheaply. Something of the sort is also going on at Esperance in Western Australia, only I understand much of the cheap land was first obtained at fifty cents an acre by an American syndicate which is reselling it to farmers at $200 an acre.

This used to be known as the Ninety-Mile Desert. The grass is tall and dry and the trees have that peculiar dark desert green about them still. Like other gum trees they imitate the non-gums in their different environments. There are gums that can soak up water like willows, gums that have leaves almost as narrow as pine needles so they hardly need transpire, gums as big, old, and rot-resistant as California redwood, gums with white bark like birch trees and mottled bark like hemlock. These look like the salt cedar of Arizona.

The Murray—Australia's biggest and best-known river—is not nearly as wide as I imagined it. It may be losing some of its normal flow to irrigation works in the citrus groves and vineyards up around Renmark and Mildura. Murray Bridge is a pleasant town, a dairying centre. We ranked beside a small public park with a colourful wooden pergola surrounded by trees and grass. Peggy made tuna fish sandwiches and we bought Coca Cola and beer in the regular Australian-size bottle. Such a bottle is enough for three, but Peggy was driving and wanted little and neither did Candi, so I was left with the lion's share of it and got terribly sleepy during the afternoon. Hence most of my recollections are of the road through the Lofties in the morning.

We topped Mt Lofty and looked back at Adelaide between hill-tops, spread out like a river delta. Then we drove through literally millions of gum trees and got the true feel of Australia for the first time. It's incredible how many gum trees there are and how little else besides gum trees. Their dusty green colours the whole country-side, their feather-like tufts of leaves springing lightly up in the air make a landscape unforgettably Australian. Contrary to the opinion of some travellers there is no monotony in gum trees. Their variety, though subtle, is infinite. I find it as easy to understand the exiled Australian's longing for them, as it is difficult to explain why his stay-at-home brother won't tolerate them near his suburban cottage.

Near the town where we stopped for lunch today Peggy and Candi caught sight of a man lying on the ground close to the edge of the road. He could have been drunk or dead; it was an unlikely place to be merely taking a snooze. By the time all this sank in we were nearer the town than him, so I stopped at the post office to report it. The clerk said it was a police matter and pointed to a man in uniform. "Don't tell me!" said the policeman. "I'm off duty now." He then proceeded to instruct me on how to find the police station.

Two police detectives called to inquire about the car. Did we still want to claim ownership and bring it back out of the desert or were we giving it up? No, I said, we weren't giving it up but neither did we claim ownership. Its owner was the insurance company, the car having been stolen, and the insurance company must decide what to do with it. One of the detectives said, "It wasn't stolen. Thistledown bought the car from you and has merely failed to pay you for it." "Who says so?" "Thistledown himself"; and they showed us his picture, twinkling eyes, beard and all. "Was this the man?" Little by little I wormed out of them these facts:

The police in South Australia had interviewed Reg personally in June. They had no trouble finding him because when our description was circulated he was serving a six-months' sentence for theft. He told them then that he never meant to steal the car. He intended to give the money to Candi when he got back to Adelaide, only he had lost her address. While the detectives were telling us all this one of them thumbed through a half-inch-thick

sheaf of documents, holding them close to his body. I didn't ask what they were, though I guessed they must refer to Thistledown; and only at the end of the interview did the detectives tell us. They were records of convictions on at least twenty other thefts!

I told the detectives there was a quotation in Lawrence's Kangaroo which exactly fitted the situation: "Every man his own policeman"; and if the word of a convicted felon is accepted against that of his accuser it would have the advantage of making work easier for the police, but if the process went on long enough Australia would get filled up with crooks. One of the detectives muttered, "It already is." He said they have five cases like this in Sydney every week.

Still Thistledown was an old man and hadn't long to live. Nothing could be served by prosecuting him. "And the insurance company?" "You haven't a hope. You said you gave Thistledown permission to take the car." "But don't you recognize fraud in this country? Here is a convicted confidence man. He induces a rich widow to let him hold her diamonds, for a valuation or something. Wouldn't that be larceny by trick?" Well—yes, but it didn't apply to automobiles.

When the detectives left I called Bagarion, our chicken-hearted solicitor, to tell him about Reg's criminal record and to ask if this wouldn't help in our case against the insurance company. Could they now continue to maintain it was a simple case of false pretences and that they weren't liable? This proved beyond all doubt that Reg had set out deliberately to swindle us of the car.

"Don't tell the insurance company that!" Bagarion warned. "They'll say that if he had such a bad police record you should never have entered into any dealings with him."

I couldn't help wondering, were there many people in the world who had such a low opinion of their own countrymen? What Bagarion was saying in effect was: "Don't sell your car to any Australian until you've had a police check made on him!"

In due course Bagarion informed us that the insurance company had decided to pay our claim. In the form we were required to sign they described the case as one of "larceny by trick." They had apparently done their own research into Reg's background and when Bagarion's letter reached them they realized they wouldn't have much chance if the case went to court. They couldn't know that Bagarion had no intention of taking them to court.

Remarkable things these solicitor's letters. If you have any grievance at all, your neighbours making too much noise, or a collision, or too high a gas bill, you get your solicitor to write a letter. What makes it all the more wonderful—if Bagarion's style was any criterion—a letter is one thing a solicitor can't write.

During the football season in Victoria a magistrate fined a man $10 plus $7.50 costs, in default seven days gaol. In the same week a judge in Sydney put a youth on a $500, three-year good behaviour bond—no gaol sentence, no fine. The Victorian offender did the unforgivable. He took a football which had been kicked over his fence and into his vegetable garden; he put it on a chopping block and hit it with an axe. The Sydney youth's offence was less grave. All he did was jump on another boy and take a running kick at his head. He crushed the boy's skull of course and killed him. In putting him on a good behaviour bond the judge said, "The thing that sticks in my gizzard is that you have not expressed one word of remorse for what you did."

Australian jurisprudence does have its extremes. The publishers of a Melbourne magazine ran an article poking mild fun at the royal family. In a purported interview they quoted Prince Philip saying the Queen nagged him and Prince Charles sold the tiles off Buckingham Palace roof to raise pocket money. They were dragged into court and solemnly charged with no less a crime than sedition. A South Australian child of nine was put on parole for nine years for a first offence of breaking and entering to steal $30. She said she wanted the money, most of which was recovered, to buy Easter eggs. Another first offender, a woman of sixty-one in Wollongong, was sentenced to fourteen days' gaol for stealing four packs of cigarettes. In the same week a youth in Brisbane Magistrate's Court admitted shooting and wounding a young girl with a rifle. The charges against him were dismissed when he pleaded, "I wanted to teach her a lesson for coming down to us in a bikini and daring me to shoot her." When a Western Australian University lecturer was given ten years for the murder of his four-year-old mentally retarded son, a public outcry went up against the sentence's severity. The child had developed the habit of poking his tongue out all the time and, said the defendant, "this affected me badly because it gave the boy the appearance of being so unnormal." A case of justifiable homicide.

Reporting crime also has its anomalies. When a pedestrian is hit and killed by a drunken driver it is always done anonymously. Unless the driver himself is killed his name doesn't appear in the newspapers until the case comes to court; and with very little trouble he can have it suppressed. Little wonder a Sydney judge could state that in nineteen years on the bench he could not recall a verdict of guilty in a manslaughter case involving a road accident.

When a Sydney man held a nine-year-old boy hostage and barricaded himself in a house against police after firing three shots at a fourteen-year-old girl, the story naturally was a front-page feature, together with a large photo of the house ringed by besieging police. But nowhere in the story was a name given for the man, the boy, the girl, a neighbour who sheltered the girl, or the divorced wife of the man who was brought to the scene to plead with him to give himself up. It would have been libellous to identify the man before his case went to court.

On the other hand an Adelaide case that did come to court and was repeatedly adjourned was faithfully reported after each adjournment. It concerned the hearing of cross-petitions for divorce. The husband (named) was suing his wife (named), alleging adultery with two men (both named with addresses). Names and details were given in the papers every time the story appeared. In the end the husband withdrew his suit and the divorce was granted to the wife on grounds of habitual cruelty.

Australia's cleverest criminals are her confidence men, her Reg Thistledowns. In 1967 Scotland Yard devoted a special supplement of its Police Gazette to them—a signal honour, one that only a handful of national rogues have ever deserved. Among those named were Dinkum Dick, Wee Jummy, Verbal, Pat the Liar, Australian Jack, The Swan, and Glasses.

Approaching another village later in the afternoon—and there are virtually no farm houses visible in the open country between villages—we passed a series of roadside grass fires, with carfuls of men running across the road to beat at them with hessian bags. Soon a fire engine showed up to help them, and in the town we saw the cause: a caravan with its rear burnt out and a burnt mattress protruding from it. The grass is as dry as powder and even a small fire is difficult to put out. It was lucky this was Saturday afternoon with plenty of manpower available.

The land looks poor, yet I understand the soil here in the Wimmera north of the Grampians is better than average for Australia. The farmers of this nation are battling a far from friendly environment: thin, poor soil, too little rain or else flood. About all they can really count on is the sun; and the midday and afternoon sun here is so hot and bright there are mirages in the fields of growing wheat and grass. Lakes appear. Distant trees shimmer and dance. Single strands of wheat, light and bright against the drabber ground, spread out sideways, widening in a wavy distortion like an image in a trick mirror as the car speeds past. I saw some real lakes as well, and billabongs with drinking sheep; galahs and green native parakeets, and roads of a quality inferior to South Australia's.

What the countryside seemed to need most was an occasional farm house. Are even the wheat farms here owned by big syndicates? We saw a camp of itinerant harvesters, their square tents in two neat rows and their big machinery close at hand. We also saw some eucalyptus oil works, Rube Goldberg contraptions of chimneys and old steam engines, that I first thought might be primitive moonshine distilleries.

When John Brown's baby had a cold upon his chest, as recounted in an old parody on The Battle Hymn of the Republic, *and "they rubbed it well with eucalyptus oil" the oil undoubtedly came from Australia. Now even the oil for Australian babies' chests is as apt to come from any of twenty-six other countries, out of leaves grown on trees from Australian seeds. Like kangaroos, Aborigines, and other things once exclusively Australian, the eucalyptus oil distilleries are vanishing, and those that remain are up to a hundred years old—dilapidated relics consisting of an array of pipes, a vat to collect the distillate, and a steam boiler patched all over with rags and clay.*

38

It is a commonplace to say the little towns are all alike. Their houses range along both sides of the road, each with its low front fence and high board fence on back and sides. Tin roofs run in a nearly straight line from peak to verandah edge. The business streets of the smallest towns still have trees to find shade under, but the large ones are open to the full glare of the sun. Such a one is Bendigo, famous in Australian gold-mining annals, a centre of the first rush which occurred shortly after California's, of a will-of-the-wisp echo in 1950, and of an eight-pound nugget literally picked up off the street in the mid-1960s. A forty-year-old carpenter was walking along the road soon after graders had been at work on it when he noticed "a great shining lump," picked it up, and found he held in his hands a solid slab of gold, seven inches by five, and an inch and a half thick. It had been freshly scraped by the grader blade. "I put it in my tucker bag and told nobody about it until I could get to the bank"—all in the best tradition of Bendigo, Australia's Golden City, where miners kept only the nuggets and threw the dust away. Three such nuggets found in 1852 weighed respectively over twenty-one pounds, nearly twenty-one pounds, and thirty-four pounds. As late as 1868 the fields could still yield a near-eighteen-pounder, after which quartz mining went on for nearly a century and finally stopped, not when the gold ran out, but when its depth was too great for economic recovery.

The Troegers lived in the centre of a large dusty paddock, iron-fenced all around. Their rented house was of corrugated iron too, a not uncommon building material in small cities like Bendigo. From the outside it could hardly look worse. Yet they had fruit trees, chickens, a galah bird which Rudi found and which spoke two languages. It startled us when we entered the house by calling out, "Don't go!"

Inside, the house was a model of German cleanliness and cosiness, with a fireplace stove in the kitchen besides an old gas stove used for cooking in summer. We gathered in the small lounge in front of another fireplace and around a low table where, in time, we had excellent coffee and hors d'oeuvres of cheese and salami. Rudi was born in eastern Germany in what is now Poland, then was crowded out of his home when his father remarried after his mother's death from TB. He and his full siblings became stepchildren. At fourteen he went to the Ruhr to apprentice as a mechanic, but was called up at the outbreak of war and spent nine years fighting or in a Russian prison camp. On his release he came back to the Ruhr and everything was changed. None of his old friends knew him. Nobody was interested in anybody else, just making money to buy a bigger TV set than the next one.

He became a trucker carting produce into the heart of the Ruhr around Essen, so highly industrialized all its food had to come from outside. There he met Greta and they married and their children were born.

He worked as a mechanic and lived in a fourth floor flat where there was no scope for the children. After twelve hours a day seven days a week he counted and distributed his pay and found he had none left over. "But it's different there now," I suggested. "No. It's just a big shiny bubble. It will blow up. I get letters. I read between." With his fingers he traced lines and pointed between them.

They began to think of migrating, their choice resting between the United States, Canada, and Australia. Rudi read a lot about Australia, said if only half were true it would be heaven. (And just about half was true.) He talked to people and their stories made it seem you could pick up money in the streets. His wife's brother was here but wouldn't sponsor them, although sponsorship meant nothing more than assuring them a roof to stay under and the promise of a job. There were no jobs to be had in America. And Canada was "a cold country and cold people." I demurred at this but he knew two German families who had been there and left to come to Australia.

Then the Australian fever began to take effect. Everybody was thinking of coming to Australia. More than any other country Australia wanted them. So they came. It cost nothing. They were put in a hostel in the Riverina, having come over in a special migrant ship with 800 other Germans, some Danes, Yugoslavs, Balts,

266

etc. West Germany was the jumping off place for east Europeans. The refugee camps became recruiting grounds for Australian employers.

The Riverina hostel would accommodate up to 10,000, of different nationalities but grouped each with his own kind. The Troegers had three rooms and board, all free, plus nine dollars a week unemployment benefits until they found work. Then, if they elected to stay at the hostel, they paid $15 a week board and room. Most people moved out after a few weeks of work. The Troegers stayed on. Rudi took jobs cleaning toilets and picking fruit. Harvesting was the only job, apart from their regular trade, that migrants were forbidden to turn down; so the hostel served as a pool of seasonal harvest labour paying $29 a week for 40 hours. There was virtually no community life in the hostel.

When they moved it was because an acquaintance they'd made on the ship found Rudi a job and offered them temporary housing in Ballarat. Housing was extremely scarce. They paid $20 out of Rudi's $28 weekly wages just for rent, leaving hardly enough to buy food. They had since moved to Bendigo and brought the rent down to $10; other expenses: $5 on a car, including replacement

267

and 200 miles a week driving costs, and $28 for food, beer, and household essentials. Clothes were variable. A school uniform for Berthe, including two summer and two winter frocks, blazer, and raincoat (but not shoes) cost $120. Both parents now worked, and he didn't argue when I said he probably earned $40-$44 a week. When he bought bread he insisted on sweet and sour (white with some rye in it). The regular Aussie bread stuck in his throat—and he opened his mouth and pointed to where it stuck.

For four years from 1945 to 1949 Rudi was a prisoner of war of the Russians working three shifts, a total of sixteen hours, in between six four-mile walks to and from the wharves of Stettin and his camp. They loaded huge cartons. Couldn't tell what was in them till one broke open. "Guess what it was," he challenged me with a wicked grin. "Cleaned used red bricks!" Other boxes had clothes in them, "old clothes you wouldn't wear." The Russian was good and kind, though, until he got drunk. Then he went crazy.

Once in camp Rudi was hungry for a smoke. (He opened his mouth and grasped his throat to show how hungry he was.) He was hungry for a smoke. A Russian general (hard g) walked through, reached in his trousers pocket (Rudi did also) and took out a package of cigarettes, put one in his mouth, lit it, and put the package back in his pocket. (In went Rudi's own hand.) Rudi approached him, said, "Tovarish General, dye-me cigarette." The General stopped, looked at him, pulled the cigarettes out of his pocket, and flung the package at him. Rudi grabbed them eagerly and put two in his mouth.

"A German general would have shot me, right there. A British or American general would maybe have shot me. The Russian gave me cigarettes. That's how they are." "Bad and good," said Greta. Rudi nodded.

"The people are so poor. They smoke mahorka. It comes from the strings of the tobacco plant. They carry it loose in their pocket. When they want a smoke they reach in their pocket"—as did Rudi—"take out a handful of mahorka. Then from the other pocket they take torn sheets of Pravda. Pravda *is their newspaper. They tear it in strips, roll the mahorka in it. Then s-z-z-t." Rudi ran his tongue over an imaginary cigarette and stuffed it in his mouth. He coughed to show how the combination of mahorka and* Pravda *must taste.*

He said he'd never hold a rifle again, and demonstrated by sighting an imaginary rifle. War was never any good; "kill people for nothing." "For money," corrected Greta. "The capitalists . . ." "No," said Rudi with a firm shake of the head, "For nothing."

He was in the Brandenburg Division, a special outfit engaged against guerillas in Yugoslavia, Poland, Ukraine. He'd seen them here in Australia, Yugoslavs, Poles, Ukrainians, Greeks, who'd fought beside him against the partisans. All afraid to go home. Had been members of the S.S. in their own countries. "S.S.?" I inquired. "Secret police," said Greta. "They run to the winning side," said Rudi. "When we're ahead they're with us. When the Russians are winning they go with them. Whichever side is winning."

On the docks at Stettin there were 2,000 ordinary prisoners, 1,000 German S.S. The food got so bad the S.S. went on strike, resisted all threats, and won. From then on the S.S. had good food, the rest just as bad. Such an incident only heightened respect for the S.S. whom the soldiers already believed were near-supermen. They were branded, however, each with his blood group letter tattooed under his arm. The German plan had been to tattoo all soldiers but they never carried it out past the S.S. Hence the Russians easily spotted them when they undressed to have their clothes disinfected. Rudi saw such a group of youngsters, seventeen and eighteen years old. Before they were identified he set to work slicking off the tattoo with a razor blade. Another German saw him, "a spy."

"What did you do to him?"

"Drowned him."

"What?"

"Drowned him."

"Drowned him?"

"In the toilet."

NOVEMBER 14: The memorable things about today's journey were Glenrowan and the smell of eucalyptus—a clean, pungent, medicinal odour—in the heat as we passed among the gum trees lining the road. It was a pleasant change from the diesel fumes belching out of the overhead exhaust pipes of the large semis. I wonder that the unions of Australia, which have so effectively closed down the movies, shops, and bars on Sunday, do nothing about the truck-driving. I even saw one carrying coal. And parallel to the railway line.

We were now on the Hume, Australia's best-known thoroughfare, the major link between Melbourne and Sydney. In the world of autobahns and freeways it doesn't fit, but measured alongside the other roads of the country it seems almost a superhighway. What it is actually is a relatively wide two-lane road of reasonably smooth surface, with passing going on as though it were three lanes. Often we were one of three cars abreast. The best thing about it is that trees are still allowed to grow beside it. Because of the trees and the absence of billboards the Hume is as pretty a cross-continental highway as one is likely to find anywhere, certainly prettier than any in the U.S.

The land is cleared, fenced, and gently rolling, the grass yellow and sometimes waving, but little livestock is visible except clustered under an occasional tree. We passed a few swagmen's camps outside the fences—a piece of canvas laid over a rope and a fire burning in front. We passed innumerable cars with their bonnets (U.S. hoods) up. I believe the first thing an Aussie driver does when he stops in the country is lift his bonnet. If an emergency, like his wife's skirt catching on fire, should make the stop necessary he'd say while jumping out: "Hang on a minute. Just let me bung up the bonnet." One of the causes of a Volkswagen owner's feeling of inferiority in a land overrun by Holdens is that he has no bonnet to raise. You never see a Volks stopped beside the road.

Eastern Victoria is Ned Kelly country and Glenrowan, where Australia's one authentic national hero made his last stand, is its centre. An ideal setting it is too for a Ned Kelly movie, the bushranger on a horse and fitted with his home-made coat of mail, galloping over rolling fields dotted with clumps of eucalyptus; its hills and distances perfect for moustached and helmeted constables running in hot pursuit. Nor, I think, would it be necessary to build a replica of the Glenrowan Inn where the constables finally closed in on Kelly. The present Glenrowan Hotel would serve excellently: it is old and rakish enough.

Professor Hobson had an interesting anecdote to tell concerning the great influenza epidemic of the first World War. Brought into the country by disabled troops returning from the trenches it spread like wildfire, killing thousands and defying all medical efforts to check it. Finally in desperation the Government of New South Wales required every person to wear a tight-fitting gauze mask over nose and mouth when in public. All over Sydney you saw people in these masks, in shops, offices, factories, on the streets; and no one went anywhere without his mask. A doctor living in Balmain rebelled and refused to wear one. He was arrested and tried and acquitted. His attorney cited an old law dating from Ned Kelly days which explicitly forbade the wearing of a mask in public. You might be a bush-ranger! Like another

270

and slightly more recent law prohibiting bathing on a public beach between sunrise and sunset it had never been repealed.

Coming back from dinner (tea in Australia) this evening in Albury we met a young fellow carrying home two large bottles of beer, plus no telling how much inside him. He said he'd been in a blue and got his right eye cut open. It had happened before to his left eye, never his right, but this time he ducked the wrong way or he'd have got it in the left again. And not with a fist but a bar stool. I said I didn't know you could buy beer on Sunday. Well he had it, didn't he? What was I doing in Australia? "Looking over the country. I figure we might buy it. We already own most of it as it is." "Well I'll tell you," he said confidentially, "I'd rather you blokes would own it than those bloody poms." He invited us home to meet his wife. Said she wasn't much to look at, tall and thin, but she was a good woman. "I'm sure she would be. You'd know how to pick one." "No," seriously, "she's not a good sort, but she's a good woman."

39

NOVEMBER 15: The region we've driven through this morning, a region of sheep, dairying, and some wheat, has been hilly and enchantingly rural. I still miss seeing houses though. When Aussies speak of filling the empty spaces of their vast continent they mean the Centre and the North, but they needn't look so far afield. Here in the shadow of Sydney and Melbourne there are a few small towns but virtually no country residents. From Yass to Canberra is some of the prettiest scenery I've seen anywhere, all rolling hills of pale gold accented with spots of dark eucalyptus green. I would think though that the bucolic surroundings of Canberra must have some effect on the legislators and civil servants; the capital is just a bit too remote, within a nation that is itself pretty remote. But it does have a magnificent setting.

NOVEMBER 16: There is space and to spare in Canberra, and well-paved roads or boulevards spanning this space in all directions; and trees growing luxuriantly along all these roads. And as you look at it coming toward the town there are houses spread out over the space. Nor are they so loosely or casually spread if the street we are on is any criterion. Our neighbours breathe down our necks on both sides. There are shops and public buildings at the city centre across the lake, a horde of traffic last evening coming out of the centre, and two inept policemen at each important intersection trying to regulate it.

Miss Cavanagh, ordinarily the most serene and amiable of maidenly women, entered enthusiastically with our cabbie into a condemnation of policemen on point duty. Much as I had been told of the Australian dislike for lawmen such bitterness I hadn't believed; but it doesn't apply to all police, just traffic officers. The cabbie said his own brother turned bad when he became one.

Perhaps as we look around more I'll see other things to approve, even signs of people really living here. Because this is my strongest impression of Canberra. I see people but they all look to be sightseers like ourselves.

The lake is pretty of course, with its straw-coloured banks and the mountain behind it; and the land is kept (or at least still is) free of everything save trees on the far side of the road; so that here at any rate one can see Canberra without its incredibly ugly houses and shops. Williams on *The Australian* told me people complain because every block of land they buy is subject to control over what they can do with it. I can only protest that the controls have either begun to be exercised too late or were never stringent enough. Elizabeth, less well-planned than Canberra, is better looking because what plan there was has been or is being carried through. In Canberra the carrying through pretty well stopped with the trees. The older sections especially, with their high fences and hedges and miscellany of outbuildings packed close against them, are not far from looking like slums. The downtown office and store buildings haven't even the excuse of being old. The town is new. But its architecture (and this I'm afraid extends to its public buildings and memorials) echoes the worst of the 1920s. Here on a new stretch of land, laid out and planned as perhaps no other city has ever been, are the monstrosities of Los Angeles's 1920s bungalows. The slapped together shopping arcades, office blocks, and stores may in time be demolished to make room for something else. But the bungalows are here for the life of Canberra, an incubus on a city that was only truly beautiful while it was as yet unbuilt. Then it had trees, boulevards, bridges, the lake, and the golden grass rolling to the water's edge, and the mountains. These it still has if you stay close to the lake and out of sight of the bungalows.

NOVEMBER 17: We began our tour of public buildings with Parliament House. We had some little trouble finding it, for it is far from being the most imposing building in town. It is a temporary structure that comes so close to being permanent, the guard at the desk, a man of about fifty, thinks he won't be around when the permanent building is opened. It will take, he said, ten years to build, and ten years before that for the legislators to make up their minds what to build. He likes Canberra. Had lived in Sydney but couldn't stand the pressure and the dirt. A shirt would get soiled almost as soon as you put it on. "The flies don't bother you?" Yes, there were quite a few little flies. This was due to the livestock all around Canberra. But the mosquitoes were worse than the flies.

273

His walls and ceilings would sometimes be covered with them. "The flies at least don't bite."

"Not these flies. But we do have biting flies. Sand flies. If one bites you below the eye you'll swell up like this." And he held his hand six inches from his face.

We saw the House of Representatives chamber and Candi had the thrill of sitting at one of the desks. Our guide addressed us with elocutionary precision, emphasizing conjunctions and putting equal stress on all syllables of a word. Then we went across to the Senate chamber and saw where Her Majesty sat to open Parliament in a scene vividly potrayed in a painting hung in the Hall of Kings. We also saw one of the sixteen extant original pages of Magna Carta in a case filled with argon capable of warding off deterioration for 2,000 years. Candi, as I say, was greatly impressed by Parliament and declared that if she lived in Canberra she would attend every session. She very much wished we'd be around when the new session opens in February.

The Anatomy Building has a comprehensive exhibit of Aboriginal lore, custom, artifacts, and history, including the presumed origin of the people. The suggestion is made that the Australoid is not merely a different race, but a different sort of man—perhaps not really a man at all—descended from a missing link of its own. This I am satisfied is pure anthropological humbug.

NOVEMBER 18: I have one more observation of Canberra as a part of my first general impressions. Walter B. Griffin designed the city but Australia made it, and only the trees and boulevards—and the lake—belong to Griffin. He could never have guessed how perfectly his plan in other respects dovetailed with the Australian penchant for suburbia. Canberra, unlike other Australian capitals, is not a city overwhelmed by a proliferation of suburbs. It is the suburbs themselves without a city.

NOVEMBER 19: We completed our formal tour yesterday by visiting the War Memorial, enthusiastically recommended on all hands as "the finest in the world," "ten times as good as any other," a place where "you could spend all day and never see half of it." We didn't spend the day but no doubt we could have. Like all Australasian war memorials this is primarily devoted to "the Great War" when Australia, her historians feel, came of age. There is no disputing something decisive happened to Australia at this time, and the profligate blood-letting at Gallipoli gave it a kind of sacred character, like a schoolboy oath sealed in blood. To the historians this decisive event was Australia's debut into the larger world of the great powers to take her own place among them.

Somehow I don't see it that way. Gallipoli was a British imperial operation aimed as much at her imperial Russian ally as her Turkish enemy. There was no particular coming of age for Australia in being merely the hand that got burnt while reaching for a British chestnut. What did happen, I believe, was the unifying of Australia in a renewed pledge of allegiance to the British crown. However strong or weak it may have been, republicanism died at Gallipoli along with several thousand republicans. Since the second World War Australia has loosened her ties with Britain, or had them loosened for her. Anzac remains today a symbol of something believed to have been fine which is irrecoverably lost.

So the symbol shines in the War Memorial exhibits, and even the Great War itself is made to appear beautiful—as it no doubt was by comparison with later and future wars. We see souvenirs of heroism, lucky accidents, humorous situations and events. Two cases with their displays of direction signs, battered helmets, rusty guns, and other mementoes of time and place produce a veritable nostalgia. The souvenirs and dioramas of the second World War and Korea are wrapped in no such glamour. Shiny and new-looking, the souvenirs appear to have been crafted especially for exhibition here or surely acquired after deliberate search. Those of the Great War have the look of things spontaneously donated and tossed thereafter into a general bin, to be resurrected later and tagged.

NOVEMBER 20: Graeme Williams's main reason for liking Canberra is on account of his kids, five and three. The eldest boy was in a Catholic school in Sydney. There were seventy in a class and the teachers were so overworked the Williamses had made up their minds to transfer the boy to a State school. In Canberra however the church schools are the equal of the State schools and the State schools are the best in the country. They come under N.S.W. Education Department supervision, but in buildings, equipment, and teachers' salaries they far surpass the rest of the State.

Williams said his wife finds the cost of living 20 per cent higher than in Sydney, and she misses her mother and brothers, but he is sure she prefers Canberra otherwise. Because of the high cost of living the rule is for wives to work, and many men have two jobs. He knows one personally who has three: milkman early morning, office clerk by day, and barman in a club in the evening. And there is, he says, little likelihood of living costs falling inasmuch as the existing retailers occupy the only freehold land in the city, and the city planners won't allow outsiders to take up leases.

We walked to town yesterday and joined other tourists shopping

275

among the restaurants, reading the posted menus. We settled on a shop specializing in fish, and shared a table with a young Anglican priest and a sheep farmer. They were in Canberra for the day on business. The farmer had apprenticed as a jackaroo, having lived his youth in Sydney, and now owns a station north of Yass—about 100 miles from Canberra. Most of the stations in N.S.W. and Victoria are owner-operated, he says, though companies have started to move into Victoria. And while it is true that absentees now own much in Northern Territory and Western Australia the first stations there were also pioneered by individuals. The big job today is farm improvement, to be able to stock more beasts. This is what all farmers are working at, supplying soil deficiencies, phosphates in particular, but especially putting in new grasses better able to resist drought and give nourishment over more months of the year. The most successful of these new grasses was developed in the last few years, and different varieties are now being bred for different localities. It's an Australian project.

The priest is the son of a sheep farmer who sometimes regrets leaving the farm. He wasn't prepared to say whether Australians are irreligious, although the farmer said they are. Besides his local church he preaches at two other small-town churches each Sunday, one at 8.00 a.m., one at 11.00 a.m., and one at 7.00 p.m. The morning service may have thirty or forty in attendance, the evening service as few as six, but he hates to quit because of disappointing the six.

Only one Australian marriage in nine is a civil ceremony. Of the remainder nearly a third are Anglican; another near-third are Roman Catholic; a quarter are about equally divided between the Methodist and Presbyterian churches. Although 30 per cent of adults never go to church, virtually the entire population professes to adhere to some religious faith at census time, 36 per cent as Anglicans, 25 per cent as Roman Catholics, 10 per cent Methodists, 9 per cent Presbyterians. In numbers the Roman Catholic Church is growing by far the fastest. Its rate of growth, too, is higher than that of any faith save the Orthodox Catholic and the Lutheran, but these together account for only three per cent of the religious population.

After lunch we visited the display of the National Capital Development Commission and saw all the good things in store for the city in the next five years: new suburbs, schools, playgrounds, parks, sewers, car parks, public buildings, and monumental edifices such as only a city with unrestricted access to the public purse can ever aspire to. The farmer had said Canberrans were self-centred, looking on themselves as a chosen people able to command anything from the Government. Canberra is to Australia, however, what Versailles was to the France of the Bourbons: its country's showcase to the world. I talked with the Development Commission attendant, a lady who has been in Canberra forty years and only recently decided she likes it here. She likes it, not because of its splendours present and future, but because it is clean and quiet and free of slums. She especially likes the neighbourhood shopping centres.

"A pity you have to drive to them though," I said. "Nobody here ever walks."

"That is so, isn't it? I hadn't realized it before. When my husband and I first moved here we used to walk everywhere. Now there's a car for every three residents and even the young people in school have to have one."

Today Peggy took the car and shopped for the weekend. Then we drove around a bit, finding it pleasant along a boulevard running south and up a hill, where the houses are large and sometimes handsome, the blocks are wider and deeper, and their lawns sweep down to the road without any footpath crossing them. After all, of what use is a footpath to a people without feet? There are fine views of the city, lake, hills, and some splendid gum trees. Here in this city where trees of every variety have been planted the gums look best of all.

NOVEMBER 21: We attended communion at the Anglican Church of St John the Baptist, one of the oldest structures in Canberra, with services dating back to the middle of the last century —long before there was a Canberra. The sermon was short and the theology, I thought, surprisingly liberal. The rest of the day was hot and very fly-ey. We ate a poor lunch of stale bread and corned beef and sketched the distant hills and the sky full of clouds; and came home to a delicious bottle of beer.

"The service was beautiful. I have come to like the Anglican services because of that. All the ritual and chanting and things. This one was especially effective because they had all the chants and prayers and Apostles creeds in the first half of the service and you went up and down on your knees all the time then. After that you sat down and they turned off the lights in the church and just left them on the minister and he gave his sermon."

NOVEMBER 22: The wealthier legations occupy hilltop estates visible to tourists but cushioned by spacious grounds from noisy neighbours. "Mount Vernon" consists of a number of red brick two-storey buildings in restoration Georgetown (Maryland) style of architecture, on a road along which scarcely any traffic goes except a rubberneck bus. For the U.S. ambassador and his staff Canberra is a serene country retreat, a place of quiet and peace for restoring nerves and catching up on sleep lost in the more exciting diplomatic posts. Many of the poorer legations, like India, Burma, and Ceylon, occupy houses in ordinary residential streets, distinguished from their neighbours only by a flag at the top of a tall staff on their front lawn and the inevitable black ambassadorial limousine parked in the drive or carport. For them, as for ordinary folk, Canberra is a place of dogs, crowing roosters, neighbours speeding parting guests by gathering round the car and talking at the top of lubricated voices, the early morning shouts and clatter of garbage collectors, and the smells of cooking onions and burning rubbish.

40

NOVEMBER 23: We left Canberra, after some difficulty repacking the car, just before noon. The yellow rolling pastureland was pretty along the road south to Cooma and the mountains were actually a vivid blue—not the greyed blue that most ordinary mountains acquire with distance. The millions of eucalyptus trees on their slopes exhale a fine aromatic mist that catches and shatters the sunlight to deepen and intensify its blueness. Cooma is a town of coffee bars, well patronized by young men and specializing in Italian and German dishes. They also have loud juke boxes which the customers keep constantly in play.

We blundered into a motel which had just had a cancellation; otherwise it would be our bad luck to have to spend a cold night camping out. The early evening air is already chilly at this nearly 3,000-foot altitude, and the town is thronged with tourists like ourselves come to see the Snowy River Project. Only they, being Australians, had the foresight to book their accommodations well in advance. The Snowy River Administration is a kind of town itself attached to the old town, and both together add up to something quite a bit more boisterous and on the move than the sleepy mountain village I'd expected.

NOVEMBER 25: Our touring caravan consists of five cars (we each drive our own), or six including the pilot's. Graeme Conybeare is employed as a draughtsman and, like other white-collar workers on the project, gets assigned to pilot a tour every so often. Riding with him is a middle-aged couple and their teen-age son. The father has been a war pilot and can't bear to drive on heights. To tell the truth I'm not very good at it myself; and this I feel is the only flaw in the auto tour idea. We travel so fast bumper to bumper eating one another's dust that we can't enjoy the scenery. Then we stop, spend ten or twenty minutes in a little building looking at models or samples of rock and sand, and are off again in a 50-mile-an-hour road race to the next little building. A bit less time in the little buildings and more time on the roads would suit me better. Graeme's a great one for rock samples, though.

The roads themselves, well made for their purpose, which was to handle the project's four-wheel-drive machinery, were not meant for high speed driving. I have never driven on steeper ones. The old road from Phoenix to Globe, Arizona, was a picnic by comparison. These mountains are hard to climb and still harder to descend. Yesterday afternoon, after dipping and twisting down a long grade to the Tumut underground power station, we lost our brakes just as we reached the bottom. They failed completely, due to overwork. Graeme grinned and said it was a lucky thing they didn't give out sooner. I think he'd have hated seeing us go over the side.

I learnt from Graeme that there are seventy regular employees of the Authority who take on this guide work as an occasional substitute for their regular jobs. They went to school to learn what to say, and went on a conducted bus tour to further familiarize themselves. Besides the seventy there are thirty-two full-time guides to handle the 60,000-70,000 tourists who visit the Snowy each year. To these 100 guides, as to the Authority itself and perhaps for aught I know to the average Australian, the important thing about the tour is the instruction given and received. I don't see it this way. To me the important thing is the spectacle and what it symbolizes for Australia. With all the instruction I have received the last two days my strongest impression, so far as the physical enterprise is concerned, is of a grandiose plumbing scheme—more ambitious, even allowing for the tremendous difference in technological standards, than the Roman aqueducts—carrying water in every direction through miles of solid rock. I am quite prepared to take the word of the American Society of Civil Engineers that this is "one of the five future wonders of the world," and to believe it a sleeping giant that can sit idle all day and presto! Five minutes after a phone call it will send a million or so kilowatts surging through Sydney's grid. But transcending the physical structure in my eyes is the sense of pride it must give Australians to see their country, their Government, take such a bold step and carry it through so smoothly and efficiently. It required a daring imagination to conceive of it. The project ranges over such a vast area and at so many different levels it requires two days just to see it all. Then the planning was a feat in itself, enlisting the engineering skills, mobilizing the manpower literally from the other side of the world, reconciling the clashing interests of State and Federal

Governments. And now here it is, proof of Australia's ability to develop her own resources, with her own hands, to her own people's benefit.

I can't say the tour has made a hydraulic engineer of me. I still find one dam looking pretty much like every other dam; and the large cross-sectional diagrams of them on the walls of the little buildings, purporting to show how the river water on one side of the mountain range is piped underground into irrigation ditches on the other side, turning underground power turbines on the way—these only left me more confused than ever, like the farmer's first sight of a giraffe: "I don't believe it!" What I'm saying is that I liked the trip and I'd have liked it better still with less education and more contemplation. Lake Eucumbene, the chief storage reservoir, source of New South Wales's emergency power and Victoria's irrigation waters, looked to my untutored eyes like a typical mountain lake. One of the most engaging things about it was the island in its centre, on which the curator of Taronga Park Zoo has freed kangaroos, koala bears, and other native Australian animals to preserve them from extinction.

Every year the farmers in the region around the north-east Tasmania town of Avoca get together in a Sunday barbecue, with beer and games and a shoot. The shoot is the real purpose of the get-together, and the object of the shoot is the wallaby—a native Australian animal similar to but smaller than a kangaroo. The farmers have a lot of fun at the Avoca shoot and, with the $1.50 bounty they receive, turn pleasure into profit. They generally manage to polish off a thousand or more of the beasts before tidying themselves up for evening church services.

The sport is not uniquely Tasmanian; it's fairly common throughout Australia. One recent Federal Government in fact even sent troops out with gatling guns to slay emu. But Tasmania's size and isolation enable the exercise to be carried on to a decisive conclusion more quickly than in the open spaces of the continent. The emu of Western Australia simply scattered before the onslaught of the Federal troops and escaped largely unscathed; in Tasmania the emu were wiped out in a single generation. An earlier generation had disposed of the island's Aboriginal population, exterminating the entire Tasmanian race.

Avoca's wallaby hunters call their outing a shoot. Actually the animals are so gentle and tame that a bullet needn't be wasted on them. A front-page photo in the Melbourne Herald *showed a hunter in the act of braining a live wallaby with a rock. "I was*

281

filled with disgust," said an organizer of the outing, "not because a wallaby was being dispatched, but because a cheap and sensational journal saw fit to print it on the front page for filthy lucre and gain." He deplored the hue and cry that had risen over the slaughter, saying that if the people who protested had their way "our young men would be nothing but a lot of city namby-pambies nursing pomeranians and pussy cats, and we would all have to go back to eating yams and lizards—if we were allowed to wring the lizards' necks."

The business of kangaroo shooting on the mainland is done more quietly, in the dead of night from a car without a windscreen, using a spotlight and a rifle with a telescopic sight. It is frankly a business—for the few cents a pound the pet food manufacturers pay for the meat. Since only the meat of the hindquarters is wanted a single hunter has to kill several each night in order to pay expenses and show a profit; and since at least 1,000 hunters are engaged in the business the annual death toll runs into the millions.

The second car in our caravan has a young honeymoon couple in it from Sunshine, Victoria. It is an old Holden that can't climb hills until it gets thoroughly revved up and it also overheats. But there was only one hill that gave them real trouble, coming back from Tumut underground power station. This was the hill where our own brakes gave out going down.

The third car holds a large contingent from Sydney. They were late arriving at the information centre and we nearly started without them after waiting forty-five minutes. They are consistently late at every stop, never dream of getting into their car until everyone else is in and waiting. They brought up the rear at first but were impatient driving behind us (this was when we were still trying to view the scenery) , so I invited them to take our place in line. Actually this makes theirs the fourth car. The third and former fourth is a Holden (the laggards have a big new Chevvy; and nothing looks bigger on an Australian highway than a new Chevrolet) occupied by an American Fulbright exchange teacher from Royal Oak, Michigan, accompanied by wife, infant, and mother and father-in-law from Chicago. The two men wore shorts and probably regretted it before the day was over. There just aren't that many shorts wearers on Australian bush roads. They all think they'd like to settle in Australia but the teacher only on condition that he wouldn't be teaching.

We lunched yesterday cafeteria style at a dining mess patronized by Project employees and slept last night in excellent single bedrooms in a large dormitory in Cabramurra. At dinner, same style, in Cabramurra I sat with a visitor from Tanzania. Saidi (his first name; he thought his last would be too much for me to cope with) is here studying the project, his visit paid for by the United Nations. The manager of the dining room is a young Londoner who came to the Snowy with the same aim that everyone else has who works here: to make a lot of money in a hurry. The only difference is that when Simkins amasses his modest fortune he plans to invest it in a book-making business back home.

Today we had a comparatively easy run from Cabramurra to Khancoban, viewing the Tumut and Tooma reservoirs on the way. Then the road from Khancoban to Geehi and the twisting Alpine Way over the Great Dividing Range to the ski resort village of Thredbo proved as stern a challenge to the mountain driver as I have met anywhere.

NOVEMBER 26: I should say something about the Yank teacher's attempts to use Aussie expressions like "garbo," "beauty," "good *on* you," "I gave it away," "fair go," "fair enough," etc.; and his unquestioning acceptance of Aussie myth: dignity of the workingman, mateship over the beer glass, amateurism in sport, and relaxed way of life. I protested they weren't Rousseau's noble savages and he opened his eyes at that in some surprise.

This morning we planned to start for Bega on the Prince's Highway but a petrol attendant advised against it, saying the road was mostly dirt and very hilly. Accordingly we went back into the Snowy Mountains, breaking new ground for the most part but finding the steep grades as much an ordeal as before. When we finally saw the last of the swift twisting descents we were put on a long stretch of single car width blacktop alternating with rough gravel. I began seriously to wonder whether we wouldn't be better off without a car in the event that we stay on in Australia beyond this year. We enjoyed our Snowy excursion, the sweep and audacity of the project and the mountain scenery, but we'd have enjoyed it more in the company of other people. As it was, each family enclosed in its own car, we were scarcely able to get acquainted with one another.

We finally reached Albury at 5.45 this afternoon only to find the motels 100 per cent booked. Fortunately we discovered a large campground in town and on the Murray, and are putting up our tent and fighting off mozzies at the present moment.

NOVEMBER 28: Camping on the Murray wasn't at all bad apart from the mosquitoes, and the mosquitoes though numerous were not terribly venomous. I woke up to the laugh of a kookaburra. At least it's called a laugh. It sounds more like the cackle of a hen laying an egg. I believe it's the first time I've seen a live one, though I easily recognized its call from the number of times I used to hear it on short wave radio introducing Radio Australia. It's a rather large bird of dark, slightly blue plumage, with a thick strong beak; not greatly different in size and appearance from the magpies we've seen nearly everywhere. In fact I assumed it must be a distinct variety of magpie until one of the other campers told me it was a member of the kingfisher family. There was another bird, too, whose call sounded so much like two words that I was sure I should remember it, but I can't. Perhaps it was a magpie; they have many different calls. One is a perfect wolf whistle.

Most of the campers, like ourselves, were overnighters only, using the camp in lieu of a motel; and this we might have done last night also except that the fierce heat drove us to seek shelter fairly early, and we happened on this motel in the Goulburn Valley just north of Seymour, sixty miles short of Melbourne. The land along the highway is open countryside, cleared and gently rolling, the grass yellow and sometimes waving, the livestock when visible clustered under an occasional tree. The towns are few and small. In a more densely settled farm country there would need to be tractor dealers and welding shops to make the roadside unsightly—not to mention triptych after triptych of billboards. On the other hand we were having trouble with the carburettor in the intense heat, stalled from time to time and had to wait for the vapour lock to break. We could get no help from a garage as they are all closed on Sunday.

NOVEMBER 29: It was a bright morning, the parched yellow fields flat and generally empty of livestock but fenced, sometimes with the rocks and stones scattered over their surface but usually with split rail posts and wire. The occasional building was cheap and hand made, tending to roof. And there was still, even within fifteen miles of Melbourne, virtually no outdoor advertising. In Melbourne we had a breakfast of lamb's fry and saw Myer's animated Christmas window displays with great crowds standing before them and all but blocking off the footpaths. Then after putting the car in storage for Reg to pick up later we had a Chinese lunch of prawns, pork, steak, vegetables, rice noodles for $1.95 (all three of us) and telephoned Mrs Thorne to wish her a merry Christmas, only to learn she had had another cerebral haemorrhage and was convalescing in the Royal Geriatric Hospital.

A central feature of the hospital routine is physiotherapy. Hence when I called I found her on her feet, though the stroke occurred only three days ago, ready to take me on a tour of the building. During the war she and her husband lived in Tasmania, in the north-west coast settlement of Stanley, where he operated a shark liver processing plant. Stanley, she said, was like Pitcairn Island, the residents descended from a few families and all bearing the same few names. Hardly anyone over forty could write. Later her husband flew regularly to one of the islands in Bass Strait north of Tasmania, and found a still more isolated community, descendants of shipwrecked mariners. Their fathers and grandfathers had practised wrecking and looting ships. Mrs Thorne refers to her husband, dead ten years and still quite dear to her, as "Daddy." Most Australian men, young and old, call their wives "Mum" and then, to differentiate, they refer to their real mothers as "old Mum."

41

NOVEMBER 30: The Commonwealth-operated car ferry to Tasmania was designed and is run more for the comfort of its crew than its passengers. My cabin was hot, cramped, poorly lighted, and noisy. The mattress on the narrow bunk was encased in heavy plastic over whose hard shiny surface the sheet slid and twisted. Dining at a high counter I had rump steak fried in fish oil, with the inevitable chips, peas, and a half tomato grilled. Afterwards, not fancying either the hot cabins or hotter chair lounge, we went out on the narrow deck and watched the ship wind its way along the shallower of Port Phillip's two channels and ultimately, at 9.50, I felt a jolt as we slipped through the rip across the heads and took a sharp turn to port into the ocean. The stars were bright; the lights of several other ships were visible in the distance.

Devonport from the sea the next morning, on the side of a low hill back of the shore, looked like an early print of Australia. Devonport's environs called New Zealand's North Island to Candi's mind. It was, she said, "not only the greenness of the countryside or even mainly that; but something about the little hamlets every now and then, like in Auckland going out along the Manukau, and the gorse bush and wild roses along the fences, and the hilliness compared to the flat brownish expanses over most of Australia." The soil was a bit drier than the North Island in midsummer, the grass shorter and not quite so green; trees were still being cut out and burnt, as though the land were being settled for the first time. Our descent into Launceston was quite dramatic. "And you remember that American lady who sat in the front of the bus between her henpecked Australian husband and the driver. What was she chewing him out for? Something to do with putting a hat on the bag rack, I think. So she'd turn her head one way and snap at her husband, then turn it the other and positively gush over the driver. He'd have to be pretty dense if he couldn't see the difference

286

between her sweet talk to him and the grouchy way she bossed her husband."

DECEMBER 1: For such a small city—less than 60,000—Launceston is remarkably impressive, Australian through and through but mellowed and smoothed around the edges. It might almost be English if it weren't so hilly. We've found a first-rate restaurant and our motel is almost extravagantly elegant, with a view looking through branches and foliage down onto a quiet, tree-shaded street. Yes, that's what makes Launceston so pretty—the trees, exotics mostly, and just coming fully into leaf. There's a fine wide river too and, says Peggy, "that one main street that we never seem to get off of, and that Chequers restaurant and its good steaks with Worcestershire sauce on them, and our walk through the park to this deserted coliseum. Also the trip down to that little spot by the waterfall where the road is all torn up by road machinery."

Although Tasmania has, I understand, fewer migrants proportionately than any State except Queensland, nearly every person I talked to today happened to be one. There was the Czech shopkeeper who settled in Melbourne sixteen years ago. After two years he came to Tasmania on holiday and liked it so well he came right back and has stayed ever since. He can't stand big cities. Hobart isn't too big, he says, but the best trout fishing is here in the north. The cashier at Chequers restaurant is Belgian; speaks Flemish rather than French. Why did she come to Tasmania? For the sun of all things! (It was pouring down outside.) Yes, people had told her Tasmania was sunny. Now her husband has arthritis; so does her boy; so do many other children on this island. She has been only to Melbourne on the mainland; didn't see much sun there either. Our waitress, from England, has lived in Sydney and would like to go back; says Tazzie is too cold. I've seen several youngsters wearing duffle coats, long out of style elsewhere, even New Zealand. Nobody seems to be doing any Christmas shopping.

Mrs McHutchinson stayed to afternoon tea and told us about Sydney's Christmas festivities. It is customary to decorate trees, she says, but artificial trees are preferred. The natural trees shed too much in the hot weather. The artificials fold up and store away. Cards are exchanged but presents rarely, except among relations. Lighted trees are stood in windows and lights are put outside a house when a party is on, but that's about all. The elaborate outdoor light displays and rooftop decorations she saw once on a visit to America, Australians just wouldn't go for. Santa Claus and Father Christmas are interchangeable, as they are in England; Kris

Kringle she has never heard of. Turkey is the preferred Christmas dinner, along with plum pudding. There is a growing trend toward a cold buffet as a concession to the hot weather; the turkey is cooked the day before.

A bigger thing than the actual Christmas Day celebration however is the pre-Christmas cocktail party. Better say parties, for I calculated Mrs McHutchinson will attend about thirty of them between the first of December and the twenty-fifth, to wit: two given by her bowling club, one by her card-playing group, eight by the neighbours of her home-unit (condominium) flat, fourteen by personal friends, two for her nearest kin, and two or three I can't now recollect. These are held in the evening or on weekend mornings or afternoons.

Sunday morning is a favourite time for cocktails and savouries; no brunch, no waffles or griddle cakes. Invitations are often informal and telephoned a day or two ahead; if for afternoon "any time after four" with the expectation of ending at six in time for tea. Evening affairs have no natural termination. Men drink whisky; women a gin and tonic or gin and soft drink, sometimes just a soft drink; young people prefer beer.

Office parties go on the whole week before Christmas, and every year there is talk of shortening them and donating the money saved to charity. A bank, for instance, will throw staff parties in its various branches which the staffs of other branches are welcome to attend; it will have a party for managers, and a party for the executives of other banks. Christmas mercifully puts an end to the festivities by which time, Mrs McHutchinson says, people all vow they are fed up with parties. She thinks they are an old custom, although, come to think of it, her parents didn't honour it. Perhaps they have been growing more popular in recent years.

Peggy asked Mrs McHutchinson if she had started her Christmas shopping yet. She said she hadn't, nor will she until the weather gets hot. Hot weather is needed to put Australians in the mood for Christmas. Then she'll have to rush like mad to do all her shopping before the weather gets too hot.

I noticed a sign "Betting Centre" and turned down an alley into what looked like a large ballroom, reaching up to a barn-like roof. Around the walls were a dozen or so chest-high counters, each manned by a bookmaker and his clerks. Odds were chalked on a blackboard behind the counter. Tasmania is the only State where off-course bookmaking is legal, and the only State entirely free of illegal S.P. or starting-price bookmaking in the pubs. The difference is one of revenue. The S.P. bookies give the State no cut at all. The legal bookies of Tasmania give the State two-and-a-half per cent of their takings plus stamp duty. But the T.A.B., with its plush bank-like offices in every neighbourhood and hamlet, hands the State a present of 15 cents out of every dollar wagered with it. Next year T.A.B. comes to Tasmania.

An estimated two thousand million dollars a year goes into gambling, nearly two-thirds of it into legalized betting, poker machines, and lotteries yielding tax revenues to the States. To encourage this painless way of tax collection the N.S.W. State Lotteries run large ads in the daily newspapers picturing a happy winner and headlined variously "This $60,000 just cost me a quid!" "Forget the camping trip, Betty—we're heading overseas!" and "Now I'll pay off Mum's mortgage!" The text of one of these ads is just as intriguing:

"Yes, today you can make your Mum's dreams come true. Call it a hunch ... call it simple luck, but the New South Wales Lotteries transformed your $1 note into $24,000, in just a matter of days. New South Wales Lotteries pay well, pay fast—and are the easiest of all to win. Every week, 17,223 people pick up cheques from the State Lotteries. Every week, an average of $621,550 is paid out. Every 9 days, there are 7,014 prizes in the big $200,000 Opera House Lottery. Choose the one that suits your purse today. It could make a wonderful change in your life—and the life of your family."

To help win one of these prizes several private companies manufacture and sell good luck charms, and they are also regularly advertised. There is Lucky Manny with its testimonial from a woman who had lost everything by fire and, since buying the charm, has won $10 in a lottery and seen her husband's health improve besides. The Lucky Hindu Lodestone is sold with a money-back guarantee. Lucky Larry comes with a dream book as an added premium and Lucky Chinese Charlie offers a system of "Lucky Numbers for racing, lotteries, bingo, etc."

Lotteries have been a source of colonial and State tax revenue for over 100 years. The oldest lottery in the world is Tattersalls; privately operated, it pays the States of Victoria and Tasmania 31 cents of every dollar their residents invest in it. Buying "a ticket in Tatts," in a typical branch with its battery of cashiers' windows and its patrons busily filling out deposit slips, has all the dignity and reverence of putting money in the bank. I felt almost virtuous

289

sliding two two-dollar bills under the cage and receiving a sweep-stakes ticket on the Doomben Cup.

Mr Carmichael the branch manager said that gambling was almost the last source of revenue left to the States. They used to rely mainly on income taxes to pay the costs of police, education, health, transport, and roads, which were and still are State respon-sibilities. The tax on real property, called rates in Australia and extremely low by American standards, belonged to cities and town-ships and paid for sewerage, garbage collection, libraries, and street lighting and maintenance. To pay the costs of defence and social security the Commonwealth levied sales and estate taxes, excise and customs duties.

Then as a wartime measure the Commonwealth took over col-lection of the income taxes from the States and refused to give it back when the war was over. It didn't much matter at the time because, in the form of special grants, the Commonwealth returned substantially the full amount the States had formerly netted after the cost of collection. Thanks to savings through the elimination of multiple collections it was also able to give the less populous States an additional bonus to help in their development. Each year however the Commonwealth kept a little more of the income tax for itself. Thus it was able to finance capital expendi-tures directly out of revenues instead of through loans payable over the life of the capital structures. Australia in consequence, despite the cost of two big wars, had a national debt charge of—

"Hang on a minute," said Mr Carmichael, and he began work-ing the levers of a large machine used in his lottery operations. "Our Commonwealth expenditures this year come to almost exactly $500 per head and the cost of paying off our national debt amounts to $7.85. I reckon that must be pretty near the lowest in the world."

This was the bright side of the picture. The darker side was that the gap between income tax collections and refunds had widened until now the States received only two dollars of every three col-lected. They levied a stamp tax on cheques, bills, receipts, every conceivable kind of commercial paper, but it still wasn't enough. Unless they legalized two-up and brought it under the tax umbrella Mr Carmichael didn't know how they could go on paying teachers', constables', and railwaymen's salaries. Their one remain-ing hope lay in the mineral royalties, which still belonged to the States. But to yield the necessary royalties, the minerals had to be mined, and mined quickly. Education, transportation, public safety, all the other essential services the States provided couldn't wait until Australian firms backed by Australian investors got around to the job of recovering the minerals and processing them in Australia. Australians were notoriously slow to invest in enterprises that didn't yield a quick return, Mr Carmichael said; they preferred lotteries.

DECEMBER 2: Jock, who taxied us to the station after lunch for our train to Hobart, said people leave Tasmania faster than migrants can be found to take their places—young people especially. He himself has no wish to leave though; life on the mainland is too fast. If he moved it would be to the north-west coast, where the pace is slower yet. As there was still time after checking our bags he suggested we have another quick look at Cataract Gorge, a magnificent spectacle anywhere else with its twin waterfalls, a few hundred yards apart, cutting through layers of rock and buried in masses of lush green native vegetation. In quiet Launceston (it is near enough to be virtually a part of the city) it borrows some of the city's quiet casualness and restfulness and seems hardly more than a family picnic spot. There is a narrow path up to an equally narrow swinging bridge across the torrent and along the sheer rock face on the other side; but, light as the outer rail was which saved us from slipping off to our doom, and prone as I am to feel dizzy looking out of the window of a tall building, I felt only peace and well-being here. The Launceston influence unquestionably.

42

The train goes south through open country, mostly flat, with distant mountain ranges on both sides. The mountains look old and not very high, though actually they are the highest outside the Snowys; Tasmania is the most rugged place in Australia, and this river plain we are on, which extends nearly half the distance to Hobart, is almost the only part of the interior which is relatively level. It is a curious mixture of old and new, cut-over gum scrub succeeding mixed farms, in turn succeeded by large sheep and cattle stations, the foothills also covered with gum scrub or with pastures fenced into separate paddocks by gorse hedges. Houses and outbuildings are few and, nowithstanding each house sprouting a TV antenna, have a pioneer look to them. The land itself, on the other hand, gives the impression of being worn out and ready to be thrown away—like the used-up land of the Carolinas, Georgia, and Alabama.

Yesterday we bought Candi another Maths book, her lecturer having left her high and dry on an island of permutations in an unknown sea of sets and groups. Sydney was as crowded and noisy as ever. We lunched at Repin's, less gustatorial than Cahill's in the Arcade, but easier to find a table, and then on to Sheppard's Bookshop. A Javanese of Dutch descent works there. His family moved to Australia in 1922 to get away from malaria. They had tried Europe and liked Australia's space and lack of hindrance to movement, spatially and socially. He still speaks with a slight accent but considers himself fully Australianized, with an Australian's right to criticize the country.

His chief criticism is of the wastage of natural resources, especially in the soil. "America perhaps could afford to create a dust bowl but Australia can't. She needs to be able to feed more people, not less. The sheep are making a desert of South Australia

as the Arabs and their goats did of the Sahara." This was an Aus-
tralian failing he criticized. Its democracy he likes. He can live
next door to Sir Henry Halpern and talk to him over the back
yard fence; not so much as formerly, to be sure. Jack is no longer
quite the equal of his master.

The greatest wastage of land resources occurs in the vast regions
of the north and west under foreign leasehold. Vesteys of London
hold some six million acres in the far north of Western Australia
on 50-year lease at rents so low—from 66 to 90 cents per thousand
acres—that any expenditure at all on soil improvement and con-
servation would multiply capital investment almost astronomi-
cally. The Emanuel Brothers, also of London, pay only from 65 to
85 cents annual rent per thousand acres in Western Australia, or a
trivial $1,390 for nearly two million acres of leasehold. No one,
least of all the absentee owners, knows how many animals are
stocked, but a conservative estimate would put some 60,000 sheep
and 180,000 cattle on the two giant properties, bringing the cost of
feed for each of the Emanuel Brothers' beasts down to 2.3 cents a
year. For the Vesteys the cost per beast might be a tenth of a cent
higher, compared to $30 up in most parts of the United States.
The profits in a good year in this tropical monsoon region are
spectacular; if the rains come on time and are plentiful the ravages
of the seasonal "dry" period are soon repaired. Every twelve to
fifteen years a "wet" comes along that is not wet enough; the land
is turned into barren desert in which you can drive for hundreds
of miles and never escape the stench of rotting corpses.

The rural townships, of which Ross would be typical, cover a
fairly large tract of ground yet appear to be merely small farm
houses brought slightly closer together. A haphazard network of
roads, some only dirt tracks, takes the place of streets. The houses
have for me the added distinction that they are the only ones I
have seen in Australia whose back yards are not equipped with a
rotary clothes hoist. They still rely on the conventional long line
pushed up with props.

Below Ross the river plain thins out and the train jolts and
sways on its narrow-gauge track as it climbs to the high point of
the line, 1,460 feet. The hills are grazed and seem to carry almost
as many sheep as the lush pastures of New Zealand. The characteristic hill form is a cone rising to a sharp peak, and the pastures are
nearly treeless.

The train descends from the outlet of Rhyndston Tunnel,
giving a view over the tops of neighbouring mountains, down a

steep winding path amidst bush, green grass, and sheep, and past
ploughed hillsides, fields of green wheat, pasture with sheep, and
pasture cut for hay, into Colebrook Valley. All around on the
valley floor are undulating smooth, nearly bald hills with strips of
windbreak willows and dark patches of gum. Beyond Colebrook
settlement and its collection of light grey buildings, piles of cord-
wood, and fences, the valley widens to accommodate rolling green
pastures in which the dead skeletons of trees stand up like white
bare bones in a surrealist landscape. Cloud shadows spotting the
green hills that reach out to the deep blue mountains enhance the
effect of distance.

At Bridgewater the train crosses the wide placid Derwent River
and runs along beside it between two rows of golden hills backed
by bush-covered mountains. At 5.30 the weather is closing in.
Clouds have settled low down the sides of the hills. The air,
though still warm, is damp. The river continues to widen in a
succession of coves with pleasure craft at anchor in them. Then
the working harbour of Hobart takes over. Tugs are tied up at the
wharves. Beyond the new highway bridge, which is set on tall concrete pillars, a small freighter is at anchor. There is a yacht club
on this side of the river and houses spread over the hills on the
other side.

DECEMBER 3: Hobart impressed Candi as being a prettier place even than Adelaide along the railway coming in, with the dooryards given over so generously to flower gardens. It too is a small city, smallest of all the State capitals; but, like Launceston, it has acquired with trees and age, and its own splendid river, a certain elegance. It isn't the oldest city in Australia but it manages somehow to suggest colonial history more than Sydney or any of the others. This could be because it isn't growing like the others and its lovely old buildings aren't being torn down to provide ground space for new.

Yet our "motel" is an impressive enough seven-storey building, a restaurant on the top floor to which we hurried as soon as we reached our flat, only to encounter a dismally tasteless meal. I had roast chicken and Peggy had chicken Maryland, and what we got was two halves of a chicken which had been stewed to make the cream of chicken soup on the general menu. All flavour had been boiled out before my half was put briefly in the oven and Peggy's was crumbed and put as briefly in a fry pan, to emerge as something near cardboard in taste and texture. Candi, who is wiser than we to the quirks of Australian cuisine, very sensibly ordered meat pie and sauce.

Today we lunched at a restaurant in the Cat and Fiddle Arcade. While we ate, the court outside filled up with people waiting for the hour to strike. Peg went out to see what happened and what did happen was this: there's the figure of a cat, a cow, and the crescent moon alongside a large clock at one end of the court. When the clock struck, the cat played a fiddle and the cow jumped over the moon; and perhaps 200 people had assembled to see it.

After lunch we procured a map and went to look at Battery Point, said to be the oldest and most historically interesting part of town. It's on a high point just up from the water and consists evidently of some of the original dwellings of Hobart town, the houses all joined together and pressing close on the footpath. There are flower beds and small patches of parkland, and splendid views of the river estuary as it opens to the sea. It is fairly hilly and nothing is identified, nor did our map which came from the Tasmanian Government Tourist Bureau help to make what we saw seem important. There is a row of stately old structures behind the riverside park that leads up to Battery Point, all still in use for warehouse and other humdrum purposes. These and other architectural gems that catch the eye literally on every hand cry out for historical identification; and on them all the Bureau sayeth naught. This could be Hobart's easy-going way.

It is also Australia's way. The first thing Lili Vitonis said when she heard I came from California was: "Those historical markers!" A stateless person until she came to Australia and eager to strike roots, Lili had immersed herself in Australia's past. "A country is not a country without a past; a person is not a real person without a country." So the thing that meant the most to her on her American visit was that California, not a sovereign country like Australia, but having a similar landscape, climate, and even a similar history—including nearly simultaneous gold rushes—had taken the pains to identify the events of its past with markers and monuments nearly everywhere she turned. I hadn't fully realized this before but now I recalled the historical society in my own small town actively campaigning to have a monument erected on the highway coming in, with a brass plaque explaining how the town got its name. In Australia I could not recall having seen a single historic spot identified.

Lili was born in Lithuania. She was child of ten when, during the Nazi retreat, every person in her village was ordered to get out or be shot. Her father was dead; her mother died on the day of evacuation; what she went through on her way into Germany she had long since forgotten. Nor did she want to remember it or the months and years she spent in a refugee camp waiting for the war to end. When at last it had ended "a rich American" came to the camp and withdrew all the orphan children to a centre of their own. She had learnt German; now every morning she had to attend an English class, and how she hated it! "You don't pronounce the words the way they look!"

Years later in Australia her small daughter asked for her help on a school essay. Still not completely at home in a language in which sound and spelling were scarcely related to each other, Lili said she wasn't sure that what she wrote would be understood. Her daughter protested: "Don't write it in your language, Mum! Write it in mine!"

At fifteen Lili had been given a wide choice of countries to emigrate to: America, Canada, Australia, Argentina, Brazil. She turned America down because the boy-friend who had been courting her and with whom she had broken was going there. She was afraid she might run into him. All she knew about Australia was that it was always summer. Or was supposed to be. She looked out at the white wintry Melbourne sky and the icy rain driving against the windows as she said this and she laughed.

She arrived in December on a refugee ship of which she could also remember little save wondering what Australia would be like.

Coming into Port Melbourne she anxiously scanned the shore. The little cottages amazed her. They were all so tiny and so decorated over with wooden lacework she thought they must be gingerbread and sugar-plum cottages out of Hansel and Gretel. *This was her first impression of Australia. Her second was of the drab, dusty monotony of the countryside along the road to the hostel at Bonegilla. "It looked like a dead country. There were no houses or people, just the dry yellow ground and dusty grey trees."*

She soon left the hostel to work as a housemaid for two dollars a week. At seventeen she became the bride of another Lithuanian, as completely cut off from natural ties to his homeland as she: no living parents or other close relatives, only a sister who was a refugee like himself, who was separated from him in Germany, and whom he finally saw again when she too migrated to Australia. Paul Vitonis's ship was the first of the refugee ships. Because it carried only Lithuanians, Latvians, and Estonians—people from the Baltic States—all of Australia's European migrants from that time on were to be known as Balts.

I asked Lili how she felt about Australia now. "Oh—" then after a moment's reflection, "Australia is a new country. It has no —what do you say?—no traditions. No yesterday. I still remember a little bit of Kaunas, the old capital of Lithuania, its old buildings, so much that was old and settled about it. In my village too. Here—it's a new country. It's what you make of it. What you yourself make of it by working in it."

And how did she happen to visit California? A sudden smile broke over her broad open face. Her sister-in-law had won a fourth prize in Tatts! She insisted on Lili sharing it with her; Paul could take care of the kids. Where would they go? Not to Lithuania. There was nothing there for them; nor in Europe either, a place of unhappy memories. England meant as little to them, and exactly as much, as Iceland or Uruguay. Should it be a week at Surfers or in Sydney, which neither as yet had seen? Too tame. All at once they had it. California and Disneyland!

As Ferenc Geisz at the bus depot said concerning no one knowing much about the local chess club, "What kind of a capital city is this?"

Geisz was a Hungarian refugee, settled first in Sydney, here sixteen years and determined to make the best of it. He's been with the bus company for twelve years, a driver up to the age of sixty; was a lecturer in geography and geology at a military institute in Budapest; has been all over Australia and likes Hobart best.

Hobart Domain

Why not Sydney?

It's not a characteristic Australian city—too international. But with its harbour it is distinctive among the world's cities—"an original city."

He says Australia has freedom but the people spend it. I asked if he meant they don't appreciate it and he muttered something about politicians and doctors being the only people who count in the eyes of Australians. He says he's a second-class citizen. There are third-class citizens: the Aborigines, he said, with what sounded like a bitter laugh.

43

In fence conscious Australia the prettiest fences of all are in Tasmania. The hedges of hawthorn, broom, and gorse, and the low walls of stone are among the graces of the cultivated landscape. Unlike the rest of Australia Tasmania has no vermin fences, those long, costly, and largely futile barriers all the other States erected against encroachments on their pastures and sheep. The rabbit fences were the first, beginning as early as 1886 in New South Wales and Queensland and around 1900 in Western Australia. Invariably they were put up too late; the rabbits were already inside the area they sought to enclose. Many of the rabbit fences were later raised to a height of six feet to keep out the dingo, Australia's native wild dog. Such was the beginning of the famous Dog Fence, hailed as the longest fence in the world. From its eastern terminus on the Queensland-N.S.W. border it runs some 220 miles west to the South Australia line, south for 140 miles, and then across South Australia between sheep and cattle country for 1,350 miles to the coast at the head of the Great Australian Bight.

The bounty on dingo scalps is two dollars outside—which is to say on the cattle side—of the fence and ten dollars inside. South Australia shared with New South Wales the cost of converting the section of the fence between their States to make it dog proof; and for thirty years shared the cost of its maintenance. In 1943 South Australia woke up to the fact that she was spending money to keep the dingoes on her side. Now New South Wales carries the burden alone.

DECEMBER 4: Our drive this morning landed us quickly in the country, after a short stretch of surprisingly modern freeway; and much of our route was through second growth gum and into hills where sheep grazed amid the trees. We sat three in one seat

300

behind the driver; behind us was a young mother, a three-year-old boy, and an infant girl; and a loquacious elderly gentleman of stocky build sat in the left front seat. He and the driver, Neil, discussed the weather pretty thoroughly including a heavy rain east of Hobart that had washed out two bridges.

We drove through mist and fog which greyed and flattened trees and hills almost, sometimes quite, to the point of disappearance; crossed a narrow bay called Pittwater and moved into thicker and steeper hills, making detours at a hotel or post office to deliver mail. We picked up a girl in jeans and dropped her shortly after. We dropped the man in the front seat and later picked up another to take his place, but this one—also elderly—was thin and said nothing except "16 shillings, right?" when he paid his return fare.

Near Tasman Peninsula we began to see the ocean, white breakers against a crescent bridge; and the strip of land tying the peninsula to the rest of the island left water close at hand on both sides: the open sea on the left and a long inlet from Norfolk Bay on the right. Neil said dogs used to be chained across this narrow neck to prevent convicts escaping from the peninsula. We passed some more farms, saw the famous unconsecrated church (because two murders had been committed in it), saw some ruins of other buildings loosely distributed over grassy hills, and discovered to my surprise we were in Port Arthur. Around our motel, which I understand is right in town, are farm houses, clumps of gum, tall grass, and a low density population of cows, horses, and chickens.

DECEMBER 5: We visited a few of the ruins yesterday—the roofless and windowless cathedral, with grass growing on the floor and trailing over the doorsills, where we took snapshots of Candi seated in a window opening. Like the guard house, powder magazine, the penitentiary, and the other relics, it was built of cut stone, and still looks firm after 130 years. It was designed by one of the convicts.

According to Terence Herlihy, Australia's second penal colony after Sydney was to have been at Port Phillip rather than Tasmania. But the first two men sent to examine the Melbourne site returned with unfavourable reports: one because he had an application pending for a freehold near Sydney and feared he would have to take one at Port Phillip if he spoke well of it; the other because there was a bonus of two years' pay in selecting another site. Port Arthur, Herlihy said, was not the oldest penal settlement in Tasmania but the one best known for the hardships inflicted on its prisoners—the Devil's Island of Australia. It was founded in

Hobart

1830 and continued in use for nearly half a century. In fact, said Herlihy, his grandparents came out from Ireland in 1877, the year Port Arthur was abandoned.

I could have guessed, before he told me, that he was a native Australian, though I don't mean to imply all native Australians are easy to spot. But his large roundish nose, round eyes, roundish chin and cheekbones in a face more square than round, and the thick sturdy frame of the southern Irishman furnished one set of clues. And the easy comfortable look he had of belonging, of owing no allegiance to any other—and most definitely not England —told me the rest. For there are native Australians of divided allegiance, including many who claim ancestry from the First Fleet, but not the ones whose forbears came from Ireland.

A little past the cathedral, still in this quiet empty space of trees and spacious lawns, is a living church, small and of white clapboard. It is all alone among the ruins; from it the grass and trees sweep to the water; and only by following a path around the head of the bay did we come to a little group of shops, a grocery and general store, a sandwich counter, a makeshift museum with a helter-skelter of mementoes from prison colony days. There are cars and guides by the hour and the day, and one merry fellow, carrying his swag over his shoulder on a stick, offered to accompany us on a foot tour. Across the bay is the penitentiary, with cells little larger than rabbit hutches. A so-called model prison—the word "model" had an ironic meaning—the hospital on a hilltop, the guard house farther along the road, all stand like gaunt futuristic monuments in an English rural landscape.

Except for the shop-keepers and guides, the residents seem not to show themselves out of their houses; and the tourists, treading softly over the thick grass and speaking in the subdued mumbles that the loneliness of the place imposes, are almost like ghosts. Everything seems enchanted, as though time had stopped; and you wander around along empty roadways, up and down hills, viewing the eyeless monuments from different vantage points, feeling all alone between sky and water in this green luxuriance of trees and grass.

Then in a cloud of dust and stones a car comes hurtling along one of the metalled roads and the spell is broken. You notice that the area between the penitentiary and the bay is a huge caravan park, with tents and caravans pressed close against the old stone walls. Smart, our landlord, says he will have no vacancies during the height of the holiday season. The campground won't have a square foot of unoccupied space. In just two weeks the buses will run every day, bringing as many as 350 people to feed for lunch. Small boys will stage mock battles among the ruins; and if they fall into worse repair nobody will greatly mind. Neil has already said he'd like to see them all cleared out, leaving nothing to recall the once dreadful horrors of this place. Another Tasmanian I've talked to, one of a group of some thirty bagpipers and their women staying at our motel, said the same thing. His eyes glistened with real tears when he thought about it. He blinked them rapidly away and added practically, "They could use the room too. It looks empty now, doesn't it? Come back during the Christmas holiday season and you'll be lucky if you can find space to park your car. That's what people come here for. They want to enjoy themselves and have a good rest. They don't want to look at the burnt-out shells of a lot of old buildings. Keep the lunatic asylum if you like." He chuckled. "The local Council holds its meetings there. But if I had my way I'd raze the rest to the ground and put in more caravan parks."

In Britain, where everyone was conscripted, Llew Brice promptly got rid of his war mementoes and avoided veterans' clubs. Here, he said, where enlistment was voluntary, the R.S.L. had a prestige value. So he joined and sent back for the ribbons and medals he'd scorned to accept in U.K. He paraded on Anzac Day and, while convinced a nuclear war would destroy everything, was coming around to the belief that there would be at least one more non-nuclear world war.

This was about four years ago. I had been reading a newspaper report on Australia's defence needs in the way of submarines, short take-off and landing troop-carriers, and a second aircraft carrier. In it a correspondent for the Melbourne Age *said the R.A.A.F. could not afford to wait for Britain's TSR2 supersonic fighter-bomber. Even with the much earlier delivery promised for the similar Lockheed F-111 it was nip and tuck whether Australia would be able to defend herself in the meantime. Brice snorted when I told him this. "The Chinese," he said, "could conquer Australia merely by timing their invasion for the Christmas holidays!"*

The Australian holiday, during which the entire nation downs tools and locks up desks, is not so much a holiday as a kind of Anglo-Saxon lent. There is massacre on the roads and to what end? So that tens of thousands of motorists can go to Canberra, filling every motel room and overflowing into Queanbeyan, Yass, and Goulburn. Will they enjoy themselves? Or are they performing a ritual, a just penance for the many guilty hours they've spent in the sheer enjoyment of their work? The smokos, the arguments over footie and the races, the unalloyed pleasure of having something useful to occupy themselves with.

Can it be that these austere holidays with their picnic hampers and beer and nothing to do save watch the kids and their fathers play are fun? Isn't this dutiful trooping en masse *from shrine to shrine, with the kids for once forced to behave themselves and act like civilized people expressly and peculiarly contrived to make the normal working routine seem by contrast more delightful? Each new award of the Arbitration Court lengthens the holiday and prolongs the boredom. The working stiffs are hypnotized into believing they've won something, and the economy over-all is kept in balance by piling on more overtime and importing more labour.*

It could be argued that with two days off every week the Australian would have holiday enough, provided he worked only eight hours each of the other five. His increasing productive efficiency

—as determined by the Arbitration Court—might better be rewarded with higher hourly wages, straight time. But I doubt whether the workingman himself would agree, and certainly his wife would not. Pass up the chance of saddling Daddy with responsibility for the behaviour of the children for three, four, maybe five weeks every year? Not blurry likely!

For himself he has never thought to question the value of longer and longer holidays. They must be good, else the employers wouldn't oppose them. The employer has to pay him for doing nothing, doesn't he? Three weeks, four weeks, perhaps in the foreseeable future as many as thirteen weeks a year. This is costing the employer money, and wresting money from him in whatever form it takes spells victory for the workingman. Besides he has been schooled into believing that any boost in weekly wages is immediately taken away by inflation. The flurry of price-rises hard on the heels of every dollar-a-week national pay increase enforces this lesson. By comparison the lengthening holidays are made to seem inflation proof.

To be sure his holiday pay is straight time whereas his ordinary weekly income includes overtime. The difference if he works ten hours, as many do, and either Saturday or Sunday, is around 85 per cent. So what a holiday boils down to is a layoff with unemployment benefits of a little more than half his regular income. The benefits wouldn't be so high on an actual layoff, but neither would he use them to stay at Canberra motels. However, with the employer paying the holiday bills, or seeming to, he can't simply stay home and mow his lawn and argue with the blokes in the pub. What kind of a holiday would that be?

What he needs to really enjoy it is nervous strain and boredom, the discomfort of a motel bed and the unfamiliarity of a restaurant meal which can't be relished, knowing what the bill will be. At the end of it all he'll have some hazy memories, a stack of colour slides that no one wants to look at, and a sizeable debt for the costs his employer's straight time didn't cover. This debt will give him an extra incentive to work hard the rest of the year at time and a half and double time.

Some seek to beat the game and escape the burden of debt by passing up Canberra's high-priced motels and restaurants, living in a caravan park in a quiet retreat like Port Arthur, and eating beans from the can. What they are doing is frankly if unconsciously recognizing the holiday for what it is, a layoff on reduced pay. They can't forego the holiday altogether but they can strive to keep it within their budget. Out of their comfortable houses, away

305

from their kitchens, they endure the heat and the flies, the barking dogs (for surely each family brings one), and the general slum conditions of an overcrowded campground. They, more than the gayer vacationists, will have cause to go back to their jobs with joy and thankfulness.

For the locals from miles away the great attraction of Port Arthur is this licensed motel's Saturday night cabaret. Here they come to sit at tables in family groups, or cosily together in chairs, and drink and dance until after midnight. Last evening's entertainers were the kilted and blanketed and sporraned Derwent Bagpipe Band who were raising money for a new set of pipes.

DECEMBER 6: Going back to Hobart this afternoon we stopped again at all the post offices and to pick up farmers' mailbags, and found it a very pleasant drive in the sunshine, passing as we did numerous bays and inlets with hills and mountains on the opposite shores. It wasn't really until we came to Sorell less than twenty miles from Hobart that the land appeared to be farmed, either in grass or crops.

DECEMBER 7: I wanted to find a certain chess player I had met among the spectators at a tournament in Christchurch. I knew he lived in Tasmania and could describe him vaguely. Though I had forgotten his name I was sure I should recognize it if I heard it. I thought if I asked at a few shops selling chess sets or chess books I might get a lead, but never did I expect the veritable outpouring of help I received; and as I said finally, "Hobart will certainly know someone was interested in finding out about its chess club!"

I started with the Tasmanian-Methodist bookshop. The genial manager plays chess, has a son who's quite a whiz, and called his son at Cadbury's. The son didn't know but thought another man there might, and offered to ask and call back. At Fuller's in the Cat and Fiddle Arcade the whole staff went to work cudgeling their brains and telephoning, and finally gave me a Leopold Kirchner to call after six. At O.B.M. the manager and his chief assistant got on two phones and routed out a G. F. Waterhouse whom I was also to call after six.

Kirchner is a migrant from Stuttgart who couldn't place my chess player but chatted pleasantly when I called. He likes Tasmania because it is out-of-the-way, and out of the big cities. Waterhouse proved to be the best informed of any I have had contact with. He knows everyone in Tasmanian chess except my man. When I said I had been rewarded in my search by the helpfulness I encountered on every side he said my description of Tasmanians applied better to Americans; if Tasmanians were exceptional it was because they saw so few new faces and heard so few new voices. But this is what he likes about Tazzie, being "in the world and yet out of it." He promised to drop over tomorrow evening.

DECEMBER 8: Like most other Tasmanians Dr Waterhouse, who migrated seventeen years ago from Kent, has not lived anywhere else in Australia. He spent the first seven years in Devonport and calls these the seven years of the locust. He says the most surprising thing is his being unable to remember anything about them. He practised dentistry and his patients had nothing to say even when he wasn't working on them. He believes they were so inbred that they had suffered reversion. He retains some of that attitude toward the Tasmanian-born in general but, having found a common bond of interest with other Hobart chess enthusiasts, is content with this quiet retreat where he can watch the rest of the world go by.

44

This morning Ferenc Geisz came around with one of the bus company limousines to drive us to the top of Mount Wellington. I think this gave me the best idea I have had yet of the general appearance of Tasmania, for I seemed to be able to see the whole of it from this 4,100-foot height. We could look down on Hobart and its suburbs along the winding bays and turns of the river, and beyond to the islands in the estuary and far down to the causeway at Sorell, and still farther to the Tasman Peninsula itself. Then to the north-east we saw mountain after mountain, not so much in separate ranges as spread out over the whole area with alpine meadows on their slopes, and in their midst in the distance a large golden valley—probably the same Esk and Macquarie Rivers plain we had come down through from Launceston.

"It was real cold the day Auntie Edie went—not all sunny like it was for us. I even think she said it started snowing as they got higher up. Anyway cold weather always makes her want to go, and the bus just kept chugging along so slowly and it was getting worse and worse, so that when they finally reached the top she nearly beat the door down getting out. But the others were still fussing with their binoculars when she got back. They all gathered round the guide, and the first things he pointed out to them in all that view were two factories—Cadbury's and one other. In the guided tours she went on these were the top tourist attractions."

Mount Wellington itself is covered mostly with snow gum mixed with sassafras and wattle; and the hills and curves going up were so smoothly graded that the climb was positively delightful —or Ferenc at any rate made them seem so.

Going down was a different story. He returned to the subject of his second-class citizenship and how, though he had been a university lecturer, Australia wouldn't even let him teach an infants' class. Not until he went back to Teachers' College for an Australian diploma. But this wasn't the reason he felt the way he did. He said the life of a teacher in Australia was impossible for him to contemplate. The pay was low and many other things were bad about it. His voice as he spoke was unemotional enough. He really didn't sound as if he minded. But there must have been some charged feeling behind it all because the car began picking up speed and soon we were on a wild ride down the mountain, whipping around curves so fast I thought the doors would pop open and fling us all out.

He reined up at the bottom and drove quietly along the waterfront. He pointed out a Hobart identity who was supposed to have made pots of money in the junk business but who has been banned for life from the race courses for flagrant bribery of jockeys. In one famous race there were only three horses running. When the two jockeys who were paid to lose couldn't hold their horses back they both tumbled off.

DECEMBER 10: The latter part of our trip by train yesterday from Hobart through Western Junction up to Devonport was over a countryside probably very like agricultural Britain, more cleanly cultivated than farther south. The bus ride today along the northwest coast was tantalizing in its promise of what we could have seen had we gone by rail. The tracks hug the water all the way to Burnie and beyond, making it virtually inaccessible except at a pleasant little town called Penguin where there is a small city park and a beach. What little we could see from the highway gave promise of spectacular scenery, with volcanic rocks and peninsulas, beaches and cliffs, rivers and dense bush all along the coast.

The first thing to greet us as we approached Burnie was the thick white smoke of a huge paper mill. And the mile and a half walk along the shore from our motel to town was without any attractive feature. The whole beautiful shoreline has been blighted, and it's all the more heart-rending because you can see what a lovely little city Burnie used to be before the paper mill started operations in 1939. It then had about 3,000 residents, a wonderful natural site of hills, harbour, blue water visible at the ends of two sets of cross streets, and a long curve of sand and narrow parkland between the railway and the shore. Today Burnie is Tasmania's third largest city, the fastest growing of all, but what a price it has paid for progress. And the State has paid a still bigger price to get the mill, if I can believe Vance Lowell, a N.S.W. apple grower I met at the car ferry dock, in much of the undeveloped land we saw and a vast area

in the south-west noted on the map as "primitive and uninhabited." The hopes of the island now rest mainly on the west coast where large reserves of tin and copper have been proved; and the water power is producing the electricity to process aluminium. These ventures too are all foreign owned.

In 1955 the Governments of Australia and Tasmania built and began operating the country's first aluminium processing plant— not from choice but because private capital for the venture could not be found. This was at Bell Bay in Tasmania, and the plant's capacity was a mere 12,000 tons. In the same year the first Australian aluminium ore—bauxite—was discovered at Weipa on Cape York in northern Queensland. This too was Government-owned, being on land technically reserved to Aborigines.

Within two years the 2,000-million-ton deposit of Weipa bauxite had been handed over to Comalco, a joint British and American concern, and the process of dispossessing the Aborigines from 2,300 square miles of their hunting grounds began. In 1961 Comalco bought the Bell Bay plant and boosted its capacity at once to 52,000 tons and later to 100,000 tons. Also in 1961 the

Aluminum Company of America acquired a controlling interest in
a second large field of 100 million tons in the Darling Ranges of
Western Australia. In 1965, ten years after the Bell Bay plant
began operating, the third and last find, consisting of 200 million
tons of high grade bauxite on 50 square miles of Arnhem Land
Aboriginal Reserve, was delivered to Nobalco, a Swiss-controlled
concern.

Until 1960 Australians spelt iron with the three letters—BHP
—that stand for British-controlled Broken Hill Proprietary. BHP
mined its iron ore in South Australia and on an island off the
coast of Western Australia; and one Federal cabinet minister
charged with natural resources development despaired of ever
finding any more. To conserve what little there was the Govern-
ment prohibited export of the raw material. The mere lifting of
this ban in 1960 produced a veritable miracle. Iron suddenly
cropped up everywhere in huge surface deposits, literally visible to
the naked eye. From being an iron-starved country Australia
became overnight one of the richest in the world, with proven
resources of 15,000 million long tons in Western Australia alone.
The discovery of iron, aluminium, and—more recently—oil came
at the close of a sixteen-year investment spree that saw nearly 4,000
million dollars of foreign funds pumped into the country and put
four-fifths of its mineral wealth under overseas control.

The city centre of Burnie is like Devonport's, a drab succession
of shops without charm or colour, with no Christmas look or
sound to them. It was Candi's last chance to buy Tasmania souvenirs but she could only regret she hadn't done so on our arrival in
Launceston. There was one store demonstrator whom we could
hear out on the street. He was hawking decimal converters—small
cardboard gadgets to use for computing exactly what any given
sum in pounds, shillings, and pence amounts to in Australia's new
dollars and cents currency.

Truth to tell, decimal currency is no longer so very new—but
perhaps it is down here in Tasmania. Anyhow there was a small
crowd around the demonstrator. An elderly lady asked why the
computers couldn't be made of plastic as the cardboard ones wore
out. "You can't buy them in plastic, madam. Plastic is too expen-
sive. People wouldn't buy them. They would stop home and never
learn anything about decimal currency." Another in the crowd
questioned the accuracy of the converter, of which the hawker had
an enlarged model on display. The hawker held the questioner up

to scorn as one who presumed to know more about decimals than the great mathematicians who had produced his converter.

We went on down across the tracks to the park on the beach; it was cold and uninviting. The few benches were unoccupied. Had it not been for the personal charity of Bert Gussey we'd simply have done time in Burnie. Mr Gussey—or Bert as he asked to be called as soon as he told us his name—is evidently on a first-name basis with everybody. He was chummy with the proprietor of the delly from which we were buying bananas, canned milk, bread, and peanut butter, having already tried the only recommended café. We met him again coming back from the park where we'd eaten our lunch. He nodded and smiled in passing, walked a few steps and turned abruptly around. His car was parked just around the corner.

In a few moments we were all in it driving to the top of a hill above the town where its factories, wharves, and ships in the harbour made what I had reluctantly to admit was a dramatic picture. At this distance even the paper mill was glamourized, its chimneys pouring out thick, palpably thick white smoke. Then we went deeper into the hinterland, a magnificent dairy country with large grassy hills in farms of 120 acres or less. Bert confidently expects the city to grow and move back into this farmland. When I remarked on how much better the country looked here than farther south he said, "This *is* Tasmania."

He took us home and introduced us to his eighty-eight-year-old mother, to his brother Dave who lives in Canberra but is holidaying here, and to Dave's wife Dolly. Contrary to my first impression, Bert wasn't one of these Australian bachelors who never got untied from his mother's apron strings. He was married back in the 1930s but his wife left him for a family friend, a Catholic who was already married and had children but couldn't get a divorce. She had nevertheless taken his name and gone to live with him in Italy. This did something to Bert, or so he thinks. Until then he had been a typically complacent, easy-going Australian, generous and free-spending in the little things but cautious in the big. To be sure he hadn't gone quite as far as his brother was to go (Dave is much younger than Bert) and become a public servant, but there were no public service jobs offering in the Depression '30s anyhow.

A few of Bert's friends proposed to set up an independent oil distributing concern in competition with the international giants that, by mutual agreement, controlled and carved up the Australian petrol market. They needed a bit more money, quite a bit

312

by Depresssion standards—$5,000—to bring their total starting capital up to $17,000. As it happened, said Bert, $5,000 was almost exactly the amount of his father's estate, left to him jointly with his mother. He persuaded his mother to invest it in the wildly risky venture and Bert himself went to work for the new company.

The company proposed to introduce an electric pump. It was to be their wedge in the door; or more accurately—as Bert put it—into the dealer's line-up of bowsers. Dealers in those days sold several different brands of petrol, which made it a lot easier for a new company to break in. They didn't have to build a lot of their own service stations; they had only to convince the independent dealers to install their pump. While one of their directors went to the U.S. and negotiated a deal whereby Bert's company became the sole Australasian distributors of the electric pump, they were equally busy at home selling stock.

"Bringing the public into joint ownership of the company proved the source of our greatest strength. The foreign corporations didn't have Australian stockholders to wish them well, patronize them, promote them by word of mouth; we did." Money from the stock sales was deposited. Operating expenses, which consisted mainly in the sale of more stock, were paid by the interest. In the end the number of their stockholders amounted to a considerable fraction of the total petrol consuming public.

They had their difficulties all the same. To protect the entrenched oil giants from upstart competition, the weights and measures departments in the several States refused at first to approve the new pump. They stalled. They said it took time to make such an important decision. And time, said Bert, ate away at the capital of the little company, as the bureaucrats well knew. They finally decided—Bert laughed when he came to this part of his story—that they would come to a decision only when the new pump had been tested.

"After all," I protested mildly, "it was only fair."

"To give the pump a test? Fair enough. The pumps were already in use in America; and what kind of test were we asked to give it? A three-month trial in the market place—provided we could induce a dealer to take the pump on such a basis and provided we could find the petrol to run through it." For this was the gist of the problem: they could only get petrol to sell when they were legally allowed to sell it, and they could only acquire this legal right after having successfully sold it for three months. Such were the nearly insurmountable hurdles an Australian free

313

enterpriser must leap as long ago as 1936 in bucking foreign monopolies.

They did somehow leap them, thanks to the support of their stockholders, who lined the shores of Sydney Harbour to welcome their first tanker, decorated with flags and blowing its whistle. Egged on by the oil giants in a last-ditch fight, the dealers threatened to boycott the new petrol. But Bert and his associates had by now been turned into fighters as tough and ruthless as their opponents. They threatened to install pumps in front of their own distributing plants and sell at the wholesale price. The boycott collapsed.

As I looked at Bert, friendly and smiling, getting plump, very smooth skin, very smooth features, I found it hard to imagine him as a hard-fighting competitor; and still harder to imagine his mother, very thin, very wrinkled, and fragile, having the audacity to back him in his wildcat scheme. They both retain a stock interest in the company and Bert in addition owns shares in Mount Isa Mines and two mines in New Guinea.

Brother Dave is a dinkie-die Aussie whose favourite expression is "snoozer," meaning bloke. He regrets the passing of old Australia and recited a ballad by Banjo Patterson about a horse racer who stiffened his mare and got stiffened. The old Aussie blood, he says, is being diluted by the hundreds of thousands of poms and other migrants.

We talked some about horses, Dave being a small-time weekend bookie. He said he doesn't really make a book; merely uses odds supplied him by wire or a special confidential sheet which costs two quid a week. He then attempts to cover himself when local punters change the odds drastically. Normally he has a year-end profit but he lost a little this past year.

His young sons came in while we were talking and mentioned some cowboy star on TV I had never heard of. I asked if they could talk American. One said he could and I asked him to do so. He said, "Yeah." I asked what word he normally used for yes. It was "yeah."

I said Candi, who was beside me, had learnt to speak some Australian. "She says 'bloody' every other word. That's Australian isn't it?"

The boys agreed.

index

Mossy Cove

Send
Her
Down,
Hughie!

Arthur
Clifford

Aboriginal 5,7,53,64,83,96,129,135-6,
151-2,187,193-4,198,203-4,208,211,
224,237,241,243-4,274,281,311. --
bark painting 135-6. --black tracker 5,192,211. --boomerang 129,224.
--cave paintings 198. --corroboree
129,224. --mia mias 224. --tree
sculptures 96. --souvenirs 243.
--Yuala (dance) 224.
Aborigines 5,53,129,137,141,159-61,
180,192-4,199,203-6,208,211,215-6,
218,224-7,236-7,241,243-4,246-7,
250,264,299,310.
Adam and Atoms 243-4.
Adelaide 3,21,37,42,51,53,89,110,
112,129,132-3,135-7,140,142,144,146,
149,158,161-2,170-1,179,183,187,190-
1,195,199,209,215,228,231,236,238-9,
249-50,256,259-60,263,295. --Hills
187. --University 132,161. --Zoo
132. Port-- 127.
Advertiser, The 138,161.
Albany 240.
Albury 167,271,283.
Alice Springs 89,129,150,190-2,194,
197-8,203-4,206,224,236,247-8.
Alpine Way 283.
aluminum 208,310-1.
America 8,17,20,31,55,62,64,78,83,
109,129,138,157-8,166,178-9,202,216,
220-1,248,250,253,266,287,292,296.
Voice of-- 165.
American 1,5,10,23,33,47,49,55,58-62,
65,67,71-3,76,81-5,89,91-2,97,102,
110,123,129-31,138-40,158-0,165,179-
80,183,194,209,216,221-2,228,250-2,
254,256,259,268,282,286,190,296,
306,310,314. --Negro 160,188,250-1.
--Puritans 178.
American Language, The 116.
Americans 8,53,55,57,94,117,129,166,
188,212-3,220,240,250,253.
Andamooka 251.
Anglican 92,276,277.
Another Country 181.
Anzac 275. --Day 18-9,21,185-6,304.
--Highway 142.
Any Questions 180.
apartheid 160-1.
apprenticeship 83.
arbitration 230. --Court 84,116-8,
253,304-5.
Archipenko 37.
Arizona 197,210,259,280. --High-
ways 137.
Arnhem Land 136,208,311.
Asia 141,163. --ns 7,10,163.
Atherton Tablelands 69.
atom bomb test 244.
Auckland 3,12,14,64,241,286. --
Domain 146.
Aussies 4-5,130,167,172,174,177-9,
185,201,212-3,228,250,256. dinkum
-- 11,236. --myth 283. --Rules (see
football).
Australasia 35,234. --n 138.
Australia, area of 141. --Day 21,141.
--,discovery of 20-1. --House 49,
156. --,population of 141. --,pro-
duction of 141. Radio--284.
Australie 188-9.
Australian 5,18-9,41,57-8,60-1,74,
78,82-5,89-90,94,102-3,108,120-4,
130-2,135,138,142,144,218-9,256,
258. --Broadcasting Commission 164-
5. --constitution 222. --flag 45,
97,102,195. --Immigration Dept. 139,
156. --Labor Party 4,10,80,97. --
myth 134-5,283. --painting 37,135.
--Quarterly 137. --,The 90,92,273.
--Woman's Weekly 28. --a 136. --s
5,57,60-1,67,80-2,84,94,103,112,
114,117-8,129,131,153,159,184,186,
188,200,219,258,287. new--- 200.
Avalon 105.
Avoca 281.
Ayers Rock.
Babii Yar 37.
Bakery Hill 46-7.
Balgowlah 37.

Ballarat 45-8,267.
ballot, preferential 254-6.
Balt 29,135,266,197. --ic States 297.
Barossa Valley 29,141,177-8.
barrack 174. --ers 23.
Barrenjoey Lighthouse 105.
barrister 56-7.
Barron Falls 69. --River 67.
Bass Strait 23,122,285.
Bates, Daisy 223-8.
Battarbee, Rex 204.
bauxite 310-1.
Bayview 105.
beer 1,13,19,46,88-9,98,145-6,176-
7,235-6.
Bega 283.
Bell Bay 310-1.
Bendigo 265,267.
Bilgola 105.
Billings, Josh 130.
Birdsville Track 51,150.
Blackman 187.
Bondi Beach 16.
Bonegilla 297.
bookmaker 80,288-9.
Bordertown 256.
Botanic Gardens (Melbourne) 44. --
(Sydney) 96,107.
Botany Bay 94.
Bounty 96.
Boyd, Arthur 37,187.
Brazilian doctor 192.
bridge, Sydney Harbor 12,16,20,55,108.
London-- 55. Roseville-- 108. Spit--
108. Iron Cove-- 108. Gladesville--
108.
Brisbane 41-2,73,76,78,80,83,86,88-
90,110,129,133,209,238-9,263.
Britain 6,78,112,131,135,159,182,186,
209,242,244,253,275,304,309. --'s 121,
159,195,304.
British 58,65,91-2,153,165,183,216,
220,258,268,275,310-1. --colony 18,
195. --Commonwealth 11,194,221. --
fiction 168. --Government 158. --
novelist 182. the-- 13.
Broken Hill 19,89,190,228,230-1. --
Proprietary 253,311.
Broome 83,89,226.
Bryan, William Jennings 92.
Bullamanka 126.
Bulletin, The 137.
Bumerang 206.
Bundaberg 67.
Burnie 309,311.
Burnside 177.
bush, the 11-2,54,125,148,151-2,239,
247. --rangers 129,270. tropical--
69. up--158.
Cabramurra 283.
Cairns 63-70,72-3,89,215-6.
California 23,38,59,133,155,209,213-
4,216,239,253,259,265,296-7. Inde-
pendent--Rangers 47.
Cambodia 209.
Campbell, Donald 190.
camp 166,193,204,225,227,283-4. --
fires 203,224. --ing 3,126,283-4.
--ground 128,147,237,283-4,303,306.
Canada 11,29-30,49,84,124,138,141,
253,266,296. --ian 66,71,179.
Canberra 58,110,129,144,151,186,208,
248,256,272-9,304-5,312.
Candi 1,4,6,13-4,16,19,39,54,74,90,
93,124,129,135-6,145-6,155,161,166,
168,170-1,176-7,185,187,217,220-1,
239,246,248-9,254,256,260,274,286,
292,295,301,311,314.
Cape York 21,310.
Capricornia 204,218.
Captain Cook 7,21,94.
Carlton 135.
Cataract Gorge 291.
Catholic 97-8,178,276.
Cecil, Lord Robert 46-8.
censorship 180-1,194.
China 8,62,121,124,163,201,209,258.
Chinese 20,120-1,163,226,284,304.
Christmas 179,285,287-8,304.
Churchill, Sir Winston 254-5.

Church Point 105.
Cincinnati, Ohio 250.
Circular Quay 11,18-9,93-4,102,107,
239.
Clinton 126.
clubs 97-8,119,158. Catholic-- 98.
chess-- 119. Cobbers-- 153. German
-- 171,176. Memorial-- 202. Re-
turned Servicemen's League--98,185.
Coal and Candle Creek 105.
Collins, Tom 54,145,218.
Commonwealth 290. British-- 158. --
Day 21,106. --Railway Lines 193,
227. --Scientific & Industrial
Research Organization (CSIRO) 192,
193,195,248.
Communist 97,117,131,182,219,256.
conscription 103.
convicts 5,21,41,160,166,177-8,233,
301.
Coober Pedy 198.
Cook 224-7. Capt.-- 7,21,94.
Cooktown 163.
Cooma 279.
copper mining 89,163,310.
Coral Sea 78.
cricket 45,133,145-6,174. --ground
142.
Cronulla 94
CSIRO (see Commonwealth)
Culotta, Nino 3,130.
Cunderdin 227.
Curl Curl 105.
Czech 17,181. --oslovakia 141.
--'s 122.
Dandenong Mountains 29.
Danielsson, Bengt 206.
Darlinghurst 84. --Ranges 311.
--ton 53.
Darrow, Clarence 92.
Darwin 89,96,151,162,182,201,208.
Deep Well 210.
Dee Why 105.
Derwent River 294.
desert 9,12,129,159-60,167,196-7
204,209-10,223-7,231,243-4,259-
60,293.
Devonport 286,307,309,311.
DDT 53.
diggers 46-8,103,178,200.
dingo 223,225,243,300.
Disneyland 59,297.
Dobell, William 96.
dogs 144-5,155,278,301,306.
Domain, the (Auckland) 146. --
(Melbourne) 44. --(Sydney) 18,
96-9,233-4.
Dry, the 162,293.
Drysdale, Russell 37,187.
Duke of Windsor (see Prince of Wales).
Duntroon 57.
Dutch 20-1,30-2,256-8.
Eddy, W.H.C. 90.
El Alamein fountain 93,99.
Elder Park 132.
election 254-6
Elizabeth 144,155,161,166-7,171-2,
174-5,215,256,273.
emu 223,238,243,246,258,281.
Empire Games Village 239.
England 6,8,49,57,60,64,72,91,114,
131,137-8,142,144,146,151,154,156,
158,167,172,174,176,179,181,186,195,
197,226,287,297,302.
English 6,37,41,54,57,72,81,96,114,
116,121,130-1,135,141,148,153,160,
174,177-80,189,195,197,206,215,222,252-
3,287,296,303. --colony 151. --mid-
lands 4,172.
Englishmen 3,4,5,50,54,57.
Esk River 308.
Esperance 259.
Eucalyptus trees 133,155,193,195,205,
210,259-60,269,272,279,292,308. --
oil 264. --timber 193.
Eureka Stockade 45-8.
Europe 33,110,129,141,158,163,169,
180,184,202-3,292,297. --an 20,113,
121,132,135,185,188,209,222,226,233,
243,251,267.

Evans Head 237.
Eventyrets og Fremtidens Land 215-6.
Exmouth Gulf 82-3.
ferries 19-20,29. ferry 102-5,256,286.
Finke 192-3,210,224. --River 210.
Fisher 223.
Fitzroy Gardens 116.
flies 75,110,128,150,155,162,226,
249,273-4,277,306. bush-- 192.
horse-- 192.
Flinders Street Railway Station 28.
Flinders Ranges 190,224,246.
Florida 216.
Flying Doctor 191,201.
Flynn, Rev. John (see Flying Doctor).
football 22-3,25-7,141-2,231,262.
Fortunes of Richard Mahony, The 217.
France 29-30,124,141,188,209,228,276.
Frankston 32,35.
Fremantle 234,239,241-2. "--doctor"
122.
French 97,177,187,189,206,215,258,287.
Freshwater 70.
Gallipoli 18,185,274-5.
galah (bird) 264-6.
Geehi 283.
Geelong 45,193.
General Motors 7,144,166. --Holden 71,
121,142.
German 215,250,258,266-8. --y 29,31-2,
158,184-5,188,250,266-9,296-7. --
Lutherans 29,178.
Ghan, the 190,192,209.
gibber 191,195.
Gladstone 67.
Gleghorn 187.
Glenelg 128.
Glenrowan 269-70.
goannas 243.
God Save the Queen 195,202.
gold (mining) 163,228,265,296.
Gold Coast 42.
Goldsworthy 82.
Goonoo Goonoo 99.
Goulburn 304. --Valley 284.
Government 7,60,68,84-5,100-2,109,
118,144,160,165,167,169,205,225,243-
4,280-1,310. --Welfare Settlements
53,204,206. Commonwealth-- 194,204,
244. --House 44.
Governor-General 44,186.
Grampians 264.
Graydon, William 243.
Great Australian Bight 223,226,300.
Great Barrier Reef 3,64,66,72.
Great Dividing Range 283.
Grey, Sir George 46.
Green Island 66.
Griffin, Walter B. 274.
Groote Islanders 136.
Group, The 181.
gums (see Eucalyptus trees).
Gunn, Mrs Aeneas 150-2.
Gymea 94.
Hartog, Dirk 21.
Hawkesbury River 105.
Hayes, Timothy 46.
Heads, the 104-6.
Henley 211.
Herbert, Xavier 204,218-9.
Hermannsburg 198.
Heysen, Hans 187.
Hick, Jacqueline 135.
Hobart 91,110,186,287,291-2,294-5,
297,301,306-9. --'sBattery Point
295.
Holland 123,188,233,258.
Hong Kong 8,12,120,195,198,243. --
jade 199.
horse racing 80,88,102.
hostel 142,153,266-7,297. Methodist
-- 187. Smithfield-- 142.
hotel 1,5,63,88,98,163,193,210,230-
2,234-6,241.
Hotham, Gov. Charles 45.
humpies 193-4,203.
Hyde Park 13,94,96.
Ickford 6. Greater-- 6. Little-- 6.
Indian Ocean 193,242.
Indians 121,215. American-- 160.

Indonesia 30,182,209,258.
Immigration Act 121.
Immigration Department 139,156.
iron ore 58,82,311.
Italy 33,163. --ian 121-2,246,279.
Jansz, Willem 20-1.
Japan 8,71,82,85,124,181,226,240.
  --ese 9,78,82,121.
Jay Creek 204,210.
Johnson, President 102-3. LBJ 109.
Joobaitch 226.
Kalgoorlie 217,228-9,243.
Kanakas 121.
kangaroo 7,12-3,19,145,151,201,223,
  238,243,246-9,258,264,281-2. --
  skin 63.
Kangaroo 53-4,93,261.
Katherine, The 151-2,190-2,201.
Kelly, Ned 129,270.
Kennedy, President 176,254.
Kentucky 179.
Khancoban 283.
Kings Cross 93-4,99.
Kisch, Egon 122.
kiwi 5,6,9,41,177.
koala bear 133,160,248,258,281.
Kogarah 94.
Kookaburra 284.
Kuranda Station 66-9.
Kuring-gai Chase 105.
Kwinana 239.
Lady Chatterley's Lover 180.
Lake Burley Griffin 110,273-4.
Lake Eucumbebe 281.
Lake Eyre 190.
Lalor, Peter 47-8.
Lancashire 141-2.
language 7,8,121,130-1,170.
Launceston 286-7,291,295,308,311.
Lawler's, Ray 134-5.
Lawrence, D.H. 38,53-4,93,261.
Lewers, Margo 187.
Light, Colonel 187.
Lightning Ridge 199.
Linkletter, Art 71.
Lismore 237.
Lithuania 296-7. Kaunas-- 297.
Now is the Hour 177.
Lockheed 304.
Lofty Ranges 256,259-60.
London 6,37,55,92,156,174,181,218,
  238,293. --er 283.
Lorimer, George Horace 37.
Los Angeles 8,119,242,273.
lottery 10,86,88,289-91.
Lutheran 92,205,276.
MacArthur, Gen. Douglas 76.
MacDonnell Ranges 205.
Mackay 67.
Macquarie River 308.
Magna Carta 274.
magpies 284.
Manchester 156,174.
mangroves 127.
Manly 8,9,16,102-5.
Maoris 5,160.
marching girls 75-6.
Marion 133.
Mark Twain 35.
Marree 190.
Mascot Airport 119.
Meanjin 137.
Mediterranean 209.
Mee, Arthur 225.
Melbourne 3,5,6,10,12,22,24-9,35-7,
  39,41-5,50-1,60,69,89,92,103,110-1,
  114,119-24,129-30,132,134-5,137,
  144,185-6,194,238-9,242,245,256,
  259,262,269,272,284,287,296. --
  Cricket Ground 45. --Cup 163. --
  Grammar 43. --University 42,44,121.
  Monash University-- 186. Port-- 23,
  123,297.
Melville Island 96.
Mencken 116.
Menzies, Robert 1, Sir Bob-- 186.
Methodist 276.
MI5 158,246.
Michigan 138.
Mielche, Hakon 215-6.

migrants 10,24-5,27,29,32-4,39-41,50,
  54-5,81-2,84,91,93-4,107,111-4,121,
  130,132,135,138-40,152,155-8,160,163,
  166-7,172,174-81,183,185,187-9,200,
  211,233,239-40,243,251,256,258,266-
  7,271,287,291,297,301-2,307,314.
Mildura 259.
milk bar 94,99-101,153.
Miller, Arthur 91.
miners 163,198-200,229-30,231.
Moomba 36.
Moonee Ponds 122,124,128.
Moorabbin 37.
Mormon 215.
Mornington Peninsula 29.
mosquitoes 3,110,162,226,273,283.
Mount Eliza 238.
Mount Isa 63,89,314.
Mount Lofty 260.
Mount Wellington 308.
mulga 193,195,205,210,243.
Murray Bridge 256,259. --River 167,
  259,283.
myalls 204,208.
myxomatosis 192.
Namatjira, Albert 5,204.
Narrabeen 105.
National Art Gallery (Adelaide) 132,
  135,187. --(Melbourne) 44. --Sydney
  96,102.
National Library 151.
New Guinea 6,74,160,209,314.
New South Wales 6,21,89,94,96,102,130,
  162,167,190-1,194,199,217,230,237,270,
  275,276,281,189,300,309.
New Year's Eve 16,36,76.
New York 19,35,108,240.
New Zealand 3-6,8,17,21,49,64,102,141,
  143,145,160,165,168-70,180,190,195,
  221,286,293. --er 122. Christchurch--
  306. Wellington-- 6,20. Whangarei-- 3.
Ninety-mile Beach 6. --desert 259.
Nolan, Sydney 37,135,187.
Norfolk Bay 301.
Northern Territory 150,162,190,194,204,
  276.
Now is the Hour 177.
Nullarbor 90,193,217,223,227,246.
Oenpelli 136.
oil 64-6,312-4.
Olympic Games 45,116.
One Day of the Year 18-9,59,186,
  211-2.
Oodnadatta 190,210,236.
Oldea 223,226-7.
opal 198-200.
Opera House (Sydney) 10,79,82,104,
  107-8. -- Lottery 289.
Orr, Sydney Sparks 90-2.
outback 68,125,132,135,151-2.
Outer Harbor 127,248.
oval 141,231.
Overland Telegraph Station 198,
  203-4.
Pacific 76,242. --coast 104. --
  Islanders 121.
Palm Beach 105.
Palm Island 64.
Papunya 204,206.
Parliament 59-60,82,99,273-4.
Passing of the Aborigines, The 225-7.
Paterson, Banjo 314.
Pearce, Mrs. Henrietta 201.
peasey stone 191,195,210.
Peggy 5,13-4,16,62,74,76,89-90,
  93,122,138-9,145-6,170-1,187,259-
  60,276-7,287,288,295.
Penguin 309.
Perth 23-4,53,64,82,110,112,114,122,
  129,133,137,148-9,158,209,217,226,
  228,232,238-43,245,247-8.
Pike, Douglas 35.
Pinchgut Island 9.
Pitchi-Ritchi 198.
Pittwater 105,301.
Poland 123,266,269.
Pollack, Jackson 37.
Polynesian 97,215.
population 35.
Port Arthur 301-2,305-6.

Port Augusta 236
Port Hedland 82.
Port Phillip Bay 23,29,72,286,301.
Port Pirie 190,224,245.
Port Wakefield 126.
Presbyterian 131,201,276.
Priestley, J.B. 182,197.
Prince Charles 262.
Prince of Wales 224,227.
Prince Philip 262.
pub 13,50,80,83,97-8,163,167,174,
  212,228,231,234,288.
Puckle Street 124-5.
Punchbowl 233-5.
Pyrmont 12,16-7,19,51,76,108.
Quaker 159,178.
Queanbeyan 304.
Queen 18,186,242,262. --'s Birth-
  day 21. --Counsel 56-7. --name 47.
  --portrait 14.
Queenscliff 105.
Queensland 3,21,25,60,63-8,74,76,
  86-9,114,121,150,152,193,237,287,
  300,310.
rabbits 192,223,225,243,258,300.
Raffaello, Carboni 46-8.
railways 29,37,94,102,120,190,
  224-5,293.
Red Lynch 66,70.
Renmark 259.
Richardson, Henry Handel 217.
Richmond 33.
Rigby's Romance 218.
right-hand-rule 139-40.
Riverina 266-7.
Rocks, The 12.
Rosebud 36.
Ross 293. --Creek 64. --River 64.
Rottnest Island 239-41.
Royal Automobile Association 128,
  141,174.
Russell, Bertrand 129.
Russia 36,163. --n 36,60,122,158,
  258,266,268-9,275.
St. Kilda 42.
St. Peters 234-6.
St. Vincent Bay 128. --'s Gulf 144.
sandflies 162,274.
San Francisco 19-20,64,119.
Santa Teresa 198.
schools 43,68,84,166,170-1,185-7,
  191,206,220-1,253-4,275.
Scotch College 43,183.
Seven Emus 218.
Seymour 284.
Seymour, Alan 18-9.
Shute, Nevil 197.
Simpson's Gap 198,205.
slang 3,8,95,103,130-2,212-3,271,
  283,314.
Snowy River Project 158,248,256,
  279,280-3. --Mountains 283,292.
solicitor 56-7,261-2.
Sorrell 306,308.
South Africa 49,151,158-60,215.
South Australia 21,29,51,133,149-50,
  156,172,177-8,190-1,227-8,249,260,
  264,292,300,311. --n 110,127,129,
  135,262. --Historic Trust 179. --
  Housing Trust 144,155-7,167,170.
Southeast Asia 30,65,209.
Spencer Gulf 224,246.
spinifex 195,210,227.
Stanley 285.
Stoney Creek 67. --Falls 70.
  --Gorge 70.
Such is Life 54,145,218.
Summer of the Seventeenth Doll 134-5.
Sunshine 282.
Surfer's Paradise 42,124,297.
surfing 84,94-6,104,130.
Susanberg 127.
Swan River 239.
Sydney 3-4,6-7,9-13,18-20,23-5,29,35,
  37-9,42-3,51-5,57,64,72,76,89-90,92-
  4,96-7,99,102,104-6,110-2,114,119-20,
  122,124,129,132,135,137,141,144,150,
  176,180,182,201,219,233-4,238-9,242,
  245,247,261-3,269,272-3,275-6,282,
  287,292,295,297,299,301,314.

Taronga Park 93. --Zoo 19,281.
Tasman, Abel 21.
Tasman Sea 3,16,20,111.
Tasman Peninsula 301,308.
Tasmania 21-3,41,50,91-2,122,209,
  248,256,281,285-9,291-2,300-2,306-9,
  311-2. --ns 51,91,303,307.
Tattersalls 32,289,297.
TB 51-3,266.
tea 14,69,142,213-4,245-6,271. Devon-
  shire-- 271.
Tennant Creek 162-3.
They're a Weird Mob 1-3,130.
Thirroul 54.
Thredbo 283.
Three Men on a Horse 87.
Timor Sea 201.
Toorak 42,45-6.
Toowoomba 68.
Torestin 38.
Torrens River 132.
Torres, Luis Vaez de 20. --Islander
  97. --Strait 20.
Town Like Alice, A 197.
Townsville 60,63-4,66,74.
trains 31-2,120,186,194,217,226-8,
  246,291-2,293-4,309.
Tree of Man 217.
Trephina Gorge 198.
tucker 13. --bag 123,210,265.
Tumut 280,282-3.
Two at Daly Waters 201.
two-up school 89,228,230-1,290.
Unley 37.
United States 6-9,20,57-62,71,91,103,
  117-8,124,130,138-9,158,166,169,179,
  181-2,185-6,188,212,219-20,222,232,
  246,253-4,266,270,278,293,313. --
  Navy 82-4.
Upfield, Arthur 5.
Veblen, Thorstein 104.
Victoria 21-2,25,27,35-47,50,58,114,
  117,120,124,127,140,149,190,193,209,
  249,262,270,276,289. --ns 51,111,
  194,228.
Victor Harbor 172.
Vietnam 31,61-2,97-8,103,209,220.
Voss 217.
waijelas 194.
Wakefield, E.G. 21.
walkabout 7,194,206.
Walkabout 137.
wallabies 258,281.
war 138,185,304. anti-- 122. the
  Great-- 18,228,270. Second World--
  61,84,135,266,268,296.
War Memorial (Canberra) 274-5. --
  (Fremantle) 239,242. --(Kalgoorlie)
  229. --(Perth) 239.
Waratah 36.
We of the Never-Never 150-2.
Weipa 208,310.
Western Australia 21,41,64,67,71,
  82,137,149,158,188,193,227,241,
  243-4,250,259,276,281,293,300,311.
Western Junction 309.
Wet, the 151,162,293.
Whale Beach 105.
White, Patrick 130,217-8.
Whitsunday Passage 72.
Whyalla 253.
Wilson's Promontory 23.
Wimera 264.
Wollongong 263.
women 17-8,24,38,101,108,117-8,
  123,127,185,190,217.
Wook Wook 127.
Woolloomooloo 20,38,51,85,93,101,104.
Woolware 94.
Woomera 129,165,246,251.
Yanks 4,14,71,138-40,179,212-3,283.
Yarra River 28,44-5,120.
Yass 272,276,304.
Yirrkala 136.

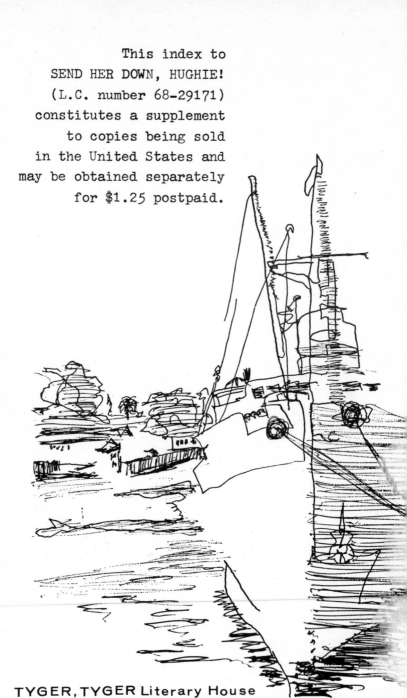

TYGER, TYGER Literary House
1546 Shoreline Dr., Santa Barbara, Ca.